Language as Symbolic Power

Language is not simply a tool for communication – symbolic power struggles underlie any speech act, discourse move, or verbal inter- action, be it in face-to-face conversations, online tweets or political debates. This book provides a clear and accessible introduction to the topic of language and power from an applied linguistics perspective. It is clearly split into three sections: the power of symbolic represen- tation, the power of symbolic action and the power to create sym- bolic reality. It draws upon a wide range of existing work by philosophers, sociolinguists, sociologists and applied linguists, and includes current real-world examples, to provide a fresh insight into a topic that is of particular significance and interest in the current political climate and in our increasingly digital age. The book shows the workings of language as symbolic power in educational, social, cultural and political settings and discusses ways to respond to and even resist symbolic violence.

CLAIRE KRAMSCH is Professor Emerita at the University of California, Berkeley. She has won the Kenneth Mildenberger Award from the Modern Language Association three times, for *Context and Culture in Language Teaching* (1993), *The Multilingual Subject* (2009) and *The Multi- lingual Instructor* (2018, with Lihua Zhang). She is the past President of the American Association for Applied Linguistics (AAAL) and of the International Association of Applied Linguistics (AILA).

T0381689

KEY TOPICS IN APPLIED LINGUISTICS

Series Editors

Claire Kramsch (University of California, Berkeley)
and Zhu Hua (University of Birmingham)

Books in this series provide critical accounts of the most important topics
in applied linguistics, conceptualized as an interdisciplinary field of
research and practice dealing with practical problems of language and
communication. Some topics have been the subject of applied linguistics
for many years and will be re-examined in the light of new developments in
the field; others are issues of growing importance that have not so far been
given a sustained treatment. The topics of the series are nuanced and
specialized, providing an opportunity for further reading around a
particular concept. The concept examined may be theoretical or practice
oriented. Written by leading experts, the books in the series can be used on
courses and in seminars, or as succinct guides to a particular topic for
individual students and researchers.

Language as Symbolic Power

CLAIRE KRAMSCH

University of California, Berkeley

CAMBRIDGE
UNIVERSITY PRESS

CAMBRIDGE
UNIVERSITY PRESS

University Printing House, Cambridge CB2 8BS, United Kingdom

One Liberty Plaza, 20th Floor, New York, NY 10006, USA

477 Williamstown Road, Port Melbourne, VIC 3207, Australia

314–321, 3rd Floor, Plot 3, Splendor Forum, Jasola District Centre, New Delhi – 110025, India

79 Anson Road, #06–04/06, Singapore 079906

Cambridge University Press is part of the University of Cambridge.

It furthers the University's mission by disseminating knowledge in the pursuit of education, learning, and research at the highest international levels of excellence.

www.cambridge.org
Information on this title: www.cambridge.org/9781108835862
DOI: 10.1017/9781108869386

© Claire Kramsch 2021

This publication is in copyright. Subject to statutory exception and to the provisions of relevant collective licensing agreements, no reproduction of any part may take place without the written permission of Cambridge University Press.

First published 2021

A catalogue record for this publication is available from the British Library.

Library of Congress Cataloging-in-Publication Data
Names: Kramsch, Claire J., author.
Title: Language as symbolic power / Claire Kramsch.
Description: Cambridge, UK ; New York : Cambridge University Press, 2020. | Series: Key topics in applied linguistics | Includes bibliographical references and index.
Identifiers: LCCN 2020015973 (print) | LCCN 2020015974 (ebook) | ISBN 9781108835862 (hardback) | ISBN 9781108798891 (paperback) | ISBN 9781108869386 (epub)
Subjects: LCSH: Language and languages–Political aspects. | Communication–Political aspects. | Power (Social sciences)
Classification: LCC P119.3 .K68 2020 (print) | LCC P119.3 (ebook) | DDC 302.23–dc23
LC record available at https://lccn.loc.gov/2020015973
LC ebook record available at https://lccn.loc.gov/2020015974

ISBN 978-1-108-83586-2 Hardback
ISBN 978-1-108-79889-1 Paperback

Cambridge University Press has no responsibility for the persistence or accuracy of URLs for external or third-party internet websites referred to in this publication and does not guarantee that any content on such websites is, or will remain, accurate or appropriate.

Contents

Figures

Acknowledgments

This book is the result of many happy serendipities. Having taught for several years a successful undergraduate course titled *Language and Power* through my German department at University of California, Berkeley (UC Berkeley), my colleague in that department, Professor Robert Holub, who had just become Dean of Undergraduate Studies, invited me in spring 2006 to give that course again within the newly instituted Discovery Course program in the College of Letters and Science. The audience would be a general audience of 18–22-year-olds from all over campus; it would satisfy their social and behavioral sciences or their arts and literature breadth requirement, and the requirements of the minor in Education and in Applied Language Studies.

These Discovery Courses, launched in fall 2005, were promoted on their website as being "deliberately designed to engage and ignite the minds of non-experts, [and] to be unforgettable." Course names ranged from: *"Physics for future presidents," "Physics and Music," "Introduction to general astronomy,"* to *"Wealth and Poverty"* and *"Questioning efficiency: Human factors and existential phenomenology"* among many others. The course L&S180 *Language and Power* was added in 2006 and was taught since then every year for twelve years. It offered the following course description on its syllabus:

> As the saying goes, "Sticks and stones/ Can break my bones/ But words will never hurt me" – but is that really so? We all know that people do things with words and that in turn words do things to people. Language can inform or deceive, seduce or insult, make us fall in love or kill our reputation. What is it about language that gives it that power? How can sounds in a conversation, signs on a page make us laugh or cry? Why are we so attached to the language we grew up with? Why can a foreign language be so sexy? What does it take to speak and be not only heard but actually responded to? How do our words remember, imagine, anticipate, respond to the words of others? And how can we acquire conversational power? This course will

explore the workings of language as social symbolic power in everyday life. We will examine the discourse of politics and the media, children's books and advertisements, psychobabble and corporate-speak, as well as the relation between language and identity, ideology, and myth.

I wish to thank Bob Holub and Alix Schwartz who gave me the opportunity to teach that course as well as my many graduate student assistants who taught recitation sections over the years: Jessica Adams, Leticia Allais, Katie Bernstein, David Gramling, Chris Hebdon, Emily Hellmich, Michael Huffmaster, Jennifer Johnson, Noah Katznelson, David Malinowski, Jaran Shin, Kimberly Vinall, Tim Wolcott. Colleagues at the University of California: Andrew Cohen, George Lakoff, Robin Lakoff, Geoffrey Raymond, James Rule, Dan Slobin, Alexei Yurchak, showed great generosity in giving guest lectures. The some 1,500 students who took the course over the years have much contributed to the ideas presented in this book with their probing questions, their vivid examples of the workings of language in their everyday lives and their willingness to engage with its paradoxes. Special thanks go to Rotem Bluvstein, Michael Bronstein, Sarah Cardullo, Rachel Fernandez, Jian Gao, Tomajin Morikawa, Lindsay Nolan and Charlotte Zhang for their insights during our coffee hours after the weekly lectures.

The book benefitted also from the feedback I received from various audiences around the world. A warm thank you to the organizers of the annual meeting of the Dutch Association of Applied Linguistics in June 2018, to Peppi Taalas of EuroCALL in Finland in August 2018 and to Melina Porto for a week-long workshop at the University de la Plata in Argentina in September 2018 where I presented parts of this book. My gratitude goes to others who invited me to lecture about language as symbolic power at their universities: Brigitta Busch in Vienna, Aymen El-Sheikh in Qatar, Claudia Finkenbeiner in Kassel, Britta Freitag-Hild in Potsdam, Muriel Grosbois in Paris, Adelheid Hu in Luxemburg, Ulrike Jessner in Innsbruck, Lotta König, Brigitte Schädlich and Carola Surkamp in Göttingen, Christiane Lütge in Munich, Bernd Rüschoff in Essen. The ideas discussed in this book benefitted tremendously from my conversations with Uwe Koreik during my semester at the University of Bielefeld on a Harald Weinrich Professorship in 2016, and with Fiona Copland during my semester at the University of Stirling on a Carnegie Centennial Professorship in spring 2017. They refined my understanding of the social and historical power of language in a German and a Scottish context. At UC Berkeley Laura Sterponi, Zehlia Babaci-Wilhite and Rick Kern generously invited me to guest lecture about language and symbolic power in their classes. The Berkeley Language Center and my colleague language teachers there provided me with a warm and sympathetic sounding board. I am particularly grateful to Rutie Adler, Annamaria Bellezza, Niko Euba, Mark Kaiser, Rick Kern, Karen Moeller, Chika Shibahara, Claire Tamen and Lihua Zhang for their willingness to engage with the ideas presented in this book. Jessica Adams and Noah Katznelson helped in finding examples for the various chapters. Special thanks to David Gramling for his generous and thorough proofreading.

In writing this book, I stand of course on the shoulders of giants. My ideas about language as symbolic power have developed over the decades not only out of my growing impatience with a foreign language education research that always seems to be missing something but also out of the growing desire to share with my fellow applied linguists the immense debt I owe to the far-sighted and intellectually generous scholars I have known in person over the span of my career and whose work has inspired me more than I can tell – among them: Pierre Bourdieu, Judith Butler, John Gumperz, Dell Hymes, George and Robin Lakoff, Paul Ricoeur, Ron Scollon, Dan Slobin and Henry Widdowson. Even though many would not recognize themselves in this book, their writings have shaped my thoughts and I can't thank them enough.

Finally, I would like to thank my dear friend and coeditor of this Cambridge University Press series, Zhu Hua, whose enthusiasm kept me going, as well as Andrew Winnard who invited us to launch this series. A vow of thanks to Rebecca Taylor, Isabel Collins and her team at Cambridge University Press who shepherded this book to production with empathy and wonderful professional attention to detail, and to my superlative indexer, Susan Storch.

As this book goes to print, the COVID-19 pandemic is raging across the globe, revealing long-standing inequalities and injustices. But it has also revealed inordinately powerful forces for social justice led by a new generation of young people, who are both socially aware and politically savvy. I hope the book can contribute to this new awareness in the years to come.

Introduction

In his classic little book *Language –The loaded weapon. The use and abuse of language today,* published in 1980 but conceived in the seventies at the height of the Cold War, the Harvard linguist Dwight Bolinger examines the way language is not only studied by linguists but put to use by language practitioners such as film and drama critics, news people who work for radio and TV networks, syndicated columnists, consultants in journalism, education and government, and language educators (among those, foreign language teachers) – in short, by professional experts, or at least specialists, in the resources of language to express, inform, teach and manipulate people and move them to action. These verbal "shamans," as he calls them, should in his view join forces with linguists, psycho- and sociolinguists to raise awareness in the general public about the nature of language. At a time when Applied Linguistics had only just taken off in the United States,[1] in this book Bolinger took linguistics out of its ivory tower and showed how the English language was being used and abused by everyday speakers and writers, but also by marketing strategists, politicians and "jargonauts" (p.125) in the real world of the time. In 1981 the book received the George Orwell Award, an award established in 1975 by the National Council of Teachers of English for writers "who had made outstanding contributions to the critical analysis of public discourse."

Bolinger had a reason to be concerned about language. While the world had overcome the onslaught of propaganda and disinformation campaigns waged by friend and foe during World War II, it was still in the throes of the rhetorical warfare of the Cold War. George Orwell (1949) had castigated communist Newspeak, but there was plenty of Newspeak on the capitalistic side as well. The rise of television entertainment and the media was fostering advertising clichés, marketing slogans, hyperboles and half-truths, and the use of language to "win friends and influence people" that Dale Carnegie had famously

1

advocated already before the war (Carnegie 1936) and that Vance
Packard heavily decried after the war (Packard 1957, 1964). These were
the brainwashing language practices of a rapidly growing consumer
culture that Bolinger and other scholars from different fields were
responding to in the 1970's and 1980's – for example Robin Lakoff
(1975), Erving Goffman (1981) and Bourdieu (1977a 1977b, 1982) in
sociology and sociolinguistics, Barthes (1972, Lyotard (1984) and Baudrillard (1983) in cultural studies.

In *Language – the loaded weapon*, Bolinger took a linguistic perspective
to examine the uses of language in the America of the seventies: the
political advertising, the sexism and euphemisms of the gun lobby and
the tobacco industry that were manipulating people's imaginations
and fabricating a social reality that was often an illusion. After a series
of "prescriptions" for practitioners to cleanse their language of abusive
features, Bolinger made the following recommendation to information
shamans: "It should be as natural to comment on the linguistic probity
of public figures as to comment on their financial probity – in both
cases they are manipulating symbolic systems that are the property of
everyone" (p.186). The book ended on a quote by John Ciardi: "Tell me
how much a nation knows about its own language and I will tell you
how much that nation cares about its own identity" (p.188).[2]

I.1 LANGUAGE AS SYMBOLIC ACTION

Today Bolinger's recommendations make us smile but they also sound
eerily prescient. Our world seems eons away from Bolinger's world of
the eighties. The advent of the Internet and of a deregulated globalized
market economy, the spread of English as a global language, and the
ever growing use and sophistication of information and communication technologies have changed the nature and role of language to such
an extent that one has to wonder whether we are talking about the
same thing. What do we mean by "language"? by "language use"?

As compared to the 1980's, our times are still concerned with speaking clearly and accurately, having equal access to the media and the
free flow of messages, and with having the ability to speak the truth,
but in ways that are different from those envisaged by Bolinger. In
many ways, the computer has diversified our criteria of acceptable
speech, democratized our access to information, amplified exponentially the flow of information, but it has also changed the nature of
truth. By changing the scale and the scope of our communications, the
digital age has fundamentally reshaped our relationship to language

and our power to be listened to and taken seriously. Social media, in particular, that idealistically claim to only want to "connect people around the globe," are now seen as creating addiction, anxiety and alienation, and as undermining democracy itself. The crude political propaganda of the Cold War has been replaced by the inordinately more subtle "persuasive technologies" of Facebook and Google.[3]

Some populists would even say that ours is not an era of persuasion, but an era of mobilization; people now move in tribes that get mobilized by the symbolic power of large-scale rallies and social media. In addition, the exacerbated competitiveness of a neoliberal market economy has increased the amount of surveillance and control of consumers, citizens and contributors to the workforce. Our language practices are being sanctioned by our "friends" on Facebook, monitored by our corporate employer in the workplace, and self-disciplined by our fear of falling out of line, out of sight or, worse, out of mind. More than ever, we feel the pressure to conform and we fear retaliation if we do not. The forms of retaliation have become more invisible: social humiliation and shame, threats to face and loss of legitimacy, spoiled reputation, social opprobrium, and the fall into irrelevance and ultimately oblivion.

This is the backdrop against which our students are learning and using language in their everyday lives. The pressure they feel is a social symbolic pressure – conveyed by words and images, online and in face to face, spoken and read, tweeted and blogged, exerting their symbolic power to influence their perceptions, memories and expectations of self and others. Language has become less a mode of information than a mode of impression management and emotional manipulation. This book aims to shift the focus from the instrumental to the symbolic dimensions of language that account for its awesome power to affect people's view of themselves and the world – language not as a loaded and potentially dangerous weapon, but language as a discourse with symbolic effects.

1.2 DEFINITION OF TERMS

The symbolic aspects of language are often occluded in Applied Linguistics by an overemphasis on the economic or material aspects of life, labor and language in a neoliberal economy. For many language learners, language merely reflects an objective reality out there, made up of money, jobs and consumer goods. But this is ignoring the symbolic nature of symbolic systems that, like language, images or music, do not just represent and inform, but act on our emotions, our identities, how we position ourselves vis-à-vis others and how we are viewed by others.

What Do I Mean by Symbolic?

Any language learner knows that language is a symbolic system, that is, a semiotic system made up of linguistic signs or symbols that in combination with other signs forms a code that one learns to manipulate in order to make meaning. But beyond that, learners generally believe that the elements of this code have meanings to be found in the dictionary, that these meanings constitute information that can be retrieved from texts and reproduced in conversation, and that the only problem in understanding and getting understood by others consists in properly encoding and decoding messages according to rules imposed by a given community of native speakers. The fact that this cultural environment has been historically constructed, socially shaped and individually manipulated by the very discourse of speakers like themselves is not something they usually think about. Indeed, they don't like to think that utterances have effects and that language has not only semiotic informative power but the much broader symbolic power to define who they and others are, and to influence perceptions, memories and expectations. The symbolic universe that language learners are entering today requires them to have a much greater awareness of the power games that are being played with language, whether in their own or in a foreign tongue (see Bourdieu 1998; Kramsch 2012b).

I will use the term "symbolic" to refer to three ways of looking at language. First, there is the linguists' view. Like other symbolic systems such as painting, music or fashion, language as symbolic system consists of units of meaning encoded in visual, musical or textual forms. In Saussure's view, the linguistic sign or symbol is a physical form (signifier) associated with a semiotic concept (signified) (Saussure 1959). That is the view shared by most learners of a foreign language.

Second, we have the anthropologist's view. For the semiotician and anthropologist, symbols do not exist out there for the take. They are always created and wielded by people who use them to address someone else. The symbols that constitute language do not represent concepts in themselves, they have to be interpreted as such by the people to whom these symbols are addressed. Indeed, they interpellate people into interpreting them. These addressees are called upon to recognize the symbols for their conventional, agreed upon meaning that comes not only from the one isolated form, but from a combination of symbolic forms that together make up a recognizable code. Symbolic relations, with their conventional meaning, their combinatory structure and their interpellative nature, build upon the lower-level semiotic ones – iconic and indexical relations, to act upon people's sensibilities and imaginations.[4] Their power to affect people is thus different from the immediate effect of a picture or a gesture. Because of their appeal to their addressees to link their form to both other forms in the system (text) and other forms in the world (context), to both universal convention and individual particularity of meaning, linguistic symbols have a variety of direct and indirect, immediate and delayed effects linked to addressors and addressees in complex and unpredictable ways.

Finally, there is the sociologist's view. Like anthropologists, sociologists are interested in the material and the symbolic culture of the societies they study. They observe and document the structures of dwellings, the ritual practices including the interactional rituals of everyday life and the meaning that members of such societies give to their practices. They note that these symbolic meanings regulate not only the conventional ritualized events of the community but also the spontaneous verbal exchanges between people and the way they go about their daily affairs. But they also note the way these meanings construct what people view as the real, the true, the good. Thus, besides the economic and material power that people have and talk about, there is a pervasive and all-encompassing layer of symbolic power that creates the very conditions of possibility of thinking and talking about material things. That symbolic power is the power of language as discourse and it has been studied in particular by Pierre Bourdieu (1991, 1998).

What Is Symbolic Power?

Symbolic power is different from physical coercion, economic domination or colonial oppression. It is the power to construct social reality by creating and using symbols that give meaning to the social world. Bourdieu writes:

> Symbolic power – as a power of constituting the given through utterances, of making people see and believe, of confirming or transforming the vision of the world and, thereby, action on the world and thus the world itself, an almost magical power which enables one to obtain the equivalent of what is obtained through force (whether physical or economic), by virtue of the specific effect of mobilization – is a power that can be exercised only if it is *recognized (reconnu)*, that is, misrecognized *(méconnu)* as arbitrary [. . .] What creates the power of words and slogans, a power capable of maintaining or subverting the

social order, is the belief in the legitimacy of words and of
those who utter them. And words alone cannot create this belief.
(Bourdieu 1991:170)[5]

Let us unpack this rather dense passage. Utterances, that is, not sentences out of the dictionary, but words uttered by someone to someone
either in spoken or in written form, are a way of exercising power
through the use of linguistic symbols. This power, says Bourdieu,
constitutes, that is, creates, the reality we usually take as given. It is
not a divine power that can create the physical world *ex nihilo*, but it
can create perceptions (visions) of and beliefs about the world that can
prompt people to take action and thus transform the world physically
and economically. How can utterances have such a power? The answer
is through their mobilizing effects, that is, through their ability to
affect, move and motivate people. But this can work only if people
acknowledge (recognize) that these words are justified (legitimate) and
believe that the speaker is naturally (arbitrarily) entitled to utter those
words. Such a legitimacy, Bourdieu adds, cannot come from the words
themselves, they come from the credibility the speaker enjoys vis a vis
his or her listeners, because of institutional affiliation, seniority,
expertise, social rank, experience and so on. In other words, authorita-
tive words must be backed by the authority of a speaker.[6]

We should also note that symbolic power is not just a question of
someone intending to dominate or to exercise power over someone
else. Because it is a social symbolic, not just a psychological power, it
manifests itself through its effects, and can be at work even if the
speaker does not intend it. For example I might not intend to exert
power over you by inviting you out to dinner, but, as we shall see in
Chapter 5, I am exerting symbolic violence towards you by putting you
under the obligation to reciprocate. In the quote, Bourdieu capitalizes
on the resources of the French language to build his theory of symbolic
reciprocity. *Connaissance* (E.cognizance) denotes a more intimate understanding of things than *savoir* (E.knowledge), that denotes a mere informational apprehension of facts. *Reconnaissance* (E.recognition) denotes
both a re-cognition, an acknowledgement of something previously
known, but, like the phrase "in recognition of someone's merits," it
is also the French word for appreciation or even gratitude. *Méconnais-
sance* (E.misrecognition) does not mean lack of knowledge, but mis-
taken knowledge. When Bourdieu speaks of symbolic power, he is
speaking of a power that can only function if it is recognized, that is,
acknowledged as legitimate, by both parties. But at the same time as it
is recognized, says Bourdieu, it has to be also mis-recognized/mistaken
or wrongly perceived as being in the natural order of things.

According to Bourdieu, symbolic systems such as words, images, music, but also fashion and living styles are instruments of knowledge and communication that serve to establish a consensus on the meaning of the social world. They add to the material world a non-material layer of signification that is composed of the beliefs and everyday practices of its members, the meaning they give to the natural and historical events they live through, the future they aspire to and that makes them share a common understanding of the social world. Symbols achieve the social integration of a group or society and help to reproduce the social order by reproducing the way the group interprets physical/economic realities. For this social integration to happen and communication to be successful, however, those who wield symbols have to make the meanings of these symbols not only recognizable to others, but taken for granted or accepted by others as "arbitrary," that is, as self-evident facts of life.

Some might think that the exercise of symbolic power in the real world is less real precisely because it is not physical, that is, it relies not on objective facts but on subjective beliefs and perceptions. This is without counting with the real objective consequences of such beliefs. Examples abound in the literature that make public shaming, the smearing of reputations and the loss of face into the source of tragedies.[7] In all these cases, symbolic power is the power to construct a social reality that can both include and exclude social actors and may even carry for them physical consequences of actual life and death. Because it is dependent on the recognition by others and on public sanction for its legitimacy, it is an eminently social form of power. While notions such as honor, duty, shame and ridicule might seem outdated for some people, they are still of crucial importance for users of Facebook and other social media, and for any endeavor whose success depends on the value of one's brand, one's name or one's popularity.

1.3   THE FUNDAMENTAL PARADOX OF SYMBOLIC POWER

One characteristic of symbolic power is its fundamentally paradoxical nature. It can appear as natural as a high I.Q. or an aptitude for languages. But a high I.Q. acquires a different meaning when it gets translated into a B.A. from Harvard vs. a B.A from a small community college; and one's linguistic abilities are given more symbolic value if one comes from a white upper-middle-class family than if one is a member of a bilingual immigrant community. Thus, the power of a high I.Q. and multilingual competence is both arbitrary (they are part of a natural endowment one has not chosen) and non-arbitrary (their symbolic power is due to one's socio-economic environment). The paradox of symbolic power is that it is non-arbitrary but people are made to believe it is arbitrary. We will find that paradox at work throughout this book. For example, as we will see in Chapter 1, the language we use as a mother tongue is not ours – it belongs to the speech community we were born into and thus constrains our thinking, but we believe it belongs to us and we are free to say what we want and the way we want. Language gives us the power to organize and classify things in the world, but it also has the power to discipline and restrict our knowledge. As we shall see in Chapter 4, discipline entails paradoxically both order and surveillance, and surveillance entails both free expression and self-censorship. Face-saving strategies can also be face-threatening acts, generosity can also be symbolic violence, compliments can also be put-downs or acts of condescension. The same words can show solidarity with and distance from or even power over others. And, in Chapter 7, we will show how the very same social media that have empowered and given a voice to so many people are being used to sell their personal data and manipulate public opinion. In short, language as symbolic power both enables and limits what we can say and think; it structures and is structured by other people's speech and thought, and, ultimately, their actions.

1.4   LANGUAGE AS SYMBOLIC POWER IN APPLIED LINGUISTICS

The relation of language and power has been amply studied by scholars from two different orientations. On the one hand, modernist scholars in linguistics, critical language education and critical discourse analysis; on the other hand, scholars in linguistic anthropology, postmodern sociolinguistics, and critical applied linguistics. The term "critical" generally indexes the social, ideological and broadly political engagement that these scholars have in common as they strive to show the crucial contribution linguistics can make to understanding the power struggles going on in public life. But there is a difference between the two groups, as I will now discuss.

On the one hand, in *Talking power: The politics of language* (1990), Robin Lakoff considers power as something that some people have and others don't. In this book, she examines "what is most traditionally thought of as the politics of language: the usurpation of language by the powerful, in one way or another, to create, enhance, and justify their power" (p.7). David Block in *Second Language Identities* (2007:26) and Bonny

Norton in *Identity and Language Learning* (2010:49) examine the workings of political power in the way that immigrants and minorities acquire the language of their host country. Here power is associated again with the existence of subordinate and dominant groups, dominance and resistance, coercion and opposition. In *Language and power* (2014:1) Norman Fairclough is interested in "increas[ing] consciousness of how language contributes to the domination of some people by others" through the use of ideologies and the manufacture of consent. He affiliates himself with Critical Language Studies within a Hallidayan systemic-functional framework. His work, associated with the field of Critical Discourse Analysis (CDA), is centrally focused on the way that power is reproduced by institutions, that is, on "the opaque as well as transparent structural relationships of dominance, discrimination, power and control as manifested in language" (Wodak 1995, cited in Blommaert 2005a:25). These four publications generally take a modernist, emancipatory approach to language and power, inasmuch as they view power as domination and as something to be resisted and liberated from.

The other group of scholars, on the other hand, takes a post-structuralist or post-modern approach, inspired to a large extent by Michel Foucault. It considers the workings of power on a larger scale, where the paradoxes of power play themselves out in more subtle and invisible ways. In *Critical Applied Linguistics* (2001), Alastair Pennycook associates power with "inequality, injustice, rights, and wrongs" (p.6) but he makes the difference between liberal sociolinguistics and critical sociolinguistics (p.55). The first assumes a "consensual view of equitable society" and believes that "language reflects society." The second assumes no such consensus. It believes that the role that language plays in perpetuating conflict and inequality must be understood and critiqued, because language as discourse not only reflects but produces unequal and inequitable social relations. In *Discourse. A critical introduction* (2005a), Jan Blommaert adopts a post-modernist approach to critical discourse analysis. He is interested less in power itself than in "an analysis of power *effects*, of the outcome of power, of what power *does to* people, groups and societies, and *how* this impact comes about" (p.1–2, italics in text). And in Duchêne and Heller's *Language in Late Capitalism* (2012), power becomes ambivalent as it has to balance the two contradictory pressures of national pride and global profit. The authors show how, in the new globalized economy, nation-states and their citizens navigate the demands of pride and profit to legitimize the two opposing discourses of the symbolic and the economic within a capitalistic framework.

While the work of sociolinguists like David Block (2018), Duchêne and Heller (2012) and Heller and McElhinny (2017) have put political economy on the map of second language studies, and reminded us of the economic forces and financial interests at work in the learning and teaching of foreign languages, the populist trends in various countries of the world are showing that economic conditions are only a trigger for much deeper cultural and symbolic power struggles. The narratives of the "forgotten-voices-of-the-downtrodden-left-out-by-globalization" are easily appropriated by populist politicians and reoriented toward age-old resentment against immigrants, racial minorities and anyone who challenges traditional gender hierarchies. The growing economic inequalities that have been brought about by globalization and have been extensively documented by sociologists like Thomas Piketty (2014), and the scholars mentioned earlier in this paragraph are being exploited by a populist rhetoric that taps into far more symbolic deficits than only economic ones, for example, lack of symbolic capital, loss of social and cultural pride, and lack of visibility on the global stage. Language becomes not only a means of economic advancement, but a means of cultural and ideological, that is, symbolic power as well. This book aligns itself with the post-modern critical tradition in the study of the relationship of language and symbolic power in applied linguistics, particularly in language education.

The field of research called "applied linguistics" emerged after World War II from the need to learn and teach English and other languages around the world.[9] It was famously defined by Christopher Brumfit as "the theoretical and empirical investigation of real-world problems in which language is a central issue" (Brumfit 1997:93). Since its inception, it has focused heavily on language learning and teaching, and Henry Widdowson has called the "problem-solving accountability" of the field an aspect of applied linguistics which "alone justifies its existence in the first place" (Widdowson 2018:142). Indeed, accountability to the practitioners is what distinguishes applied linguistics from theoretical linguistics or psycho- and sociolinguistics, even though scholars in these fields are also called upon to consult with practitioners in the real world.

Why then, when a growing number of applied linguists have expanded the notion of language, language learning and language use towards post-structuralist, ecological and even post-modern approaches, are language teachers, administrators and textbook publishers still adhering mostly to a code-centered, structuralist view of grammar and vocabulary learned and practiced in communicative activities? (Kramsch and Zhang 2018). To start exploring this complex question, I focus in this book on an aspect of language that has been consistently silenced in language learning and teaching, namely the social symbolic aspects of language, those that have to do not just with the capacity to make yourself understood but with the capacity to make yourself listened to, taken seriously, respected and valued – namely symbolic power. As we shall see throughout the book, the issue of language as symbolic power cuts across theory and practice, language use and language learning and is thus central to the mission of applied linguistics.

One caveat is in order, however – a caveat that I always state explicitly on the syllabus of the course on which this book is based (see Acknowledgments). While I draw on scholars from sociology, philosophy, and cultural studies such as Bourdieu, Foucault, de Certeau, Bakhtin and Butler, in addition to scholars in linguistics and applied linguistics, it is beyond the scope of this book to offer an in-depth critical discussion of any one of these authors. They have been chosen here because they have in many ways responded to one another's theories regarding the specific relation of language and symbolic power, and they have helped me conceptualize the arc of an argument that goes from structuralist/functional linguistics to post-structuralist applied linguistics. Chapter 9 opens up avenues for further critical readings of these scholars' rich and multifaceted writings.

1.5 LANGUAGE AS SYMBOLIC POWER IN LANGUAGE EDUCATION

As a particular area of applied linguistics, language education has to deal with three issues of concern: normativity, ethics and political answerability. Throughout the book, we will be discussing each of these issues and the questions they raise regarding the distribution of symbolic power in educational settings.

Normativity

Because of globalization and the explosion of social media, the issue of normativity has become one of the central issues in the teaching of modern languages. Which grammatical, semantic, pragmatic norms should be taught to prepare learners for today's multilingual world? One of the current approaches to language education, developed by the New London Group under the term "multiliteracies" (New London Group 2000), has emphasized the teaching for meaning and the multiplicity of perspectives in the meaning-making process. Under the banner of multilinguality and diversity of learning styles, of social and cultural identities and norms of language use, it has broadened the concept of the monolingual native speaker and has challenged the preeminence of the verbal over the multimodal in the making of meaning. The concept of multiliteracies has been applied to the teaching of foreign languages as relational pedagogy (Kern 2015:233); it has focused on the embodied nature of learning and the need to pay attention to the psychological and emotional dimensions of a language learner's subjectivity (Pavlenko 2000; Kramsch 2009a; Dewaele 2010; McNamara 2019).

However, because many language educators still hold a structuralist view of language, they are primarily focused on how linguistic signs make conventional meanings, not how speakers and writers get into power struggles over their interpretation. They engage their students more in the construction of various semiotic processes of an iconic, indexical or symbolic kind than in the arduous process of negotiating a social meaning *addressed to someone in some unfamiliar social context.* Symbolic power struggles emerge from this presence of the Other, who might interpret things differently and might not even see the need for negotiating anything. Pierre Bourdieu captured this dimension of language in a quote that has inspired applied linguists such as Bonny Norton (1995), Aneta Pavlenko (2004:48) and others who fight for immigrants' and other minorities' "right to speak" and to "impose reception," Bourdieu writes:

> Language is not only an instrument of communication or even of knowledge, but also an instrument of power. One seeks not only to be understood but also to be believed, obeyed, respected, distinguished. Whence the complete definition of competence as *right to speak,* that is, as right to the legitimate language, the authorized language, the language of authority. Competence implies the power to impose reception. (Bourdieu 1977:645, cited in Thompson 1984:46–47)

By "legitimate language" Bourdieu meant standard Parisian French as it is taught in schools and recognized as the only respectable way of speaking in French public life, but every community has its own legitimate ways with words that it imposes on its members. What has often been misunderstood in anglophone readings of Bourdieu is his insistence on the cognitive aspects of this power to "impose reception." In order for speakers to impose reception, they have to activate cognitive schemas of perception and appreciation that are shared with their listeners.

> Symbolic acts always assume acts of knowledge (*connaissance*) and recognition (*reconnaissance*), cognitive acts on the part of their

> recipients. For a symbolic exchange to function, the two parties have to have identical categories of perception and appreciation. (Bourdieu 1998:100)

The issue of normativity in language education is bound up with the power struggle between native and non-native speakers of the language who might not share identical categories of perception and appreciation. Who has the legitimacy to impose their rules for the proper use of language and the appropriate use of silences? The native speaker? The educational system? The mass media? The social media?[10]

Ethics

The second issue that is surfacing in language education, ethics, is linked to the issue of normativity. Deciding which norms to teach and implement is not just a question of observing the linguistic rules and conventions of a speech community; it is adhering to the moral values that those rules represent. Perceptions of grammaticality and social appropriateness are immediately coupled with judgments of social worth, euphemistically concealed behind instrumental or aesthetic reasons. One day, a male Spanish colleague teaching his native language at an engineering school in France asked his female students what a Spaniard had to do to seduce a French woman. They all agreed: "*Il faut qu'il parle bien*" [he has to speak well]. Not sexy behavior, not grammatically correct sentences, but "*parler bien*," that is, speak with eloquence, tact, class, what Bourdieu would call "distinction." Speaking grammatically correctly was clearly not enough.

Indeed, the moral universe of language education is likely to vary from one educational culture to another. In Europe, Michael Byram's critical cultural awareness or *savoir s'engager* is based on the following common moral values: willingness to engage with otherness in a relation of equality, focus on effectiveness not identity, importance of negotiation, capacity to take part in public debate, to argue and to resolve conflicts in accordance with the principles of democratic law (Byram 2008). But in Singapore ethics are viewed differently. Language education like all education is based on the moral responsibility to "fully realize the value of your human capital on the global stage" (De Costa et al. 2016:697). Within an educational system that privileges individual achievement and competition, the moral values are: self-reliance, innovation, creativity, boldness and a willingness to take risks and to accept responsibility for one's actions. Economic incentives for learning the language of the Other are seen as no longer sufficient, students have to align themselves with "the moral imperative to strategically exploit language-related resources for enhancing their worth in the world" and become "linguistic entrepreneurs" (ibidem). In China, historically the learning of foreign languages has tended to raise questions about the learners' "morality" because it was associated with the danger of westernization (Gao 2018a, b). But recently since the Chinese Dream speech delivered by President Xi in late 2012, language education is seen as acceptable or even desirable, provided it can be construed as an asset, rather than a liability, in the nationalistic project (De Costa et al. 2016:700). To what extent can the language teacher teach different cultural moralities? And what is the ethical responsibility of the teacher in the classroom regarding students' speaking rights, the right to talk about controversial topics, to criticize the textbook or to disregard institutional expectations?

Political Answerability

The third issue that most language educators shy away from – at least in the classroom – is politics. Some educational institutions actually prohibit their teachers from discussing politics in language classrooms for fear of creating division. But it is one thing to discuss party politics and another to discuss historical and social power relationships. In his book *Aux bords du politique* (1998:15), the French philosopher Jacques Rancière makes the distinction between *la politique* and *le politique*. In both cases, the word "politics" (from Gr.*polis*, city) denotes the exercise of power in the "reasoned management of the interests of a community" (*gestion avisée des intérêts d'une communauté*). But *la politique* has come to refer to the fight among political parties for winning elections or from a leader for taking and maintaining the power to govern. It also refers to the geopolitical game of gaining, using or wasting political capital vis a vis other nations, using your leverage to obtain favors, making alliances and generally serving the interests of your country and of international peace. *Le politique*, by contrast, refers to the exercise of symbolic power as the very principle that regulates the possibility of living together (*vivre ensemble*) in a shared community. Language educators have the responsibility of exploring the workings of *le politique* in the daily verbal and non-verbal transactions that their students will conduct in everyday life as soon as they leave their classroom.[11]

The recurring question is then: What are we teaching languages for? Increasingly the focus on linguistic accuracy, appropriateness and fluency is not sufficient to participate in the complex symbolic worlds of today. Current calls among applied linguists for bringing back literature (Hall 2015; Paran and Robinson 2016), translation (Kramsch and Huffmaster 2008; Cook 2010; Laviosa 2014), reflexivity (Byrd Clark and

Dervin 2014), and critical intercultural awareness (Guilherme and de Souza 2019) in language education are responding to the concerns of people who are learning a language not just for instrumental reasons, but because they want to understand something about language itself and how it is being used and abused in our global times. They can be shown that symbolic power can be reflected upon and talked about in the classroom, whether it be through literary texts or newspaper reports, through the analysis of real conversational data, or through a joint reflection on the very dynamics of classroom interaction. Such a reflection can lead them to become researchers of their own language use and that of the people around them.

I.6   ORGANIZATION OF THE BOOK

The book is divided into three parts: Part I discusses the power of symbolic representation. It draws on linguistic and semiotic insights into the workings of language as one symbolic system among others. It shows how the use of linguistic signs gives us the power to categorize, signify and interpret the world, and to construct and manipulate meanings that will make us respected as legitimate speakers, narrators and architects of larger discourses that are both within and beyond our control. Part II deals with the power of symbolic action. It draws on sociolinguistic and critical applied linguistic research on the social interaction rituals of everyday life. It shows the many ways we do things with words and exercise symbolic power and even symbolic violence on others even if we do not intend to do so; it considers a special case of symbolic warfare, that is, the weaponization of language to fight political opponents, and various forms of resistance. Part III turns to the power to create symbolic reality. It draws on post-structuralist and post-modern theories of language as discourse and on their manifestations in today's digital communication practices. It shows the power we wield as users of the new technologies not only to create identities and disseminate information but also to engage with and respond to acts of symbolic violence in new and unexpected ways. The concluding chapter summarizes the argument made throughout the book and considers implications for applied linguistic research and practice.

Each chapter opens with an introductory incident that encapsulates the theme of the chapter and provides a rhetorical structure for its discussion. It then shows how this theme has been conceptualized by some of the major post-structuralist scholars who have studied the relation of language and symbolic power from a variety of disciplines: linguistics and sociolinguistics, communication and media studies, semiotics and social semiotics, information technologies and network theory, discourse analysis and CDA. It provides in-depth analyses of relevant examples taken from current politics and from everyday life.

Much of what is presented in this book does not assume any prior knowledge on the part of the reader. Some readers will recognize elements of language studies that they know already from having taken a course in linguistics or sociolinguistics. Although the book is not meant as a textbook for language teachers, it provides an opportunity to revisit some of the notions that applied linguists have traditionally associated with communicative language teaching, but are seen here as imbricated in relations of symbolic power. By linking each of these elements to the notion of symbolic power, I hope to further enrich the remit of language educators and make the teaching and learning of languages more relevant to the complex world they are preparing their students for. Some additional readings are suggested at the end of each chapter. A glossary is given at the end of the book.

SUGGESTIONS FOR FURTHER READING

This book views language as discourse and as such it aligns itself with Hanks (1996), Johnstone (2018) and Scollon et al. (2012) by focusing on meaning-making practices in their social context. For a deeper understanding of Bourdieu's theory of symbolic power, see Bourdieu (1977a, 1977b, 1991, 2000). Symbolic power intervenes in all the areas researched by applied linguists. As a field concerned with solving problems associated with the acquisition and use of language in the real world, applied linguistics is a field of research extensively documented in Simpson (2011) and Chapelle (2012). A good insight into the uses and abuses of symbolic power can be found not only in interactions in real life, but also in plays and prose such as the classics Beckett (2012), Dürrenmatt (1973), Jackson (2008), Kafka (1971), Miller (1971), Osborne (1993) and Pinter (1988).

PART I
The Power of Symbolic Representation

1 "I Speak, Therefore I Am"

WHAT'S IN A WALL?

Consider the following incident of the Trump presidency that divided the country and partially paralyzed the U.S. government in December 2018 and January 2019. One of the major promises of candidate Trump on the campaign trail for the U.S. presidency was that he was going to build a wall on the southern border of the United States to keep out what he called: "Mexican rapists, drug dealers, criminals" and other illegal immigrants.[1] The idea of a border wall was the brainchild of his political advisers who were looking for a mnemonic device to make sure that their candidate – who hated reading from a script but loved boasting about his talents as a builder – would remember to talk about getting tough on immigration, which was to be a signature issue in his nascent campaign. "How do we get him to continue to talk about immigration?" they said. "We're going to get him to talk about how he's going to build a wall (Gunderman, 2016)."

During his presidential campaign, Trump made his plans to build a "beautiful solid border wall" a central part of his platform: "I will build a great wall – and nobody builds walls better than me, believe me – and I'll build them [sic] very inexpensively. I will build a great, great wall on our southern border, and I will make Mexico pay for that wall" (ibidem).

A feature of Trump's rallies in 2016 and 2017 were crowds chanting "Build that wall!" After his party's defeat in the midterm elections of November 2018, the president appeared to back away from his promise, alternately referring to the planned wall as a "steel fence" or a "steel slat barrier." Indeed, the debate in which Trump and the Republican leadership engaged with congressional Democrats and which led to the longest government shutdown in history seemed to be an argument about language. In his morning tweets, Trump sought to blame the media for the discrepancy and said he still envisioned an "*all concrete*" wall in some areas but that a "*see through*" *barrier* at the

U.S.–Mexico border would be more appropriate in other areas based on what he had been told by "experts at Border Patrol." In mid-December, Trump further shifted his stance, arguing in a tweet: "we are not building a Concrete Wall, we are building *artistically designed steel slats*." Then, in a Christmas Day appearance in which he blamed Democrats for the government shutdown, Trump described the border barrier as "a wall or fence, whatever they'd like to call it." Senator Lindsey O. Graham (R-S.C.), one of Trump's close confidants, said that the president is seeking "a physical barrier along the border in places that make sense," asserting that "the wall has become a *metaphor for border security*."

By January, as the government shutdown was already in its fifth week, the new speaker of the House, Nancy Pelosi "quietly but directly called Mr. Trump out on his lying and 'fearmongering' about immigration ... and mocked his planned border wall as a 'beaded curtain' and 'a manhood thing for him.'" But more importantly, Donald Trump's linguistic waverings on how to name the wall became a symptom of political waffling that got both parties angry. For the Democrats, a wall was "immoral, un-American, and ineffective." For Trump's supporters, Donald Trump was breaking his campaign promise.[2]

Trump's semantic wavering also gave rise to multiple speculations as to the meaning of his obsession with the wall. Democrat columnist Frank Bruni wrote:

> It's funny that we are still talking about the physical features of what President Trump wants or will settle for on our country's southern border – about whether it will be concrete or steel, solid or slatted, a fancied-up fence or, in Nancy Pelosi's hilariously acerbic dig, a "beaded curtain." Because it's not really a wall that Trump is after, if indeed it ever was. It's a victory for victory's sake. It's a show of his might. It's proof of his potency.[3]

Republicans interpreted all this renaming of the wall as a negotiation opening. Mick Mulvaney, the acting White House chief of staff, said that while he thought the shutdown was "going to drag on a lot longer," Mr. Trump's shift in wall materials could provide a semantic opening to advance the talks. "If he has to give up a concrete wall, replace it with a steel fence in order to do that so that Democrats can say, 'See? He's not building a wall anymore', that should help us move in the right direction," Mr. Mulvaney said on NBC's *Meet the Press*. "If that's not evidence of the president's desire to try and resolve this, I don't know what is."[4]

In the end, some voices started to emerge that interpreted the debate about the wall as a symptom of something much bigger.

> The wall has become a metaphor to Mr. Trump and his millions of supporters. It represents a divide between "us" and "them", a physical demarcation for those who refuse to accept that in just a few decades, a majority of the country will be people of color. Mr. Trump promised it in 2015, in the same speech in which he announced his candidacy and called Mexican immigrants rapists, criminals and drug traffickers. His goal was to exploit the anxiety of voters in an increasingly multicultural, multiethnic society. Mr. Trump's wall is a symbol for those who want to make America white again. (Ramos 2019)

Three months later, after the president declared a national state of emergency but did not get from Congress the money he needed to build this wall, he backed off his threat to "close the entire border with Mexico" and announced: "We're really making progress at letting people know this is an emergency" and the Secretary of Homeland Security conceded that the focus on the wall was, partly, a stunt.

> Well, I think part of that is just a – it's an optic. To have the president stand in front of the wall indicates immediately to any viewer that he's at the border. But I think his message is about the dual crisis [security and humanitarian] and how we need Congress to act, to give us the authority to address [it].[5]

If I have dwelled rather extensively on this incident, it is because it illustrates many of the aspects of symbolic power that we will be dealing with in this chapter. Only a recognition of the symbolic nature of the wall can explain the intensity of the current debate and the virulence of the sentiments expressed. Will the United States be a monolingual and monocultural white nation or a multilingual multicultural society? What is at stake is not only the very identity of the nation but what the critic Abrahamian calls "the coming of the global citizen" (Abrahamian 2015). The very idea of national borders has been made complicated by technology and globalization. The real walls, Abrahamian argues, are not at a border, but in the digital, commercial, political forces that control us.

The term "symbolic" can have four meanings in its relation to language and power. The first is that language, like music or painting, is called a symbolic system because it is composed of signs and symbols that combine together in a rule-governed, systematic way to make meaning. The four letters of the sign w-a-l-l combined with the two other words in the string "build-that-wall" evoke in the minds of the listeners the concept of a prototypical structure erected to protect some people in and keep other people out. But symbolic systems not only refer to the real world, they structure things in people's minds by categorizing them (category: wall), making distinctions (wall vs. fence) and evaluating them (a beautiful wall). Thus, symbolic systems are at once structured (by syntactic, lexical, discourse rules), and they themselves structure our representations of the world. In this chapter, we first examine how this symbolic relation to things is what gives humans a power to represent reality that other living species do not have.

The wall incident also gives us a glimpse into a second meaning of the term "symbolic," namely the power of symbols to create semiotic relations of similarity, contiguity or conventionality with other symbols, that listeners interpret as such. For example, a wall can be imagined as "tall" because /tall/ sounds like or rhymes with /wall/ (iconic relation of similarity); it can be envisaged as solid and sturdy because of its close association with the sturdy walls of a house and with their function to protect and defend a family (indexical relation of contiguity); but a wall can also be seen as just an arbitrary word out of the dictionary, that might be called *mur* in French or *Mauer* in German (symbolic relation of conventionality). How the utterance "Build that wall" will be interpreted – whether iconically, indexically or symbolically – will depend on the relations the speakers and listeners create between the words uttered and other words or signs produced in that particular context, and in past or imagined ones.[6]

There is a third meaning of the term "symbolic" to be gleaned from this incident. The meanings given to the wall by the various actors are more or less conventional/arbitrary, more or less nonarbitrary or motivated by the actors' desire to pursue their own political interests. The power to manipulate the meaning of signs and to impose those meanings on others and make them "stick" is a symbolic power, because it acts not through physical force but through our mental representations as mediated by symbolic forms. As we shall see in the rest of this chapter and in Chapter 4 these representations will become embodied in the rituals of everyday life, including such rituals as electoral rallies at which the rhythmical "Build that wall!" slogan is chanted in unison by the crowds and reproduced by the media. The power of suggestion of these words does not come from such utterances alone, but from the indirect institutional legitimacy of the people who utter them as supporters of a *legitimately elected* president of the United States.

Finally, there is a fourth meaning to this incident that is rather puzzling. For all the hoopla about how to name the wall, Donald

Trump does not seem to care how it is called, provided he can declare that he will "build-a-wall" and declare the mission accomplished once it is "done." But what will be done? He recently admitted that words don't matter: "Wall or fence, whatever they'd like to call it" and "Never mind how you call it: a wall, a barrier, a fence, sleet slats. These are only words. What counts is action. I am a man of action." We have the uneasy feeling that his words are becoming unmoored from their conventional referents, so it becomes difficult to know how to interpret what he really means. Is it all symbolic posturing? Metaphoric spectacle? Display of potency? Reality TV?[7] We will need to examine the term "symbolic" as applied to the construction of meaning, and to its relationship to truth.

I discuss each of these four aspects of symbolic power – the power to signify, the power to interpret, the power to manipulate, the power to construct meaning – in the remainder of this chapter.

1.1 THE POWER TO SIGNIFY AND CATEGORIZE

Signification, Value, Indexicality

The challenge of meaning-making has been captured by linguists who study the structure of the linguistic system and cognitive linguists who study the relation between speaking and thinking. Most language-teaching textbooks take a Saussurean view of language. The linguistic sign, we are told, is formed of two parts like the two sides of a sheet of paper – the signifier or sound-image and the signified or concept. As "a two-sided psychological entity," it links together not "the material sound, a purely physical thing" and a specific object in the world, but "the psychological imprint of a sound, the impression it makes on our senses" and "an abstract concept" (Saussure 1959 p.66). So, if the teacher holds up a piece of chalk and says "This is a chalk," she is not quite correct. The sound /'tʃɔːk/ does not denote this particular piece of chalk, but rather it evokes in the minds of the learners the concept of a chalk that is in this case long, round and white, but might be in other classrooms thick, square and yellow and still be called "chalk." The combination of the sound /'tʃɔːk/ and its concept constitutes its signification. Linguists point out the important fact that the meaning of a sign lies not only in its signification (the relation between signifier and signified) but also in its value, that is, in its difference from other signs (e.g., it is similar in function, say, to a pen or a magic marker, but different from an eraser).

In addition to the structural aspect of signification and value, semioticians distinguish between two kinds of signification – denotative and connotative – to account for meanings that are referential and associative respectively. One might think that a piece of chalk has only a straightforward denotative meaning as "device for writing on blackboards" until someone says: "You want some chalk? Don't you have a laptop?" and you realize that using chalk to write on a blackboard might connote old-fashioned teaching practices. As Saussure says: "In language there are only differences" (Saussure 1959, p.120). Chalk, ballpoint pen, typewriter and computer *denote* different writing technologies, but they *connote* different degrees of technological sophistication.

If connotation is a term used by semioticians, indexicality is a term used by linguistic anthropologists to refer not just to conventional semantic associations of the Saussurean kind, or loose connotations, but to whole ways of talking that mirror the social stratifications found in society and the social, cultural and political views that speakers and writers hold. The phrase "order of indexicality" coined by Michael Silverstein (2003) refers to "stratified patterns of social meanings to which people orient when communicating" (Blommaert 2005a:253). For example, the word "invasion" at the southern border indexes on one rational level the entry of large numbers of people seeking asylum in the United States; on another, more emotional level, the word can index the take-over of territory, a hostile and illegitimate entry, or even an attack on our country by foreign armies out to kill us. The way people talk indexes much about who they are and which position they hold in the increasingly stratified American society.

Categories of the Embodied Mind

If words have the power to evoke abstract concepts like "chalks" and "blackboards" in someone's head, it is because these concepts are organized into cognitive categories that orient our thoughts according to the specific logic of a given language, for instance instruments vs. surfaces (writing on a blackboard), walls vs. screens that we have experienced through our minds and bodies. Anthropologists like Edward Sapir argued that "language is a guide to social reality," that it even "conditions all our thinking about social problems and processes" and that "the worlds in which different societies live are distinct worlds, not merely the same world with different labels attached."(Sapir 1949:69). Others went further and suggested that the language we speak not only guides, but determines the way we think, indeed makes us prisoners of the concepts it evokes in the mind (Whorf 1956).[8] This is without taking into account the work of interpretation and translation that we consider in the next section. As cognitive linguists like George Lakoff (1987, chapters 4 and 18) or Dan Slobin (1996) have argued, it is not that the way we speak determines the way we think, but that in order to speak at all, we need to think in categories that are (unconsciously) recognized and accepted by the members of a speech community. These categories are both linguistic (the way we speak) and cognitive (the way our mind works) and they are deeply embedded in our bodily experience (Johnson 1987; Varela et al. 1991).

Lakoff's Idealized Cognitive Models

For example, Trump's use of the sign /'wɔːl/ in "I will build a great wall" was available to him from the English language, but it came already organized into cognitive categories that went beyond just "support/ protection." The idealized cognitive model evoked by the word "wall" encompasses experiential categories like "inside/outside," "container/ contained," "inclusion/exclusion," "Self/Other." It elicits images of the Great Wall of China, Israel's border wall with the Palestinian territories, the Berlin Wall, all built to prevent invaders from coming in or, in the latter cases, residents from going out. The president started talking back his characterization of the wall ("I never proposed 2000 miles of concrete wall from sea to shining sea") and started proposing alternative names such as *steel wall, steel fence, steel slats, see-through-barrier*, in the hope that by changing the signifier he could change the signified in people's minds. But that did not take into account the power of the cognitive categories associated with these signifiers. They all evoked an idealized cognitive model of a prototypical barrier meant to keep out strangers, foreigners, outsiders, in short, people not like us, to protect Us against Them. Not only did this model contradict the model evoked by the Statue of Liberty welcoming immigrants to the shores of the New World, but, given the context in which Trump used the term, it seemed to restrict the Us vs. Them to white U.S.-born Americans vs. brown-skinned Latinos. It was perceived by many as a xenophobic and racist cognitive model.[9]

1.2 THE POWER TO INTERPRET

As Saussure sought to delineate the domain of linguistics, he distinguished between *langue*, the abstract linguistic system found in grammar books and dictionaries, and *parole*, the living language used by speakers and writers in everyday life. Because of the rule-governed nature of *langue* and the idiosyncratic nature of *parole*, he restricted the domain of linguistics to the study of *langue*. But if we consider language not just as linguistic system, but as communicative practice, we have to recognize that in practice *langue* and *parole* are inseparable. The symbolic forms or linguistic signs that constitute language as a symbolic system can be viewed by speakers and hearers either as type-level forms that are part of *langue*, that is, an abstract system, or as token-level relations that are part of *parole*, that is, actual utterances in context (Hanks 1996:45). As abstract types these signs are arbitrary, that is, they have no natural relation to what they designate, and their meaning depends entirely on social convention. Saussurean linguists study types and their structure. Sociolinguists and linguistic anthropologists study tokens and their use. As tokens of language use, these signs are non-arbitrary; they have iconic, indexical or symbolic relations to their objects (p.84).

Peirce's Interpretants

Whether an object is read as an icon, an index or a symbol depends on what the semiotician C.S. Peirce called "the interpretant," namely a second sign that enables a person to interpret the first (Van Lier 2004:68). For example, the sign "wall" might create in the minds of listeners another simple sign, for example, "STOP," or a larger signifying discourse, for example, "anti-immigration policies." This other sign, or interpretant, constitutes an "ideological horizon" (Hanks 1996:43) that helps the person make sense of what s/he hears. As the first sign stands for a concept or ideal type of object, the relation of that type to its specific token in the real world will be interpreted as being more or less similar to other tokens (or iconic), more or less contiguous to others (or indexical), or more or less conform to the type (or conventional). For example, upon hearing "I will build a wall," some people might imagine this wall to be iconically similar to the Great Wall of China keeping hordes of enemies at bay, and they might feel a sense of patriotic pride. Others might associate it indexically with caravans of poor asylum-seeking families and feel outraged. Yet others will remain on the conventional level of the dictionary or of conventional wisdom and take the utterance as an objective statement of fact. As we shall see in Chapter 4, one of the political strategies for negating the effects of symbolic power is taking words for their literal meaning alone and ignoring their indexical value. By trying to change the type-level form of the sign "wall" to make it more acceptable, rather than considering the token-level form of the sign's ideological horizon, Trump chose to remain on the symbolic conventional aspect of the sign and deliberately ignored its more contextual – iconic and indexical – aspects. In any case, as a token of the English language, the utterance "I will build a wall" will be interpreted by the listeners against the ideological horizon of their experience and knowledge of the world. It will therefore inevitably elicit a personal reaction (fear and hatred of immigrants or outrage at the one who uttered those words).[10]

Semiotic vs. Symbolic Relations

It is important here to distinguish between semiotic and symbolic relations. First, these three kinds of semiosis (meaning making process) are in a hierarchical relation to one another, the symbolic relation being the highest and including the indexical and the iconic. For example, the symbol *"wall"* can refer to an object made of brick-and-mortar but it cannot avoid evoking lower semiotic levels, such as an image in the mind, or association with other symbols like *"exclusion"* or *"protection"* depending on one's political views.

Second, while all three semiotic relations need to be interpreted, symbols are addressed to someone and require that addressee's interpretation. While icons have an immediate and direct impact on the viewer, symbols have more complex meanings precisely because they can also be read iconically and indexically. Hence the need for a relational thinking and interpretive power that chimpanzees, for example, do not have. People might disagree on how to interpret the indexical relations evoked by the word "wall," but the symbolic power of an utterance such as "build that wall!" repeated in unison at a campaign rally depends on the supporters recognizing the legitimacy of the author of these words in a democratic society. This legitimacy is also supported by the crowd's belief in what the philosopher Paul Grice (1975) has called "the cooperative principle" in conversation understood as exchange of information. At first glance, it seems as if Donald Trump consistently flouts Grice's four basic maxims of quantity (don't say more than required), quality (be clear), sincerity (be sincere) and relevance (be relevant), in the same manner as he revels in breaking all expectations of normal social behavior. He repeats himself and says much more than is required to convey his message, his use of words is vague and obfuscating, his sincerity is questionable and so is the relevance of his utterances to the good of anyone else than Donald J. Trump. But upon second thought, Trump's very disregard for Gricean maxims is a sign that his discourse is not meant to inform his supporters, but to appeal to their emotions, fuel their outrage and present himself as a savior above the norms of civil discourse.

Third, symbols function in combination with other symbols (Saussure's combinatory or syntagmatic principle) to form symbolic systems or codes. When combined with the indexical meanings of these other symbols, they are likely to develop not only idealized cognitive models of concepts, but "metapragmatic" or "metacultural" models of social reality as well, that is, recognizable types of persons or objects in recognizable situations (Silverstein 1976; Wortham 2006:32).[11] A wall to keep "Mexican rapists, drug dealers and criminals" out of the United States is one such metacultural model that Trump supporters adopt and with which they frame any news they hear about the wall. It has also, as we know, prompted some to take violent action against Latino immigrants and other minority groups in the United States.[12] Thus, while all three semiotic relations make meaning, they make it in different ways and with different effects.

Sapir's Condensation Symbols

Saying that symbols are conventional systems of reference is not to say that their meaning is arbitrary. As mentioned in the last section, a symbol at the type level is arbitrary, but the same symbol at the token level is not arbitrary at all. The word "wall" might be arbitrary as a symbol of the English linguistic system, but in Trump's mouth that same word carries with it all the iconicity and the indexicality of its context, and it is the result of the speaker's deliberate choice of words. Trump knew what reaction he would elicit from his supporters by having them repeat the phrase: "Build a wall." That phrase became more than a conventional linguistic symbol. It became what Edward Sapir called a "condensation symbol, whose actual significance is out of all proportion to the apparent triviality of meaning suggested by its mere form" (Sapir 1934:493). Sapir explains the two different kinds of symbolism. The first is referential symbolism, manifested in "oral speech, writing, the telegraph code, national flags and other organizations of symbols which are agreed upon as economical devices for purposes of reference" (Sapir 1934:493). The second type of symbolism is condensation symbolism "a highly condensed form of substitutive behavior for direct expression, allowing for the ready release of emotional tension in conscious or unconscious form." He adds: "In actual behavior both types are generally blended" (Sapir 1934:493).

Any symbol can become a condensation symbol. Even seemingly purely referential educational practices as conventionalized spelling and standard pronunciation, can easily become the object of violent debates and substitutive forms of emotional expression among educators and the public at large. In the case of Trump's wall, it is interesting to see how a simple phrase, "build a wall," scribbled on a notepad by his advisers as a purely mnemonic device to remind the presidential candidate to talk about immigration at his rallies, could be turned into a condensation symbol so potent that it caused the government to shut down for more than a month, taking hostage in its symbolic grip both the president and the nation at large.

Condensation symbols can emerge especially in times of danger and threat. For example, before September 11, 2001, wearing an American flag pin on your lapel meant nothing more than that you were an American. The flag referred to a nation called "the U.S.A." and that was the nation you belonged to. After the attacks on the World Trade Center, the lapel pin ceased to be simply a sign, it became a condensation symbol for patriotism and even national loyalty. The fact that Barack Obama did not wear an American flag lapel pin when he campaigned for the presidency in 2007 raised eyebrows and Republicans started putting into question his loyalty to the United States. Some, like Donald Trump, insisted on seeing his birth certificate. Obama relented and started wearing the pin again, but it is interesting to read what his reasons had been for not doing so.

> WATERLOO, Iowa – Democratic presidential candidate Barack Obama, D-Ill., said he will no longer wear an American flag lapel pin because it has become a substitute for "true patriotism" since the Sept. 11, 2001, terrorist attacks. "My attitude is that I'm less concerned about what you're wearing on your lapel than what's in your heart," he told the campaign crowd Thursday. "You show your patriotism by how you treat your fellow Americans, especially those who serve. You show your patriotism by being true to our values and ideals. That's what we have to lead with is our values and our ideals, [...] The truth is that right after 9/11 I had a pin. But shortly after 9/11, particularly because we're talking about the Iraq war, that became a substitute for I think true patriotism, which is speaking out on issues that are of importance to our national security."[13]

Here we have the clash between two symbolic systems: on the one hand, pins, flags and other symbolic devices that can quickly become shibboleths, that is, words or objects used to test your legitimacy and exert control over you as a member of a social group; on the other hand, symbolic action such as speaking out on important issues and leading with values and ideals. In a sense, Obama is discarding the use of concrete objects like flags and words and prefers to focus on verbal action as a sign of "true patriotism." This is the opposite of what Trump does when he insists on seeing Obama's lapel pin and birth certificate in order to give him legitimacy. The controversies over lapel pins and border walls are part of larger symbolic political struggles that are increasingly consuming the public sphere as people and nations are trying to accommodate to the new global realities that threaten the integrity of nation states.

1.3   THE POWER TO MANIPULATE

We have seen how a populist politician, backed by the power of the presidency, has the power to transform a string of conventionally accepted linguistic signs like "to build a wall" into a powerful condensation symbol that won him the election in 2016. The fundamental ambiguity of symbolic reference that can be interpreted in different ways, as type or token, and as iconic, indexical or symbolic relation, enabled him to switch in and out of levels of interpretation, and eventually impose onto others the meaning that best suited his interests – in this case, the liberty to flout linguistic expectations and to make words irrelevant.

Barthes' Myth

The French semiologist and literary critic Roland Barthes conceptualized the way that a referential symbol becomes a condensation symbol, which he called "myth" (Barthes 1972). Myth, he said, is a linguistic sign whose meaning has been slightly displaced from a first semiological chain consisting of: signifier + signified = (arbitrary) sign, to a second semiological chain composed of the first sign, that now becomes the signifier of this second chain, combined with a totally non-arbitrary, highly motivated signified to form a non-arbitrary second sign. Consider, for example, Barthes' famous example of the cover of the June/July 1955 issue of the French weekly *Paris-Match* featuring a Black African youngster saluting the French flag at a big military show in Paris. The first semiological chain links a signifier s1 (a photograph) with a signified s2 (West African youngster, called Diouf from Ouagadougou (Burkina-Faso), shown saluting the flag) to form a sign S (saluting Black African youngster). The second semiological chain empties S of its historicity; it makes S into a new signifier s'1 (saluting Black African youngster) linked to a new signified s'2 (subject of the French colonial empire showing allegiance to the French flag) to construct a new S' (French imperiality).[14] Barthes called this new S' "myth," in order to underscore its dubious relationship to historical reality and factual truth. With his promise to "build on the southwest border a 'great, beautiful' wall that 'Mexico will pay for' in the name of 'border security,'" Trump plays with two semiological chains: the first referential chain of facts (building a wall jointly with Mexico to ensure security at the border) and the second symbolic chain of myths (a *"Wall"* that *"Mexico"* will *"pay for"* for greater *"border security"*). It is that second chain that indexes for Democrats an unacceptable manifestation of xenophobia, vengeance and nationalism.

Myth, Barthes says, is "speech stolen and restored," that is, speech emptied of its historicity and of the fundamental ambiguity of its many connotations. Indeed, it transforms connotation into denotation and imposes on the addressees only one denotational meaning. Trump's reference to his addressees as "the-American-people" mythifies the sign "people" by deliberately ignoring its many other meanings such as "national community," "U.S. citizenry," "multilingual/multicultural society," and imposing only one meaning or myth, namely "America-first populists." But of course such a symbolic transformation by a single actor may become part of public meaning or standardized interpretation only if the "semantic manipulator has sufficient power, authority, prestige or legitimacy to make his interpretation stick" (Turner 1975:154). As we know, such a legitimacy is often contested and not only in the higher echelons of political power. Whether between parents and children, teachers and students, native and non-native speakers, bosses and employees, and even among children in the playground, meaning is constantly being negotiated. But, unlike what many language educators may think, the negotiability of symbolic forms is due not so much to the imperfect fit between the form and the content of an utterance, but mainly to the multiplicity of alternatives and the range of interpretations, manipulations and choices available to social actors.

Semiological Manipulation

As a semiologist, Barthes' was fascinated and angered by the increased use of publicity for marketing purposes that was slowly taking hold in the Europe of the 1950's. Having attended the Steichen photograph exhibition "The Family of Man" that was showing in Paris at the time, he was angry at seeing human beings, who had slaughtered each other across the globe during World War II only a few years back, now depicted as a "family." The exhibition, which featured human beings in all walks of life, born and dying, playing and working, laughing and crying, was technically superb and the desire for peace that its title conveyed was admirable, but for a Frenchman, who had just lived through five years of fascist Vichy ideology under the motto "Travail, famille, patrie" [Work, Family, Fatherland], the family metaphor was tainted. He felt that it had become a conservative "myth" designed by the American exhibit producers to counter the socialist myth of international brotherhood and was thus part of the symbolic warfare that the United States was waging against the Soviet Union. In the same manner that this exhibit projected a politically conservative message, the young African on the cover of *Paris Match* projected a colonialist message, meant to reinforce the symbolic power of the French colonial system, and the PANZANI ad for Italian pasta reinforced the power of free market capitalism (Barthes 1977:33). All three images were part of a system of domination that used symbolic representation to further its political and ideological agenda.

Of course, myths as manipulative symbols are not only used for nefarious purposes. At the end of his essay "Myth Today," Barthes acknowledges that the mythical imagination is one of the essential characteristics of the human species. The power to create myths is the basis not only of obfuscating propaganda and murderous ideologies, but also the source of religious faith, poetic beauty and literary truths. In fact, says Barthes, myth can only be countered with other myths, not with objective facts. As a literary critic, Barthes felt that verbal art had a responsibility to "say the world" as it saw it, rather than persuading the world how it should be or how people should see it. Hence his quest for non-instrumental, non-interested uses of language. He believed that there could be in certain literary forms a "zero degree" instrumentality (Barthes 1982). His dream of a language that would just express the world, not try to manipulate, persuade or seduce it has been shared by many poets and artists. It has produced some of the most moving poetry, precisely because, as Auden wrote about the death of W. B. Yeats,

> [. . .] poetry makes nothing happen: it survives
> In the valley of its making where executives
> Would never want to tamper, flows on south
> From ranches of isolation and the busy griefs,
> Raw towns that we believe and die in; it survives,
> A way of happening, a mouth.
>
> (Auden 1940)

1.4 THE POWER TO CONSTRUCT MEANING

Indeed, what is then the difference between a PANZANI pasta ad, which makes us see tomatoes, cheese and nutmeg in a different way and makes us dream of Italian beaches, sun and *dolce vita* while we are eating our spaghetti, and a beautiful poem that moves us to tears? Don't both appeal to our senses and our imagination, one through visual, the other through verbal symbolic forms?

Jakobson's Poetic Power

It was around the time of Barthes' *Mythologies* that the linguist and semiologist Roman Jakobson started searching for the stylistic principle that myths and literature had in common (Jakobson 1960). What makes a text "literary?", he asked; what is this literariness (*literaturnost'*) that is common to poems, advertisements and political slogans and gives them the power to touch people and move them to action? After identifying six components of the communicative situation – the addresser, the addressee, the message, the contact, the channel, and the content, he came to the conclusion that it was the focus on the message itself, its self-referentiality, that distinguished the literary text from other forms of text. The literary quality of a poem, ad or slogan appeals to both the perceptual and the symbolic self by drawing attention to its symbolic structure. Consider, for example, the following short poem by Emily Dickinson (1993:13):

> A word is dead
> When it is said,
> Some say.
> I say it just
> Begins to live
> That day.

This poem refers to a familiar *content* (words spoken, people speaking) and to an *addresser* (the lyrical I) making *contact* with an *addressee* reader/listener (some say, I say) through the *channel* of the printed page. But what makes this poem particularly striking is the way it draws attention to its style: the way the words are arranged on the page, the carefully crafted parallelisms, the rhymes, the choice of simple vocabulary. There is nothing arbitrary about the signs on the page. The choice and alignment of the words obey the principle of equivalence of any linguistic utterance, that is, the slots in the first sentence are filled by linguistic structures that fit into the syntax of the English language, that is, subject (a word), verb (is), predicate (dead). But there is one major difference: the word "said" in the second line (instead of "uttered" or "written") does not depend only on an idea the poet had in her head, but was deliberately chosen to rhyme with "dead" in the first line and to contrast with "say" in the third. The word "dead" itself at the end of line 1 anticipates the antonym "live" at the end of line 5, thus creating a dynamic tension within the poem that is both stylistic and ideational. It is through this poetic structure that we understand the poem to be about the life and death of language as used by speakers in everyday life. What makes this text a poem is not exclusively its referential content, but the dynamic style of its message. Indeed, Jakobson notes that while "dead" (a predicate) and "said"(a verb) are not equivalent paradigms in linguistic terms, they are equivalent in sound, position and shape (four letters), in the same way that the words "dead/said" that start the poem are the (negative) equivalent of the words "to live/that day" that close the poem. Because it is a poem, we tend to interpret these signs as symbols with a deeper metaphorical meaning than just their referential truth. For instance, we may attribute significance to the simplicity of its vocabulary as a metaphor for the simplicity of truth.

The Power of the Political Slogan

To what extent is the symbolic power of this poem any different from that of advertisements, slogans or political pronouncements? Consider, for example, the following slogan chanted by Trump and his supporters at the many rallies he has conducted as president:

TRUMP:	And who is going to pay for the wall?
CROWD (ON CUE):	Mexico!
TRUMP (CUPPING HIS EARS):	Again. WHO is going to pay for the wall?
CROWD:	MEXICO!
TRUMP:	Yeah! We are going make MEXICO pay for that wall!

The rhythmic repetition of the rhetorical question and the chorus response of the crowd provide an additional meaning to what originally might have been heard as a statement of fact. Making Mexico "pay for the wall" is no longer just meant as having Mexico foot the bill, but as a way of punishing Mexico for supposedly sending its drug dealers, rapists and criminals across our borders and making Mexicans "pay for their crimes." The effect is not achieved through its truth value but through its incantatory resonances. As Jakobson (1960) noted, in poetry the principle of equivalence is projected from the axis of selection onto the axis of combination, that is, the choice of words and their sequence on the syntagmatic axis is not determined by their paradigmatic referential content (their dictionary definitions), but by the formal properties of the exchange (rhythmic chanting and repetition building up to a crescendo of popular frenzy) similar to an audiolingual sentence completion drill. What Trump is doing by using such a rhetorical strategy is to turn "Mexico" into a myth (a country of criminals). "Pay" no longer denotes a monetary procedure but gets turned into a metaphor that indexes revenge and punishment. Indeed, Mexico never agreed to foot the bill and the U.S. Congress never appropriated the funds. But the rhythmical to and fro of the mob's slogan enacts the ritual beating that Trump vows to administer Mexico at its southern border and is of one piece with the physical abuses of asylum seekers that are happening there.

The Power of Genre

What's the difference, then, between Trump's and Dickinson's discourses? It is useful to remember that symbols, myths and poetry are not symbolic in themselves, but are interpreted as such. We are moved by the poem because we read it *as a poem*, and do not expect it to report on facts and objective truths. We expect poems to put us in a certain mood, to reveal truths that cannot be expressed directly in so many words. By contrast, we don't usually read a presidential statement for its poetic qualities, unless we are discourse analysts or communication scholars. In marketing publicity, we are ready to be persuaded, even seduced by the product an ad is selling and to go and buy it, but its mythic quality had better be concealed (as in Packard 1957) or else we might not buy the product.

That is where we go back to the expectations of the speech community we started with in the Saussurean model of language. We have seen that the meaning of a word is to be found not only in the link between the sound-image and the concept it represents, but also in its value as compared to other words within the same speech system. Furthermore, when seen as communication, these words are not just labels but cognitive categories that index other words that people use to interpret what they hear. This is why a speech community is necessary not only to create a linguistic system called English or French, but also to interpret the use of this linguistic system in communicative practice. When Saussure wrote that "The community is necessary if values that owe their existence solely to usage and general acceptance are to be set up, by himself the individual is incapable of fixing a single value" (Saussure 1959:113), he suggested that the individual cannot fix the meaning of any given word without knowing what the context, that is, the situation, the genre, the participants, expects it to be.

In the case of Dickinson's poem and Trump's political statement, it is the *genre* that embodies the expectations of their respective speech communities and that determines how these two texts will be interpreted. Hence the uncertainty about the speech genres of some of Trump's pronouncements and the dismay of the media at the president not speaking the truth. By conflating the genres of the business deal, the religious exhortatory, the political stump speech, and the TV show, Trump is disrupting the very basis of his speech community and its common interpretation of events.[15]

1.5 "EIN TISCH IST EIN TISCH." REALLY?

In each of the sections so far we have seen that the power to signify, interpret, manipulate and construct meaning through signs does not come from just referring to objects in the world. It comes from being aware of the relation between the two parts of a sign and of its relation to the other signs that it evokes in people's minds. But most of all it comes from having the power to have those signs recognized and accepted by members of a speech community. It is ultimately the community of language users that is the only social guarantor of a linguistic system, even if scientists, marketing strategists and poets constantly try to push the boundaries of language to make it say new things.[16]

The story by the Swiss author Peter Bichsel "*Ein Tisch ist ein Tisch*" [A table is a table] (Bichsel 1969) is a humorous illustration of what it means to push those boundaries. An old man in a gray coat, gray hat and gray trousers leading a lonely life in some furnished room in a little gray town decides one day to bring about some change in his life by renaming all the furniture in his room. After all, he thinks, the French call a bed "lit," a picture "tableau" and a chair "chaise," so why can't I? So he starts calling his bed "picture," the chair "alarm clock," the table "carpet," and the newspaper "bed." In the morning he stays longer in the picture, sits on the alarm clock and eats his breakfast on the carpet while reading the bed. This discovery made him all excited. At last life was becoming interesting! Soon he had invented a whole new language that gave him so much pleasure that he hardly went out anymore. After a while, he did go out, but he had to laugh when people said "Nice weather today" or "Are you going to the football game?" for he no longer understood what they were talking about. Not only could he not understand other people, but he could not share his excitement about his new discovery for they couldn't understand him. So he stopped talking. In the end, he only talked to himself and didn't even greet people anymore.

This story, written in 1969, was a staple text in beginning German language textbooks in the U.S. before the advent of communicative language teaching because of the simplicity of its language. It was meant also to counter the belief of many beginning learners that words are just a bunch of labels for the familiar furniture of the universe. It would be viewed today as a cautionary tale for anyone who wants to learn how to communicate in a foreign language. However, it raises a more complex question that language teachers have avoided asking: What prevented the Swiss people from learning the old man's language? After all, they were willing to learn French or English in school, so why couldn't the old man teach them his language? What does it take to change the linguistic habits of a speech community? Chapter 2 attempts to respond to these questions by further discussing the power of social actors to represent social reality.

SUGGESTIONS FOR FURTHER READING

As the father of structuralism, Saussure (1916, chapter 1 and chapters 4–5) is essential for understanding the linguistic sign and the post-structuralist critics of Saussure in the 1970's and 19'80s. Deacon (1997, part I) offers a necessary semiotic supplement to Saussure that helps understand how symbolic power comes into the picture. C. S. Peirce (1992, 1998) is a notoriously difficult read, but van Lier (2004) offers an accessible overview of Peircean semiotics. The classical essay on language by Sapir (1949) adds the anthropological perspective. Together these four readings provide the foundation for a discussion of the symbolic in symbolic power. Sapir's essay on the status of linguistics as a science (1949) and Whorf (1991) are crucial to understanding the relation of language, thought and our embodied self. Lakoff (1987, chapter 18), Kramsch (2004), Slobin (1996) and the papers in Gumperz and Levinson (1996) show that language relativity is today a well-accepted phenomenon that adds to the complexity of communication across cultures. For a good discussion of orders of indexicality and the metapragmatic organization principle, see Blommaert (2010, chapter 2). Voloshinov (1973) is not an easy read, but he provides a crucial backdrop to Bakhtin, discussed in Chapter 9, and so does Schultz (1990). Those interested in myth and how it remains at work in the present day should read Barthes (1972, 1977), Ricoeur (2016), as well as Basso (1990) and Hyde (1998).

2 The Power of Symbolic Representation

"LA RAISON DU PLUS FORT..."

In his 1988 book *Portrait of the King*, Louis Marin, a contemporary of Foucault and Bourdieu, analyzes the source of the King's absolute power under the reign of Louis XIV (1662–1715). Drawing on Pascal's commentaries, Marin asks the following questions: How does (brute) force become power and what role does discourse play in this transformation? What does the discourse of power look like? For this, Marin considers the following fable, published by Jean de la Fontaine, the well-known poet at Louis XIV's court in Versailles, in his collection of fables (1668–1694) and used since then in every schoolbook in French public schools.

> Le Loup et l'Agneau
> La raison du plus fort est toujours la meilleure:
> Nous l'allons montrer tout à l'heure.
> Un Agneau se désaltérait
> Dans le courant d'une onde pure.
> Un Loup survient à jeun qui cherchait aventure,
> Et que la faim en ces lieux attirait.
> Qui te rend si hardi de troubler mon breuvage?
> Dit cet animal plein de rage:
> Tu seras châtié de ta témérité.
> — Sire, répond l'Agneau, que Votre Majesté
> Ne se mette pas en colère;
> Mais plutôt qu'elle considère
> Que je me vas désaltérant
> Dans le courant,
> Plus de vingt pas au-dessous d'Elle;
> Et que par conséquent, en aucune façon
> Je ne puis troubler sa boisson.
> — Tu la troubles, reprit cette bête cruelle;
> Et je sais que de moi tu médis l'an passé.
> — Comment l'aurais-je fait si je n'étais pas né?
> Reprit l'Agneau; je tette encore ma mère.

— Si ce n'est toi, c'est donc ton frère.
— Je n'en ai point. — C'est donc quelqu'un des tiens;
Car vous ne m'épargnez guère,
Vous, vos bergers, et vos chiens.
On me l'a dit: il faut que je me venge.
Là-dessus, au fond des forêts
Le Loup l'emporte, et puis le mange,
Sans autre forme de procès.

The Wolf and the Lamb
The reason of the more powerful is always the best.
We will show it presently on the following case.
A Lamb was drinking at a brook
That was flowing downstream, pure and clean.
From the woods comes a wolf in search of adventure
His sharp hunger had drawn him to the scene.
Who makes you so bold as to muck up my beverage?
The creature snarls in rage.
You will pay for your impudence!
— Sire, the lamb replies, let not Your Majesty
Give in to unjust anger,
But instead please consider, Sire:
I'm drinking – just look –
In the brook
Twenty feet below Your Majesty, if not more,
And therefore in no way at all
Can I be muddying Your Majesty's drink.
— You are muddying it! insists the cruel beast.
And I know that, last year, you spoke ill of me.
— How could I do that? says the lamb.
I was not yet born. I am still suckling at my mother's breast.
— If it wasn't you, then it was your brother. All the worse.
— I don't have a brother. — Then it's someone else in your clan,
For to me you are all the same – a curse.
You, your shepherds and your dogs.
I've been told: I must take revenge.
And with that, deep into the wood,
The wolf drags the lamb and eats him up,
Without further judicial ado. (my translation)

Like Aesop's fables from which they are inspired, La Fontaine's fables use animal protagonists to illustrate human foibles and follies, and the power struggles that ensue. For example, the fable of "The frog who wants to make herself as a big as an ox" and ends up inflating herself to death makes fun of people who want to be someone they are not.[1] In "The fox and the crow," the fox manipulates the vanity of the crow to make him lose the cheese he holds in his beak by persuading him to show what a lovely voice he has; it makes fun of those who listen to flattery.[2] While in these two fables, the moral of the story comes at the end, the moral of "The wolf and the lamb" is given to us up front: "The reason of the more powerful is always the best/ We will show it presently on the following case." Indeed, readers might not understand the moral of a story in which a wolf eats up a lamb. Isn't it what wolves are wont to do? Where's the problem?

2.1   THE REASON OF THE MORE POWERFUL

The problem as stated by Marin is this: Why does the wolf need to argue with the lamb over more than twenty lines before he actually pounces on him and devours him? Why does he need to justify himself with moral arguments, find a reason to use the overwhelming physical superiority that he evidently has? Let's look at how he does this.

It is made clear from the start that the wolf is hungry and wants to kill the lamb in order to still his hunger. But he starts by engaging the lamb in what amounts to a rational, judicial procedure in order to justify his action. First, he accuses him of temerity or impudence, that is, not only for muddying the water but for behaving as if he were as entitled as the wolf to drink from that stream, thus framing his behavior from the start in terms of symbolic power differential. By declaring the water of the stream his property ("*my* beverage"), the wolf makes the lamb's crime a crime of *lèse Majesté*. The wolf adds insult to injury by using the derogatory second person pronoun *Tu* ("*tu seras châtié*"). The answer of the lamb addresses both accusations with unimpeachable deference and submission: physically the lamb cannot possibly muddy the wolf's water since he is drinking downstream from him; symbolically, the lamb gives all the signs necessary to show himself inferior to his accuser "*Sire... Votre Majesté* [Your Majesty]." Combined with the second person plural form of the pronoun, the third person form of address is here the ultimate sign of respect from a subject to his sovereign or a servant to his master (see "*Madame est servie*" [Her ladyship is served]). Unimpressed by the lamb's polite and rational arguments, the wolf brutally re-imposes his representation of things ("You are muddying it"), further using the insulting *Tu* form. His tactic from now on is going to seek to reverse the public perception of wolves and lambs by portraying himself as the victim, thus eliciting in the reader feelings of compassion that will attach them to him, not to the lamb.

If the first accusation had to do with an alleged attack against the wolf's authority, the second has to do with his reputation (his symbolic self), as he accuses the lamb of badmouthing him in the past. The lamb responds again with impeccable factual logic: "I wasn't yet born." The third accusation shifts from blaming the message to blaming the messenger: "If it's not you, then it's your brother" and again the lamb's response remains at the level of facts ("I don't have a brother"). After these three false accusations, the wolf changes tactics. Broadening his grievance to the lamb's social and cultural identity in a shepherd economy, the wolf moves from blaming the individual messenger to blaming the messenger's family and clan ("you, your shepherds and your dogs"), all of whom he sees as threats to his royal absolute power. But having expanded the scope of his grievance, it becomes difficult for the wolf to justify his impending attack on a newborn lamb. Since the facts don't provide him with the legitimation he seeks, he has to resort to a higher authority – *On me l'a dit: il faut que je me venge* [I have been told: I have to take revenge].

The colon is key here. The indeterminate pronoun "*l'*" (it) in "*On me l'a dit* [I have been told it]" points anaphorically both backward and forward. Both "You are a curse, so I have been told (backward anaphora)," and "I've been told that I have to take revenge (forward anaphora)" – in both cases, Public Opinion and Reasons of State, attributed to an impersonal "*On*," prevail. The King has to take revenge to save his honor, but he can also deflect responsibility onto his counselors and ministers.[3] This action becomes a matter of national honor and national security. And he can always plausibly deny that his action was self-interested. Indeed, it is important to note that the wolf's revenge is not a psychological sense of vindictiveness or thirst for payback; it is rather the reestablishment of a balance of power between the two parties, the shepherds and the wolves, and their respective reputation or honor. In La Fontaine's fable, "*On me l'a dit*" becomes the "filter bubble" through which anything the lamb might say is heard and received. Having smeared the reputation of the lamb and discredited his family and his people over nineteen lines, the wolf's discourse has undermined any objective facts the lamb might adduce. It has prepared us for line 20 that legitimizes the wolf's killing of the lamb by placing the responsibility on the institution of the Monarchy itself. The dialogue was from the start clearly not about water drinking rights, but about the honor of the Monarchy as institution.

Thus the stated moral of the fable: "The reason of the more powerful is always the best" is less a prescriptive statement than a faithful description of the way that symbolic power functions. The powerful, says Marin, need reasons to legitimize their power.[4] Brute force without justice can be contested, gratuitous violence can be criticized, disputed. But by using the discourse of justice, that is, by representing himself as an unjustly hounded victim, the wolf adds an imaginary layer to brute force, and thereby gains what is called "power." Brute force needs to appropriate for itself the discourse of justice, to stand for justice and to be taken as judicially equitable. In order to do that, the wolf has to refrain from pouncing on the lamb immediately. He has to use language, that is, linguistic signs, to represent himself and act upon the imagination of both the lamb and the readers. The purpose of this representation is not to speak the truth, but to create a symbolic world in which his action (i.e., his killing of the lamb) will be legitimate. A moral world, that both the lamb and the readers will buy into by virtue of its axiological rhetoric.[5]

One might wonder why the lamb is portrayed as responding to the wolf's accusations in this way, when he should know that any such response will be taken as an act of overt defiance. This lamb, despite his young age, sounds like a Cartesian product of the Renaissance. First addressing the wolf as "Your Majesty" and "Sire" shows that he knows his place in the social structure and has already learned with mother's milk the art of flattery. Then, he sticks to the facts and his talking points, which shows him to be rational and logical. But his quick wit and logical repartees may be perceived as "throwing shade" on the wolf, that is, expressing subtle contempt for the wolf's baseless accusations. His insistence on his innocence could be seen as making the wolf look like a fool. One could wonder whether La Fontaine himself, by cautioning his readers against the abuses of the King's power, might not be reinforcing the absolute nature of that power under the motto: "All publicity is good publicity," even for the killing of an innocent lamb. Certainly, the popularity that the fable has enjoyed among young public school children in France since the seventeenth century suggests that they accept as a fact of nature the reasons given by the powerful to justify their actions.[6]

Power can only be exercised with the complicity of those upon whom it is exercised. The lamb is complicit by engaging the wolf into a rational dialogue of truth, the reader is complicit by accepting the premise of the moral stated at the beginning. The power of both the wolf and the poet is exercised through the imagination – the representation, aroused by language, of what could happen, how brute force could be deployed, what destruction could be wreaked for anyone who dares challenge it. Some critics have noted that the outcome is all the more cruel because the dialogue has raised hopes that in the end the wolf might be persuaded by the lamb's arguments. That this does not happen because the argument was made in bad faith makes the moral of the story all the more ambiguous. Are the reasons given by the more powerful wolf the best because they are good reasons or because he is the strongest, as in the English proverb "might makes right"? La Fontaine, living as he did at the court of Versailles at the height of Louis XIV's reign, was not about to put the power of the sovereign in doubt. He himself admired the King and would have condemned those who believed that the King's power was subject to logical and legal negotiation.[7]

2.2   FROM REFERENCE TO REPRESENTATION: SAUSSURE AND BEYOND

We have seen that language and other symbolic systems enable people not only to refer to things in the world but to represent them in our minds and to communicate these representations to others. Saussure schematized this in the form of the famous two heads connected by two dotted lines moving from A's brain to A's mouth, then from A's mouth to B's ear and on to B's brain and vice versa (see Figure 2.1).

What moves back and forth between A and B is not the sound-image nor the concept, which are both psychological entities, but their encoded symbolic representation. Speakers hope that the representation that reaches the other's brain is the same as the representation that was in their own, but the process of representation is complex and ambiguous.

Upon rereading the fable of "The wolf and the lamb," we can see how complex this process is. First, the wolf's words are meant not only to refer to drinking water but to elicit a mental schema in the lamb's

Figure 2.1 Saussure's two talking heads (1959:11)

mind – a mental schema of guilt and responsibility that is both psychological and affective. We can hear the cognitive disbelief and emotional indignation of the lamb in his response: "How could I do that? I was not yet born." The legitimation of the wolf's symbolic power requires the wolf to manipulate the lamb into believing he is guilty of muddying the water and thus make him complicit in his own death through shame.[8] And so the readers are also asked to legitimize the reasoning of the powerful. Second, the wolf is portrayed as performing the power of the King towards his subjects. We are dealing here with a second meaning of "representation," that of putting on a show, of staging or constructing a social reality through words. Not only does the wolf construct a dubious narrative about the lamb, but the poet himself constructs this narrative to edify or caution his readers. Third, the wolf manages to persuade the lamb not only to address him as one would a king (*Your Majesty*), but to see in him the representative or delegate of a higher power, be it God or the State (*L'Etat c'est moi*). That act of delegation is expressed by the ominous and vague pronoun "*on*" ("*on me l'a dit*") that serves as the ultimate justification for the wolf's action. I return to these three forms of representation in Sections 2.3–2.5.

The fact that even an absolute monarch like Louis XIV needs to provide legitimate reasons for his actions or else the people will not accept his authority is the ultimate moral of the story. Indeed, the exercise of symbolic power is not about objective truth but about whether one can get people to agree that it is true. The reason that the wolf and the lamb don't agree on the meaning of the French verb "*troubler*" (as in *troubler mon breuvage* / to muddy my water) is that they each have different interests in that encounter. For the lamb, who is merely interested in quenching his thirst, *troubler* means concretely "to muddy the water." The wolf, eager to assert his authority and to legitimize his impending killing, "to muddy the water" means to question his authority. Despite Saussure's idealized speech situation, that sees the structural relation of the signifier *troubler* and the signified (troubled water) as the two sides of a sheet of paper, the fit between the two is far from perfect because of the different interests and motivations of the two speakers.

Beyond the gap between signifier and signified, the process of representation encounters also a gap between the concept in head A and the concept in head B. This gap is illustrated in Saussure's schema by the two dotted lines that bridge the distance between the ear and the brain of each of the interlocutors, and between head A and head B. However hard the interlocutors try, that distance will remain. The impossibility of a perfect fit has been seen as an eternal absence that no act of communication can completely abolish. We have seen that symbols are open to multiple interpretations depending on how they are read, that is, which interpretant is chosen to disambiguate them. Literary critics like Derrida (1978) talk about the meaning of a word as being constantly "deferred." And Bakhtin showed eloquently that truth can only be gotten at indirectly through allegories, metaphors ... and fables (see Chapter 9). The impossibility of perfect representation and yet the unavoidable necessity to try to close the gap lead to symbolic power struggles not only between kings and their subjects but between people in everyday life.

2.3   THE POWER OF SYMBOLIC REPRESENTATION

Not all exchanges are as insidious as the one between the wolf and the lamb. In everyday life, we are constantly engaging in small exercises of symbolic power. We have seen (in the Introduction) how symbolic power is "the power to construct reality" and to have others recognize/accept this reality, that is, misrecognize its constructed nature. We don't usually like to think that what we say about the world is anything else than what the world really is. How can a common greeting like "Nice weather today, eh?" construct the weather? Isn't it just stating what is? We are ready to admit that the question is more than a statement of fact; that it is a greeting, a way of making contact (phatic communion), being friendly. But surely the weather is a fact that is independent of my talking about it?

Well – yes and no. For sure, I do not make the weather by talking about it. But by drawing someone's attention to it, by passing judgment on it, by not saying that it rained the whole of last week but only saying that today is nice weather, as well as through my tone of voice, my facial expression and my body language, I give the weather a *meaning*, I influence the perception of my interlocutor as to its importance, as well as to the fact that I speak English, and that I use English like a native speaker. I am in a sense, albeit on a more modest scale than Bourdieu's definition seems to suggest, displaying symbolic power, that is, the "power of constituting the given through utterances, of making people see and believe, of confirming or transforming the vision of the world and, thereby, action on the world" (see Introduction). The "eh?," that seeks recognition, acknowledgement and complicity in my assessment of the weather could be seen as an exercise of symbolic power in constructing people's representation of the social world by "mobilizing" their attention, their solicitude, their feelings and their belief that talking about the weather as a form of greeting is the most natural and legitimate thing to do. And if the encounter is between a man and a woman, the whole utterance could be understood as the power of the pick-up line.[9]

Or consider the following anecdote. My 2-year-old German grandson tried to get me to take him out for a walk by using the only two words he knew: "*Schuhe anziehen*" [put on your shoes]. But Oma didn't seem to be paying attention, so he insisted with a plaintive voice: "*Oma, Schuhe anziehen!*" Oma then slipped on her shoes but didn't budge. He got really upset, pulled at her coat and cried: "*Schuhe anziehen, Oma!! Schuhe anziehen!!!*" Clearly, the representation evoked in his mind by the words he was using (going for a walk) was not the same as the one Oma had upon hearing these words (putting on shoes). Of course she had understood what he *meant*, but had decided to respond to what he *said*, because she really didn't want to go out. After a while, she decided to respond to his desire rather than to his words. She gave him a big hug and took him for a walk. Who would deny that already at that age a child knows how to engage in symbolic power struggles with adults?

Despite Saussure's diagram and the folk belief that language is just the "conduit" for the exchange of information (Reddy 1993), words and their representations do not travel, unscathed, from a mouth to an ear. They are affected along the way by emotions like desire, self-respect, pleasure or displeasure, by memories of former interactions and expectations of future ones. They are also the object of small or big power struggles between people with different interests like the one between Oma and her grandson. These subjective factors have objective effects and one recognizes their power indirectly from their effects. Oma didn't realize the importance that the child attached to the phrase "Schuhe anziehen" before he started crying. In fact, he was only ventriloquating what he had often heard his mother say and was disconcerted to find out that it didn't have the same effect on his grandmother. Even though his sentence was perfectly correct and comprehensible, his words failed to mobilize her, so he had to mobilize her through other means.

Precisely because we have to use linguistic, gestural, visual symbols to communicate with others, we are, with every utterance, playing with our and others' symbolic representations of the social world. In the following, I return to the three meanings of the notion of symbolic representation we encountered in the analysis of La Fontaine's fable in order to tease out their broader theoretical significance: representation as cognitive schema, as staged performance and as social and political ritual. In the following, I use the term "representation" both in the French sense used by Bourdieu ("mental representations" and social/ cultural "objectified representations") and in the English sense.[10]

2.4 THREE WAYS OF LOOKING AT SYMBOLIC REPRESENTATION

Representation as Mental/Bodily Schema – Lakoff, Johnson ▬▬▬

The first meaning of representation is the one we usually associate with "image in the mind." From a psycholinguistic perspective, we could say that "representation" is another word for epistemic and affective "schema," a concept studied in language education mostly by scholars interested in the teaching of reading. In Cook's words, "schemata are mental representations of typical instances [...] used in discourse processing to predict and make sense of the particular instance which the discourse describes" (Cook 1994:11). Cognitive science theory, however, has reminded us that the mind is "embodied" (Varela et al. 1991) and that the idealized cognitive models (Lakoff 1987: chapter 4) that we encountered in the previous chapter are not disembodied representations, but are very much anchored in the physical dimensions of our body or "body-in-mind" (Johnson 1987; see also Slobin 1996).[11] Representation in this first sense has, therefore, the following three characteristics:

Representation renders something which is absent present. In the same manner as a photograph, a portrait or a statue render present someone absent, imagined or no longer there, so words give presence to distant or absent people or things. They can even substitute/be a metonymy or a metaphor for the real person (see condensation symbols in Chapter 1). In Schiller's *Wilhelm Tell,* the hat of the governor prominently displayed on a staff in the town square had to be greeted by passers-by as it stood for or was used as a symbol of the governor himself. Similarly, some Christians cross themselves when walking by a church, thus re-pre-sent-ing, that is, making Christ and the cross "present again" through the symbol for Christianity.

Representation as embodied cognition. As already mentioned, representation is an activity of the embodied mind and the learning of a first or a second language is also the learning of a particular relation to our body (see Kramsch 2009a). As Bourdieu writes:

> We learn bodily. The social order inscribes itself in bodies through this permanent confrontation [of our body and the world], which may be more or less dramatic but is always largely marked by affectivity and, more precisely, by affective transactions with the environment. (Bourdieu 2000:141)

But what Bourdieu and cognitive scientists mean by body is more than just our head, hands and feet. It means at once:

- the space of the body (perceptions, sensations, emotions, feelings);
- the time of the body (memories, desires, anticipations, projections); and
- the reality of the body (actual/virtual reality, imagination, words made flesh, e.g., violent actions provoked by violent words).

Representation is both a construction of the embodied mind and a tool to manipulate other people's representations through slogans, flags, emblems, badges, crosses and so on.

Representation organizes social reality. Through the lexical and syntactic categories it provides, language as representation organizes reality into, say, animate and inanimate entities, insiders and outsiders, males and females, and classifies them, hierarchizes them, sequences them to yield a world that makes sense to us. Words give shape to inchoate thoughts. This is the principle behind the Sapir-Whorf hypothesis of language relativity that was mentioned in Chapter 1.[12]

In *Women, Fire and Dangerous Things*, George Lakoff uses Borges' description of a fictional Chinese encyclopedia as a memorable example of the power of language users to organize reality. This encyclopedia, titled *Celestial Emporium of Benevolent Knowledge,* gives a taxonomy of the animal kingdom that can only make us laugh.

> On those remote pages it is written that animals are divided into: (a) those that belong to the emperor, (b) embalmed ones, (c) those that are trained, (d) suckling pigs, (e) mermaids, (f) fabulous ones, (g) stray dogs, (h) those that are included in this classification, (i) those that tremble as if they were mad, (j) innumerable ones, (k) drawn with a very fine camel's hair brush, (l) others, (m) those that have just broken a flower vase, (n) that resemble flies from a distance (Borges 1966, p.108). (Lakoff 1987:92)

Such a representation is disorienting. It produces a bodily reaction of helplessness precisely because our mind, our perceptions, our whole mind-and-body experience is thrown off. Our embodied mind expects the rationality that comes with alphabetical order, the hierarchy it implies, the subcategorizations of the term "animals" that it suggests – but all those expectations are flouted in this Chinese encyclopedia. We desperately struggle to find the logic behind the words and to fathom the intention of the writer. Lakoff comments: "Borges, of course, deals with the fantastic. [But] the fact is that people around the world categorize things in ways that both boggle the Western mind and stump Western linguists and anthropologists" (ibidem). Also among Westerners, scholars from different intellectual traditions expressed in different languages cut up reality in different ways, sometimes making it difficult to participate in international research projects even if everyone speaks English (Kramsch 2009b; Zarate and Liddicoat 2009).

Representation as Staged Performance – Goffman, Foucault

Closely related to representation as mental and embodied schema is representation as staged performance. In this sense, as Goffman has shown (1959), the presentation of self in everyday life is both a presentation and a representation of how one wishes to be seen, exemplified today by the self-profiling on Facebook and other social media. The capacity to influence other people's representations of oneself and the addiction to these representations caused by the need for constant public sanction are one example of the insidious and invisible symbolic power exercised by language and pictures in online media (see Chapters 7 and 8).[13]

As spectacle and performance, representation brings about what it represents (see Chapter 4). According to Bourdieu, representations are "performative statements *which seek to bring about what they state*, to restore at one and the same time the objective structures and the subjective relation to those structures" (1991:225, my emphasis). For instance, talking about people's regional or ethnic identity as displayed through such indices or criteria as language, dialect and accent, Bourdieu says:

> [We should not] forget that, in social practice, these criteria are the object of *mental representations*, i.e., acts of perception and appreciation, of cognition and recognition, in which agents invest their interests and their presuppositions, and of *objectified representations*, in things (emblems, flags, badges, etc.) or acts, self-interested strategies of symbolic manipulation which aim at determining the (mental) representation that other people may form of these properties and their bearers. [...] Struggles over ethnic or regional identity [...] are a particular case of the different struggles over classifications, struggles

over the monopoly of the power to make people see and believe, to get them to know and recognize, to impose the legitimate definition of the divisions of the social world and, thereby, to *make and unmake groups*. (pp.220–221 emphases in the original)

Bourdieu clearly shows in this quote how mental/perceptual representations, coupled with acts and strategies of symbolic manipulation, can have performative effects in not only creating prejudice and discrimination, but in shaping social groups and prompting them to action.

In *Discipline and Punish* (1977/1995), Michel Foucault gives a dramatic illustration of the power of these two forms of representation – as staged performance and as mental/bodily schema – through a graphic comparison of the public execution of Damiens the regicide in 1757, and the daily schedule of prisoners in the House for young offenders in Paris in 1837. On the one hand, we have the excruciating description of the torture and execution of Damiens, who attempted to kill Louis XV while he was travelling. This description or staged representation by the *Gazette d'Amsterdam* of April 1, 1757, is quoted by Foucault as follows:

> On 2 March 1757, Damiens the regicide was condemned "to make *amende honorable* before the main door of the Church of Paris" where he was to be "taken and conveyed in a cart, wearing nothing but a shirt, holding a torch of burning wax weighing two pounds"; then, "in the said cart, to the Place de Grève, where, on a scaffold that will be erected there, the flesh will be torn from his breasts, arms, thighs and calves with red-hot pincers, his right hand, holding the knife with which he committed the said parricide, burnt with sulphur, and, on those places where the flesh will be torn away, poured molten lead, boiling oil, burning resin, wax and sulphur melted together and then his body drawn and quartered by four horses and his limbs and body consumed by fire, reduced to ashes and his ashes thrown to the winds." (Foucault 1995:3)

The detailed representation of the execution in the Amsterdam Gazette is meant to elicit and solidify in the minds of the readers a mental schema of overwhelming monarchical power, of "imbalance and excess" in the same manner as the ritual performance of Damiens' execution in the public square was meant to act not as a deterrent, but as an edifying spectacle that would instruct the masses, build their spiritual strength and restore their faith in the King's absolute power. As Damiens had disrupted the divine order of the cosmos by trying to kill the representative of God on earth, so was the ritual of punishment intended to make the world whole again. As Foucault writes: "The condemned man represents the symmetrical, inverted figure of the king" (p.29). The body of the condemned becomes the place where the vengeance of the sovereign is applied, the anchoring point for the manifestation of the King's power.

Hence the symbolic meaning of each of the details given. By melting wax and sulfur together, the two ingredients of the King's seal, and pouring the mixture into Damiens' wounds, the sovereign puts his mark, brand, sign, royal seal on the body of the condemned. Yellow bee's wax, yellow green sulfur, gray lead, yellow olive, dark brown resin are all natural elements that return the body to the earth that, according to the Bible, it comes from. Sulfur used to fumigate and disinfect is applied here as a ritual of purification. The musculature that holds the body together – breasts, thighs, calves – is taken apart. The body itself is drawn apart by four horses and quartered at the image of the four points of the compass, like the macrocosm. The dismembered body is then burned to ashes and the ashes scattered to the winds to ensure that it is not only not remembered but rendered invisible, nameless, erased altogether from human memory. The regicide's punishment is a ceremonial celebration of the restoration of world order disturbed by the criminal act – a re-activation of monarchical power.

Foucault argues that such a spectacle of sovereign power had not only a mental representational, but also a performative effect on the masses. It taught them who they were, by making them into the subjects the King wanted them to be. In the same way as a theater play or a fable represents, that is, stages or performs human actions and their consequences, so did the "spectacle of the scaffold" hold up to the people, as in a mirror, "the affirmation of [monarchical] power and of its intrinsic superiority" (p.49) and of the role they as subjects had to play in that performance.

On the other hand, and by contrast, the *Rules for the House of young prisoners in Paris* published eighty years later by a certain Léon Faucher (1838 cited in Foucault 1995:6–7) made use of another kind of symbolic representation to punish and reeducate young offenders. No longer did the display of power impose itself directly through physical force and corporal punishment. Over the eighteenth century, brute force like the one displayed in Damiens' execution increasingly failed to edify the masses and to legitimize the power of the King. People slowly turned away in disgust at the barbarity of the sentence. Foucault describes the change in the way power was exercised, namely from external physical destruction to internal self-discipline. By 1837, young offenders were being reeducated to the power of law and order by being held to a strict daily schedule of activities that represented and taught them self-discipline under strict surveillance. Here, for example, Art.17 and 18 of the *Rules for the House of young prisoners in Paris.*

> Art.17 The prisoners' day will begin at six in the morning in winter and at five in summer. They will work for nine hours a day throughout the year. Two hours a day will be devoted to instruction. Work and the day will end at nine o'clock in winter and at eight in summer.
> Art.18 *Rising.* At the first drum-roll, the prisoners must rise and dress in silence, as the supervisor opens the cell doors. At the second drum-roll, they must be dressed and make their beds. At the third, they must line up and proceed to the chapel for morning prayer. There is a five-minute interval between each drum-roll.

Prayers, work, meals, school, bedtime were regulated hour by hour. The schedule, posted on the walls of the prison for all to see, was the public representation of a disciplinary voice that the prisoners were to make their own not only by performing its words, but by monitoring their progress as well. Slowly they would internalize the rules and exercise their own surveillance. The rigorous discipline imposed on criminals and delinquents was meant to bind criminals not through visual and mental images of physical retaliation and retribution, but through the reasoned performance of textual rules and regulations, controlled and monitored through panoptic observation and evaluation.

Representation as Delegation – Hanks, Bourdieu

The third meaning of representation is the one we generally use to denote the process of standing for someone else. A social group delegates someone to represent the group, people elect their representatives in government, political candidates stand for their constituencies, CEOs for their corporations, teachers for their academic institutions, parents for their families. We have seen how in La Fontaine's fable the wolf's ultimate argument relied on his claim to represent a higher Reason of State that forced him to take revenge for perceived wrongs.

Delegates exert vicarious power, they are the incarnation of a bigger, invisible authority that gives their words and actions legitimacy. One could say that any member of a language community stands for the community that invisibly monitors the communicative competence of its members, that is, what it is feasible, appropriate and systemically possible to say, and what is in fact done with this language (Hymes 1987:224). The symbolic power of an individual is always a delegated power exercised invisibly by institutions, even though that power is constantly contested by individuals who, like the old man in the Bichsel story (Chapter 1), try and push its boundaries.

Representatives not only stand for, they also speak for, entities that are larger than the individual. Although we don't tend to think of it that way, as speakers we wield symbolic power by virtue of using communicative practices usually associated with representation as delegation. In the following paragraphs, I look at four of these practices: vicarious speech, hurled speech, reported speech and oracle effects.

Vicarious speech. In many instances of everyday life, speakers speak for others, and depending on the context, this can be accepted as normal or seen as offensive. When a teacher says to her 6-year old students: "Let us be quiet now," this is understood as totally appropriate, but if she says it to 22-year-old undergraduates, it might be understood as condescending. When a mother addresses her infant in a high-pitched voice, "Does she wants her milk now?", she is using motherese to give voice to an infant who cannot yet speak; it is heard as a legitimate exercise of motherly solicitude. But when a man responds to a female colleague who complains about being treated unfairly at work: "There she goes again!" in the presence of other male friends, the use of the third person could be perceived by the woman as offensive, for he is not directly addressing her but indirectly putting her down by addressing his male friends *about her.* This is the reason why such speech is sometimes presented as a teasing ("I was only joking"), rather than an insulting strategy, thus allowing the participants to save face while providing the speaker with an alibi (see Chapter 4). This is also why in some families children are taught never to talk about someone in the third person *in that person's presence.* This kind of communicative practice has been studied by linguistic anthropologists as a form of hurled speech.

Hurled speech. William Hanks (Hanks 1996:259–265) has studied "hurled speech" as discourse between two parties that Hanks calls "the instigator" and "the pivot," performed within earshot of a third party that he calls "the target." Like gossip, such discourse is usually meant to denigrate the target through speech that, albeit directly addressed to the pivot, is indirectly "thrown at" the target, who is meant to overhear it. Thus, for example, two women at the market are engaged in gossip face to face, when the target comes into view. The instigator says to the pivot mockingly, in a loud voice that can also be overheard by any passer-by: "Wow! Where are you going? You've dressed yourself well" and the pivot answers: "Oh there's someone I need to see!", their subsequent laughter implying sexual wrongdoing. Hanks comments: "The attack is invasive of the target. It attempts to dominate the target by subordinating her to the accepted values of the group, values like family propriety, monogamy and muted attractiveness in daily public settings" (p.263). Once attacked the target can confront her attackers directly, but she risks physical confrontation or what may be seen as unseemly behavior for a woman; or she can ignore the attack, but this might backfire, leaving the audience to believe that she indeed has a lover at the market. But, if she is accompanied, she might in turn use her companion as a pivot to reciprocate in kind, for example by throwing back hurled speech at her attacker such as "The poor dog, it doesn't see its own tail, it sees only the tail of others" (p.264).[14]

Speech and thought (re)presentation. Discourse analysts have identified various ways in which speakers manipulate the speech of others and thereby exercise various degrees of symbolic control over them. This has been seen in terms of narrator's representation of speech or action as an indicator of narrator control. For example, in Franz Kafka's short story "Give it up!", the narrator uses a not only vague, but narratively coercive way of describing a man seeking directions from a policeman on how to get to the station. "He spotted a policeman and asked him the way." The policeman answers: "You are asking me the way?" and the man answers: "Yes, because I don't know it." When we look at the various ways the initial request could have been reported, we notice that the narrator chose the one that gave the man the least amount of symbolic power. Direct speech representation ("How do I get to the station?") would have given the man maximal narrative agency. Indirect speech ("He asked him how he could get to the station") or free indirect speech ("He approached the policeman. How could he get to the station?") would have reduced the man's narrative voice but retained the specificity of his request. By choosing to merely represent the speech act performed ("he asked him the way"), the narrator constrains the autonomy of the man and puts it squarely within his own narrative control. As Mick Short comments: "as we move from [the first to the last form of representation], the contribution of the character becomes more and more muted" (Short 1996:293).

Oracle effect. The fourth instance of representation as delegation is what Bourdieu calls "the oracle effect" of political or ecclesiastical speech. In the same way as the oracles of the Pythia in Delphi were interpreted by the priests as the words of Apollo himself, so are politicians today said to usurp the voice of the people to speak not only to and for the people, but in lieu of the people; and so do pastors, clergymen, and well-intended kindergarten teachers who use "we" rather than "I" to show their identification with the individuals in their care. The oracle effect is to give the impression that one is both the messenger and the interpreter of the message, that is, that one is not only a symbolic delegate of the people, but the people itself.

> The oracle effect [...] is what enables the authorized spokesperson to take his authority from the group which authorizes him in order to exercise recognized constraint, symbolic violence, on each of the isolated members of the group [...] I am the group. I am an incarnation of the collective and, by virtue of that fact, I am the one who manipulates the group in the very name of the group. (Bourdieu 1991:211)

Bourdieu calls this kind of representation "usurpatory ventriloquism" (p.211) or "legitimate imposture" (p.214). It would be wrong to take these negative terms as a condemnation of these practices. On the contrary, Bourdieu always seeks to show that symbolic power is the name of the social game that people who are the delegates of powerful entities like the Government, the Church or the Academy have to play, and not only corrupt politicians, untrustworthy clergymen or dishonest intellectuals.

Populist politicians are only an extreme case of representative delegates that don't just speak for the people but actively construct the people in whose name they speak. Which means, in the case of representative democracy, the people are both the constituency they are speaking for and the audience they are speaking at, the latter containing potential recruits for the former.

In sum: Whether it be a mental embodied schema, a staged performance, or an act of delegation, symbolic representation is a view of the world that encapsulates our innermost desires, perceptions, memories and aspirations and is therefore prone to manipulation by self and others. In other words, it is what makes us into social actors in a symbolic power game that constitutes the realm of the "political" (*le politique*) in the broad sense of the term (see Introduction).

2.5 THE POLITICS OF REPRESENTATION

The Bakhtin scholar and literary critic Michael Holquist reflects on the reasons why Bakhtin, as a Russian orthodox Christian and a Soviet communist, was so interested in parable and allegory. Faced with the "increasing gap between his own religious and metaphysical ideas and the Soviet government's ever more militant insistence on adherence to Russian Communism" (Holquist 1981:180), Bakhtin developed a theory that Holquist calls "dialogism" (Holquist 1990), which sees human utterances as being by definition a contest, a struggle between one's voice and the voice of others. The words we use have been used by others in other places at other times, says Bakhtin; they carry with them a historical baggage that affects their meaning in the present.[15] Dialogism is a theory of language that does not start with the linguistic sign, as in Saussure, but with the duality of self and other, indeed self in other and other in self in every word that we utter. In Holquist's formulation: "I can appropriate meaning to my own purposes only by ventriloquating others" (Holquist 1981:169).

But this ventriloquation is inherently conflictual, as "individual consciousness never fully replicates the structure of the society's public values" (p.179). Faced with this fundamental contradiction built into the very fabric of language, every utterance seeks to make meaning indirectly not only in trying to understand events, but in trying to persuade others of our understanding. This gap between my representation of things and that of others is precisely the essence of politics understood as the power game of political interests (*le politique*; see Introduction). "If we begin by assuming that *all* representation must be indirect, that *all* utterance is ventriloquism, then it will be clear [...] that difficulties *do* exist in moving from epistemology to persuasion. This is because difficulties exist in the very politics of any utterance, difficulties that at their most powerful exist in the politics of culture systems" (pp.181–182), that is, in the clashes between value systems.

By suggesting that all utterances are political, that is, represent conflictual value systems, Holquist and Bakhtin rejoin Bourdieu's views on the power of symbolic representation. We can summarize these views as follows:

- In language, "relations of communication are always, inseparably, power relations which, in form and content, depend on the material or symbolic power accumulated by the agents (or institutions) involved in these relations" (Bourdieu 1991:167).
- Language reproduces material/physical distinctions into symbolic distinctions.
- It imposes ways of representing and classifying persons, things and events and makes these classifications seem natural.
- It makes these representations stick through the power of suggestion.
- Because the power of suggestion appeals to our emotions as well as our cognition, the clash of representations is inevitably associated with moral values (Johnson 1993).

– Symbolic power strives to remain invisible and misrecognized as such.
– Ultimately, the clash of representations is part of the permanent struggle to *define* reality (Bourdieu 1991:224).[16]

SUGGESTIONS FOR FURTHER READING

To further understand the gap between Saussure's head A and head B, see Kress (1993) for his discussion of the arbitrary vs. motivated nature of the linguistic sign, and Derrida (1977:18) for his notion of deferment (or *différance*). Goffman (1959, 1967, 1981) is a must to understand the presentation and representation of self in everyday life. Berger and Luckman (1966) is a classic for understanding representation as the social construction of reality. This social construction passes inevitably through the body and the embodied mind. Those interested in how cognition is intimately linked to (bodily) emotions, interests and desires should read Lakoff (1987), Johnson (1987), Varela et al. (1991), Gumperz and Levinson (1996), Kramsch (2009a). Very useful discourse analytic tools to interpret the representation of symbolic power in plays and prose can be found in Fowler (1996), Short (1996) and Simpson (1997). Interpretation of the *tu/vous* distinction in La Fontaine's fable will be greatly illuminated by reading the famous essay by Brown and Gilman (1960) on the pronouns of power and solidarity.

3 Narratives of Power — The Power of Narrative

"PFUI! GARSTIGER STRUWWELPETER!"

When I studied German in France and moved to Germany in the early sixties, the first books I discovered were some of the traditional children's books that were being read by German parents to their children. My knowledge of German was good enough for me to enjoy the adventures of mischievous boys like Max und Moritz and the abundant cartoon-like pictures that accompanied the stories. But the book that intrigued me most was *Der Struwwelpeter* [Disheveled Peter], written and illustrated by the doctor and psychiatrist Heinrich Hoffmann for his 3-year-old son Carl Philipp, and published in Frankfurt in 1845 under the title *"Der Struwwelpeter. Lustige Geschichten und drollige Bilder für Kinder von 3 bis 6 Jahren"*[Disheveled Peter. Funny stories and humorous pictures for children between 3 and 6 years old] (Hoffmann 1986). The book contains nine stories about unruly children and their punishment for bad behavior, for example, the story of little Pauline who plays with matches, Conrad who sucks his thumb, Kaspar who will not eat his soup and Philipp who fidgets on his chair. The book was an immediate success both in Germany and abroad and has been translated in more than 40 different languages.[1]

At the time, I took an anthropological interest in those stories and took them for the cultural icons they had become in German culture. They were, in my view, representations of over-the-top punishments that today one could only laugh at. It was only when I came to the United States in the late sixties and encountered the indignation of my American friends at my reading such "authoritarian" and "violent" stories to my children – even for fun – that I realized there might be more to these narratives than I thought. Indeed, while corporal punishment was still alive and well in many rural schools in the southern parts of the United States, it had largely become politically incorrect in many urban schools and families in other parts of the country,[2] and cases of "child abuse" were very much in the public consciousness

(Hacking 1999b, chapter 5). But then, I thought, why were American children exposed to so many violent films on television? And why were many brutal Westerns not equally politically incorrect?

My children were by then five and three, and I was trying to get used to American child-rearing practices: do not let your children play outside without any clothes on; do not scold them, do not spank them; do not make them feel guilty; always give them a choice of what to wear, what to eat and what to do. But it didn't seem to work. My children just wouldn't do as they were told; in my view they were unruly and ill-behaved. A well-intentioned neighbor suggested I consult a child counselor. After listening to my story, the counselor looked at me and said with a calm voice: "'Mrs Kramsch, you have a communication problem'." I burst out laughing: "What do you mean? Should I speak louder? Slower? In a different language?" I came out of the counselor's office thinking: "*Ils sont fous, ces Américains!*" [Those Americans are crazy!][3]

It was clear that the counselor and I had quite different representations of what it meant to raise a child and I certainly did not understand the symbolic value of "good communication" for an American. What I perceived as a challenge to my authority as a mother, he seemed to take as a technical problem; where I saw it as my responsibility to transmit our family values to my children, he seemed to suggest that I adopt the clear, precise, informative communication style of a tape recorder. Why couldn't he see that my problem as an immigrant to the U.S. was my loss of control over my own children? But what exactly had I lost and how did I lose it?

In this chapter, we continue our exploration of the power of symbolic representation to shape people's perceptions of the social world. We examine in particular how children's books represent and transmit social and moral values. This will lead us to consider the role of narrative representation in shaping children's symbolic identities and, ultimately, their actions.

3.1 A NARRATIVE OF POWER: DER STRUWWELPETER (1845)

The picture on the cover page is startling. A strapping young lad standing on a pedestal, arms extended and legs apart, looks at the reader straight in the eye, his hair like a lion's mane, his fingernails like animal claws. This is "Disheveled Peter," who has refused to have his hair cut and his nails trimmed for almost a year. The expression on his face is serious but inscrutable: Is he proud? Dejected? Sad?

On the front of the pedestal, decorated on both sides with aesthetically pleasing pictures of scissors and combs, we can read the following inscription.

Sieh einmal, hier steht er,	Look at him! Here he is!
Pfui! Der S t r u w w e l p e t e r!	Pfui, disheveled P e t e r!
An den Händen beiden	On both his hands
Ließ er sich nicht schneiden	He has not let anyone cut
Seine Nägel fast ein Jahr;	His nails for almost a year;
Kämmen ließ er nicht sein Haar.	He has not let anyone comb his hair.
Pfui! ruft da ein jeder.	No wonder everyone says: Pfui!
Garst'ger Struwwelpeter !	Ghastly disheveled Peter!

The book, written for 3–6-year-olds, is not meant to be deciphered by children who have not yet learned how to read. It is meant to be read aloud by parents or grandparents, who perform the text while pointing to the pictures and encouraging children to repeat the words after them: "Pfui! Ghastly disheveled Peter!" The text refers to two practices that children are known to dislike – haircut and nail trim, but that they have to undergo if they are to be respected by others in their community. By representing these practices and the opprobrium incurred for neglecting to perform them, the child is socialized into identifying with the person uttering these words and hopefully becomes that very person when he grows up. In Bourdieu's terms, the child develops a habitus that will value a neat and clean appearance by having his hair and nails cut in the proper way. How does this story achieve this?

"Sieh einmal" ["Look!"]. Addressed directly by the parent in the second-person singular intimate form of address, the child is enjoined to turn his attention to his delinquent counterpart. "Hier steht er" ["Here he is"] is on the page, visible to the child's scrutiny and stigmatizing judgment, together with the derogatory compound name: "Struwwelpeter". This coinage affixes the epithet "strubbelig or struwwelig" ["disheveled"] to a boy called Peter and makes it into an intrinsic attribute: "Peter-the-disheveled." A living boy called Peter thus serves as a negative image or "myth" (see Chapter 1) of what the child will become if he doesn't do as he's told. The child is invited to point to this boy while exclaiming: "Pfui!" – a kind of hurled speech addressed to this negative image (see Chapter 2). By adopting this discourse, the child embodies the values of his parents with proper manners and acceptable behaviors. The amount of exclamation points enhances the indignation that such bad behavior deserves. The symbolic power of the stigmatizing "Pfui!" is increased by the avowed complicity and social consensus of all well-behaved persons ("ein jeder" ["everyone"]) who cannot fail to cry out, like the child: "Pfui! Ghastly Struwwelpeter!"

Pierre Bourdieu has used the term "symbolic violence" as a synonym of symbolic power to underscore the fact that the power to construct social reality "does violence" to persons and practices by persuading them to change their behavior. In this sense, the story of Struwwelpeter, read aloud at bedtime by a loved parent, does violence to the child by mobilizing not only his or her cognitive understanding but his emotional self as well, that is, his embodied mind (Johnson 1987). The child recognizes his own desires (not wanting to have his hair cut), and in part he empathizes with Peter, in part he rejects him for fear of being called names and suffering the same fate as the boy. The representation of bad behavior is meant to help replace the natural desires of the child with the self-discipline of the cultured adult who has internalized the values of the surrounding middle-class culture.

Symbolic violence is nowhere more visible than in educational endeavors where to educate is to *e-ducere*, that is, to lead out of a state of dangerous desires to a state of cultured discipline.[4] But in the case of Struwwelpeter and the other anti-heroes in Hoffmann's book, is this violence physical or symbolic? Each story in the book represents a different incarnation of the disheveled Peter archetype and the punishment the character gets for his/her bad behavior. I want to examine in particular four other characters in the book – Pauline, Konrad, Kaspar and Philipp, and how their story reinforces the message we get from the Struwwelpeter case. I first summarize each of the four stories; I then explore in each case the nature of the offense, the nature of the punishment and the workings of symbolic power.

The Very Sad Story with the Matchbox

Aesthetically displayed across two pages, we have a story in rhyming verse that starts with "*Paulinchen war allein zu Haus'/die Eltern waren beide aus*" [Little Pauline was alone at home/ both parents had gone out] and that serves as a commentary to four graphically illustrated scenes:

1) Pauline, dragging her doll, spots a box of matches on the dresser and decides to strike one as she has seen her mother do, while in the same frame Minz and Maunz the cats raise their paws in warning: "Father has forbidden this! / Miau! Mio! Miau! Mio! / Don't touch! Or else you will go up in flames!."
2) Pauline doesn't listen to the cats / "the match burns with a lovely light / exactly the way you can see it in the picture." The

cats again raise their paws in warning: "Mother has forbidden this!"

3) "But alas! Her dress catches fire, her apron burns, you can see the flames / her hand is burning, her hair is burning / Indeed, the whole child is burning!" The picture shows Pauline engulfed in flames, arms outstretched, her mouth opened to a scream. The cats continue to wail and scream for help.

4) The last picture shows the two little kitties sitting on both sides of a neat little pile of ashes, their tears running in two dainty rivulets around two little red shoes. The text reads: "Everything is totally burned / The poor child, skin and hair / Only a little heap of ashes remains / And two shoes, so dainty and fine... Where, oh where are the poor parents?"

Unlike Struwwelpeter of whom we are told directly the nature of his delinquency but not the punishment he received, Pauline's story is a vivid narrative of what happens to children who play with matches. But what lesson is the child supposed to take away from that story? At three years of age, most children are not able to comprehend what it means to die, let alone to be burned alive. Moreover the attractive images with their flowery framings, the memorable rhymes, the repetitions and refrains, the predictable outcome, the jolly metaphors and the aesthetic staging of Pauline's remains transform a gruesome fate into an entertaining story. So where is the punishment?

The Story of the Thumbsucker

This story too is told over two pages with four illustrations corresponding to the four episodes of the story. Like Pauline, Konrad finds himself alone one day, his mother having gone out for errands. Despite her warnings not to suck his thumb or else the tailor will cut it off, Konrad sticks his thumb in his mouth as soon as she is gone. Suddenly the tailor jumps into the room and rushes towards the thumb-sucking boy. The third picture features an outsized tailor with an outsized pair of scissors slicing Konrad's thumbs as if they were paper; we see drops of blood falling into a puddle on the floor. "Alas! Now it's klipp and klapp / the great big scissors cut Konrad's thumbs / the great big sharp scissors!! Hey! You should hear Konrad screaming." In the last picture a dejected Konrad stands facing the reader, arms outstretched, displaying two hands with missing thumbs. The text reads: "When the mother returns home / Konrad is in a pretty sad state / There he stands, without his thumbs / Both of them are gone."

As in Pauline's story, the punishment for disobeying parental injunctions is severe: physical death in the first case, disfiguration in the second. And yet, apart from the drops of blood and Konrad's screams, the boy is not represented as being in physical pain. And when his mother comes back home, he is said to be "in a pretty sad state," but not to be hurting very badly. We didn't see Pauline's physical suffering while burning to death and so it is here – we are invited to look at Konrad, not to feel his pain. So here again: what kind of punishment is this?

The Story of Soupy Kaspar

This story is told in four illustrated episodes, the last one of which is smaller than the other three for reasons that will become clear. Kaspar, a healthy, fat boy with red and healthy cheeks, used to eat his soup well when it came to the table. But one day he decided he didn't want to eat his soup. He stomped the floor screaming: "I won't eat my soup! No! I won't eat any soup!/ No, I don't want any soup!" The next day, he was already much thinner and yet when the soup arrived on the table he went into the same tantrum again: "I won't eat my soup! No!. . ." on the third day, "alack and alas! Look how thin and weak Kaspar has become!" and yet the same happened again: "I won't eat my soup! No! / I won't eat any soup! No! I don't want any soup!" "On the fourth day at last, Kaspar was as thin as a thread / He weighed at most a half a pound/ And on the fifth day he was dead." The first to the third pictures show an ever-thinner Kaspar; the last picture features only a soup tureen with "soup" written on it and placed on a tomb with a cross that says "Kaspar."

The story of Kaspar, who over four full days refuses to eat his soup and on the fifth day dies of hunger, is equally intriguing. From the cross in the cemetery with his name on it to the soup tureen placed prominently on his tomb, we know exactly what the misdemeanor was, but we are uncertain about the legitimacy of the punishment, which seems to be out of proportion with the crime. Moreover Kaspar, like Pauline and Konrad, doesn't seem to suffer physically even though his body changes shape as he becomes thinner and thinner. The Struwwelpeter stories have horrified present-day educators as creepy and bizarre (e.g., Radeska 2018), and that story seems to be one of the more bizarre, if it is meant to encourage children to eat their food.

The Story of Fidgety Phil

With the story of Fidgety Phil, the intriguing nature of these stories becomes even more apparent. Philipp, a fidgety 4- or 5-year-old, is trained, like all children in well-to-do middle-class families at the time, to sit still at table and develop well-brought up table manners. In three graphic tableaux, we see that Philipp does not behave as expected. The first tableau sets the scene: At a time when the family was expected to dress up for dinner, we see a formally dressed mother, father and son sitting at a round dinner table, covered with a white tablecloth, having their evening meal. All three have white napkins; the parents have their napkins on their laps, Phillip's is tied around his neck. On the table are a loaf of bread, a tureen of soup, a bottle of red wine, plates, silver, two glasses half-filled with wine. The Mother, wearing a fancy dress and a flowery hat on her head holds up a lorgnon and observes what is going on, deferring to her husband to reprimand the boy. On the left of the picture, the Father, in topcoat, high collar and silk cravat, is seen in profile holding a knife upright in his right hand. He appears to address the boy who faces him on the right of the picture, but in fact he addresses the reader:

> "I wonder whether Philipp
> will sit still today at table?"
> Thus spoke with an earnest voice
> The father to his son,
> And the mother gazed silently
> around the table.

The father's opening statement, hurled at the misbehaving "pivot" in the third person, seems to refer to Philipp's past misbehaviors, but as we can see on the picture, that statement must be understood as sarcastic or even offensive because it is obvious that Philipp is not sitting still at table. Indeed, he is shown in that first tableau as gripping the table and pushing his chair backwards and forwards, while the father reprimands him: "Philipp, I am most displeased!" This can only end badly. In the second tableau, we can see the results.

> Look, dear children, look,
> what happens to Philipp!
> You can see it up there on the picture.
> Look! He swings much too wildly.

Philipp hangs on to the tablecloth, falls backwards, dragging with him plates, bottle, bread and soup bowl, which crash to the floor. Philipp "screams but to no avail." Surprisingly for a modern reader, the mother still doesn't say anything, and this tableau concludes only with: "Vater ist in grösster Not" ["Father is in dire need"]. Finally, the third tableau shows the full consequences of Philipp's misbehavior. The Mother stands upright, still holding her lorgnon to survey the disaster;

the father also stands, with arms raised in the air as he stomps the floor in anger. Philipp has disappeared under the tablecloth, buried under broken plates, scattered forks and knives, spilled soup and shattered wine bottle and soup bowl. The last lines of the story are the most surprising to the modern reader:

> And the parents stand there,
> Both are terribly angry,
> for they have nothing left to eat.

We understand the child's bad behavior, but its effects are unclear. It seems that the parents are the ones being punished, as they no longer have anything to eat. Philipp has not suffered physically, he has only fallen under the table cloth. How are we to understand all this?

3.2   WHAT STRUWWELPETER *IS REALLY ABOUT*

The stories in *Struwwelpeter* seem to be about physical violence and its potential to serve as a deterrent to children's bad behaviors. Indeed, they have been called "morbid" and "scary" (Radeska 2018). It is difficult today to grasp the educational value of such outrageous forms of corporal punishment; they seem to elicit less fear than uneasy laughter – the same kind of laughter that seized Foucault upon reading Borges' fictitious Chinese encyclopedia (Foucault 1970:xv). Surely our children can't believe *that!* In our disbelief we tend to fall back on stereotypes: "antiquated child-rearing," "child abuse," or even "typically German authoritarian practices."

If, however, we read these stories through a symbolic lens, their meaning becomes clearer and so do the forms of punishment they represent. In the same way as La Fontaine's fable of the "Wolf and the lamb" was not about a wolf eating up a lamb, but about the exercise of symbolic power to legitimize political power (Chapter 2), so do the stories in *Struwwelpeter* represent the symbolic violence exercised by a society's culture to inculcate in children its social and moral values. What these bad boys and girls lose through their transgression is not so much their physical lives than the perception by others of their symbolic worth, their social presence as respectable, legitimate members of a social group. A social symbolic analysis can illuminate the deeper meaning of these stories.

By playing with matches, Pauline is avowedly imitating what she has seen her mother do several times, but she fails to heed the warnings of her two cats who act here as surrogate parents and who, like a Greek chorus, urge her explicitly not to do so or else she will "go up in flames." What happens to Pauline, however, is not just that she dies of physical death but that she is no longer *visible as a social being* and that her parents are nowhere to be seen ("Where oh where are the poor parents?"). The little pile of ashes represents her ultimate and definitive disappearance, that is, exclusion from the social community. In fact, Pauline's name doesn't even figure in the title of the story that seems to focus more on the matchbox than on the girl.

Konrad, who disobeys his mother's injunctions, gets his thumbs cut off, but in the last picture the illustrator represents him standing there, like Struwwelpeter, his hands spread out for all to see, castrated and shamed. While he is represented in the very same posture as in the first picture, the two situations are radically different. In the first, he is recognized by name as a member of the family and addressed as such ("'Konrad!' spoke the Mother"); in the last, he is displayed alone to face the reader who becomes his judge. His mother is not there to comfort him. The point here is not to commiserate about the fate of the child, but to pillory his abnormality, brought about by his disobedience. Konrad's punishment is to be publicly seen as abnormal and forced to carry this stigma for the rest of his life. In fact, even his name becomes changed in the title to the derogatory name "the Thumbsucker."

If Pauline was punished through absence and Konrad through shame, Kaspar gets punished through the progressive loss of his identity as a full member of his family. His rapid and drastic reduction in size illustrates his growing irrelevance. While Pauline's name will be forgotten, Kaspar's name will be remembered by the inscription on the cross but only in conjunction with the soup bowl that is prominently placed on the tomb and will be forever associated with it. Indeed, the title of the story refers to *Suppenkaspar* ["Soupy Kaspar"], yet another derogatory nickname meant to tarnish his social identity, as it did to *Daumenlutscher Konrad* ["Thumbsucker Konrad"].

Philipp's story picks up on the themes of punishment through exclusion, shame and loss of social identity. His punishment, which seems at first sight harmless enough, reveals upon closer inspection a more serious form of sanction. Philipp has not only dragged down with him the tablecloth with all the food, he has in fact "starved" his parents. Physically considered, such a statement is laughable, as one could say that the parents can always pick up the pieces or replace the spilled food. But the symbolic reality is anything but funny. By depriving his caregivers ("who now have nothing to eat any more") of the means of exercising their homemakers' role, Philipp has shattered the foundations of the family that provides for his very existence. His disappearance under the tablecloth echoes that of Pauline, Konrad and Kaspar who are also rendered socially invisible or differently visible. The name he is given in the title, *der Zappel-Philipp* ["Fidgety Phil"], is emblematic of this stigmatization.

The punishment in these four stories is therefore only superficially a physical one. What we see at work here is a symbolic power that strives to create in the minds of children a representation of the social reality they will grow up into. This reality is inculcated through do's and don'ts that children have to internalize if they want to become legitimate members of a cultural community and representatives of this community's values. Unruly children reflect badly not only on themselves as worthy group members, but also on their parents. In small tightknit communities of neighborhoods in small German towns around 1840, parents were held responsible for bringing up well-behaved offspring that would enhance the symbolic capital of their family. A boy who would not behave at the dinner table would shame his family in front of friends and neighbors ("What will the neighbors think?"). A girl who would do something forbidden would incriminate her mother ("What will people think of the way I brought you up?" and "How could you do this to me?"). The very reputation of the family would be at stake with their children's misdemeanors and that meant that they might not be able to rely on the trust and support of their neighbors in times of need. Read in this light, the stories in *Struwwelpeter* don't sound as outlandish as they seem. Shame and stigmatization are still practiced nowadays, even when they are no longer coupled with physical punishment (Riezler 1943).

The social values of docility, obedience, respect of norms and social conventions promoted by the *Struwwelpeter* stories correspond to a conservative period in German history, *die Biedermeierzeit,* ushered in by Metternich after the Vienna Congress of 1815 that put an end to the Napoleonic wars and to the French influence in Europe. The post-Napoleonic Restoration was a time when Germans discovered their rich folkloric heritage of folktales, collected by the Brothers Grimm across the German countryside, their folksongs and local dialects, at a time when the educated middle class was gaining in power. Family customs and traditions, such as Christmas trees and Christmas carols, were valued and promoted, and children's education was part of a Protestant ethics of social stability and continuity.[5] This would explain the main concern in Heinrich Hoffmann's stories with inculcating in children a sense of community and warning them about the consequences of violating the norms of that community.[6]

Different times call for different stories. Let us examine now two children's books that have been equally influential in shaping generations of children into an understanding of language as symbolic power, this time in the United States.

3.3   *FROM* THE LITTLE ENGINE THAT COULD *(1930)* TO THE CAT IN THE HAT *(1957)*

Two classical American children's books are equally reflective of the ideology of the period in which they were written: *The little engine that could* by Watty Piper, published in 1930, and *The cat in the hat* by Dr Seuss published in 1957.

The Little engine that could opens on a familiar picture around Christmas time in the United States. A long freight train is making its way up the mountain, its cars filled with toys and dolls as Christmas gifts for children who live on the other side of the mountain, when all of a sudden its engine breaks down. The toy clown jumps off the train and flags down a shiny yellow passenger engine that comes along. The yellow engine says it has much more important business than helping carry toys over the mountain and refuses. He then asks a black freight engine that passes by, but that engine too has more important things to do. A big rusty engine comes along but says he is too old. In the end, a little blue switcher engine agrees to help. "I think I can" he says and hitches himself to the task. As he puffs up the mountain, he repeats "I think I can I think I can" and, as he triumphantly rolls down on the other side, he exclaims: "I thought I could I thought I could" and saves the day.

It is easy to see how this story captured the imagination of generations of American children raised on the notion that with determination and hard work "you can get it if you really want it," and that the future belongs to the young entrepreneurial spirits who live up to the challenges that come their way. The refrain "I think I can" brings together the quintessential American faith in youthful individualism, ingenuity and resourcefulness, while remaining faithful to the older values of compassion and solidarity in times of need as well as to the Christian tradition of gift-giving at Christmas time. The book reflects the optimistic spirit of the New Deal under Franklin D. Roosevelt following the Great Depression of the 1930's. The symbolic power of this story is evidenced by its enduring success in the United States and more recently in the strong resonance of American voters to Barack Obama's campaign slogan "Yes, we can."

The Cat in the Hat is one of the first of the many children's books published by Theodore Seuss Geisel, under the pen name of Dr Seuss, in quite a different period in U.S. history. The late fifties and sixties were marked by a reaction against any form of authority. Its radical political agenda fought for civil rights, women's rights, minority rights, reproductive rights and the right to civil disobedience and conscientious objection to the military draft. The spirit of anti-authoritarianism permeates Dr Seuss's *The cat in the hat.*

Peter and Sally, two well-behaved 6- and 4-year-olds, are sitting at home and watching the snow fall outside while their parents are away. The story is narrated in the first person by Peter, the older of the two children.

> "The sun did not shine
> It was too wet to play
> So we sat in the house
> All that cold cold wet day [. . .]"

As they are getting increasingly bored, in marches the cat with a big red and white hat. The cat both horrifies and seduces them by doing all the things their parents would disapprove of, for example: eating cake in the bathtub while the water is running, washing the walls with Mother's best dress, messing up the kitchen. What will their parents say when they return? After a day of mischief, the cat says not to worry and proceeds to clean the house and put everything back in its proper place for when the Mother comes home. Peter and Sally can only marvel. The cat in the hat has shown them the power of mischievous creativity and imagination while ultimately respecting the values of cleanliness and orderliness of the middle-class world they live in.

> "Then we saw him pick up
> All the things that were down
> Then he said "That is that"
> And then he was gone
> With a tip of his hat.
> Then our mother came in
> And she said to us two:
> "Did you have any fun?
> Tell me. What did you do?"
> And Sally and I did not know what to say.
> Should we tell her the things that went on there that day?
> Should we tell her about it?
> Now what SHOULD we do?
> Well. . .
> What would YOU do
> If your mother asked YOU?

Thus ends *The cat in the hat*. Turning to the readers and bringing them into the action is a subtle way of exercising the symbolic power of suggestion in the education of children in the late fifties/early sixties. It engages the children in contemplating various modes of action and in making moral choices. *The cat in the hat* offers a glimpse into a parallel world of unconventional and even illicit behaviors and activities in the margins of established norms – a child-centered world of fantasy and "fun" from which adults might be excluded. Unlike some Anti-Struwwelpeter variants that were published in the 1960's and 1970's in Germany and that featured children turning the tables on adults and taking their revenge against persons in authority (see note 1), *The Cat in the Hat* does not encourage children to subvert the norms of social discipline in the name of anti-authoritarian education, but instead it bypasses norms by proposing that children can find a space of their own in the realm of the imagination and in playing with language and crazy pictures.

This theme has been used since then to promote intercultural tolerance and understanding (e.g., Seuss 1953; Berenstain and Berenstain 1994) and has been picked up again in recent years in books that reflect the multiethnic urban environments in which many American children live today. For example, in the award winning *Last stop on Market Street* by Matt de la Peña (2015), a little boy and his grandma enjoy the pleasures of a bus ride in multicultural downtown San Francisco. Complaints by the child about the rain and the dirt in the streets are met by the grandmother with humor and creativity rather than with rebuffs.

Through all these books, children are socialized into recognizing the nature and function of symbolic power through engaging with its verbal and visual representation. They learn how to find their place in a social order that they will uphold, even as they sometimes seek to subvert it. And the stories they are told stake out the range of their own power in acting upon their environment and affecting the course of events.

3.4   *DIFFERENT TRIBES, DIFFERENT SCRIBES*

We saw in the Introduction that symbolic power is the power of making people see and believe a certain view of the social world, by mobilizing their hearts and minds, and appealing to their belief in the legitimacy of words and those who utter them. The children's narratives in this chapter have potentially that power. They seek to obtain through entertaining stories the child's observance of social norms that would have been obtained in earlier days through force and corporal punishment. In the same manner as the *House of young prisoners* in Paris around 1837 reeducated young offenders through written regulations that modelled the orderly conduct of a normal citizen's daily life, the *Struwwelpeter* stories educated young children in Germany around 1840 through entertaining negative models of behavior with which they could identify because they represented the reverse of a world they recognized as legitimate. Like the French regulations that represented an improvement over the more brutal forms of physical punishment depicted by Foucault in the execution of Damiens 80 years earlier (see Chapter 2), being read *Struwwelpeter* on the lap of a grandmother represented a more humane and literate form of child-rearing than in earlier historical periods where children would have been beaten into obedience. The disciplining processes represented in *Struwwelpeter* however had the desired effect only if their intended addressees were invested in them cognitively and emotionally, if they recognized themselves in them and accepted the worldview they represented as legitimate. With changing social conditions, the same children's stories were likely to have a different effect.

The horrified reaction of many parents in the sixties to the *Struwwelpeter* stories is evidence of the changed socio-cultural conditions and values of urban communities at the time. By the 1960s' in Germany, these stories were interpreted as an unacceptable authoritarian form of education; they elicited disgust or laughter, not fear. Today, they are read as cultural exotica. Similarly, in the United States, the stories of the 1930's and 1960's no longer transmit the values they illustrated at the time they were published. The *Little Engine that Could* has become a national myth and the anti-authoritarian *The Cat in the Hat* remains popular as a cultural icon of the educated middle class but has been mostly replaced by pixel videos and cartoon-like fantasies in the lives of children today. With regard to the effectiveness of these stories as instruments of socialization, not all teenagers today would find heavy-handed shaming preferable to a quick and honest corporal punishment for misdemeanors.[7]

We find a similar shift in the value of social and cultural diversity in children's books since the fifties. While intercultural books like *The Sneetches* by Dr Seuss (1953) and *The Berenstain Bears' New Neighbors* by Stan and Jan Berenstain (1994) seek to promote tolerance to cultural diversity because "deep down we are all the same," recent multicultural books like *Last Stop on Market Street* by de la Peña (2015) strive to celebrate diversity for its own sake and for the richness of experience it offers.

3.5 *FROM MORAL PRESCRIPTIVISM TO ETHICAL PERSPECTIVISM*

The diversity of children's books already discussed is a good opportunity to reflect on the moral worlds that children are being raised in through such books, and on the ethical responsibility of parents and educators. The moral values that were transmitted through *Struwwelpeter* in nineteenth-century Germany and through the various American children's books in the twentieth century were meant to develop in young children a habitus that would conform to the morality of the time and to the child's social class, and to endow children with the symbolic capital that would make them and their families legitimate and respected members of their communities. These values are, however, historically contingent and they vary from culture to culture. Should parents and other educators transmit unquestioningly the normative values of the institutions of which they are members: the Family, the School, the Church? To what extent can they deviate from the dominant discourse of their society and challenge the authority of custom and convention?

Questions of morality are generally posed in stark binary terms: either you obey the rule or you get punished; either you solve the problem or you are part of the problem; either you play the game or you are a social outcast. Morality in our day has often turned into political correctness or into moral relativism and expediency (anything goes as long as it "works"). Clear-cut rules of behavior, like clear-cut rules of grammar and stereotypical cultural conventions are convenient, but they cannot guide us any more in the complex encounters that now take place in multilingual, multicultural families, workplaces and classrooms (Kramsch 2014). We realize in hindsight that the symbolic power of any institution is precisely to remain invisible, and to make people believe in its monolithic nature, its permanence and arbitrariness – to persuade people that it speaks with one voice; that it is consistent and predictable; and that it is natural, not historically constructed.

By contrast, a post-structural ethics of symbolic power is a dialogic process that takes paradoxes in stride and makes people aware that the sources of symbolic power are not singular but multiple, not unitary but diverse, not permanent but changing and conflictual. Nowadays children can grow up in a family with strict moral values, move to another city and attend a school with loose entrepreneurial values and end up in a workplace whose co-workers hold a diversity of ethical values that require tolerance and an historical and multidimensional perspective. How should language educators best prepare them for such a life trajectory?

Symbolic power theory calls for a theory of ethics that takes into account the diverse, historical and subjective nature of norms and the need to understand the world from the perspective of others – ethical perspectivism rather than moral prescriptivism. As we shall discuss in Chapter 9, this does not mean that all perspectives are equally valid for a particular time, place and historical reality. While members of institutions have to abide by the norms of the institution that tend to have the effect of uniting its members under one code of conduct, they also have to be aware of the historicity of those norms and to contribute to possible changes within their institution. For this, they have to become aware of the heterogenous nature of institutional structures and their inherently paradoxical or conflictual nature. For example, the *Struwwelpeter* stories are quite clear about children's misbehaviors and are meant to promote compliance with social norms, but their attractive pictures and flowery illustrations, together with the rhymes and memorable lines, also encourage a spirit of mischief and poetic creativity that fires up the imagination and glorifies subversive behavior. Similarly, a strict educational system can at once spawn conformity and resistance – a paradox that might prompt students later on to turn against the system when the opportunity arises.[8]

But if one could argue that it is parents' responsibility to inculcate in their children the moral values that they hold dear, what kind of moral values is it the responsibility of the language teacher to transmit? The question has become more acute in recent years with the increasingly multicultural composition of communities and classrooms. Several suggestions have been made. Many Anglo-American educators tend to favor social and political responsibility (Byram 2008; Macedo 2019; Chun forthcoming). Their motto would be: Open up the classroom; engage students in service learning; encourage them to find examples of the relevance of the subject matter to real life; engage them in political action. Many French language educators, by contrast, tend to advocate an epistemological or scientific responsibility rather than social engagement, and if engagement, then in the form of social contestation or critique rather than political activism (see discussion in Beacco 2013; Coste 2013).[9] Their motto would be: Sharpen your students' social and historical consciousness; reflect with them on the power of the written word; spark their interest in language and their critical appreciation of texts.

The French philosopher Paul Ricoeur, who was steeped in both French and American educational traditions, promoted an ethics of personal responsibility rather than morals of conviction based on institutional rules (see Kerlan and Simard 2012). His philosophy echoes in that respect the dialogic ethics of Mikhail Bakhtin and of Judith Butler that will be discussed in Chapter 9. In his essay "The task of the political educator" (1991), Ricoeur argues that the educator has to mediate between the three different levels that we call "culture": the techno-economic level – technical efficiency, economic profitability of learning languages; the political-ideological level of entrepreneurial neoliberalism, that is, human capital development and multilingualism as symbolic capital; and the ethical level of intercultural mediation. He clearly favored this last form of ethical responsibility. "Ricoeur's reflection on the tasks of the political educator can remind language teachers how important it is not to let themselves become technocrats of the classroom, or promoters of an ideology of language commodification or professional expertise, but to draw instead on their personal experience as multilingual multicultural mediators." (Kramsch 2015:100)

3.6 THE POLITICAL POWER OF NARRATIVE

As we leave the politics of representation for the politics of action in the next chapter, narrative provides a bridge between representation and action through the way it constructs the space of the possible, and the way it serves to define the identity of the social group with which the adult will be identified.

The narrative genre is the quintessential tool of symbolic power. On the one hand, as Jerome Bruner stated eloquently in his canonical article "The narrative construction of reality," "narrative is a form not only of representing but of constituting reality" (Bruner 2002:5). It does so in various ways:

- It presents us with a mental model of the patterned way events occur over time (the absence of parents leads children to mischief; one mischief leads to another). This patterning makes for outcomes that seem reasonable and thus legitimate.
- Its protagonists are endowed with intentions and reasons for acting the way they do, even if they are cats or steam engines. This engages the listener's emotions, memories, fantasies.
- It encourages interpretation of actors' motives and actions.
- Because of its breach component (e.g., transgression, disobedience, crisis), which makes the story worth telling, it has a problem-solving quality to it that creates suspense and captures the listener's attention.
- Because a breach presupposes a norm, a narrative is necessarily normative, it has a moral dimension.

- Single narratives "accrue" (p.18), that is, they contribute to and eventually create larger cultural narratives or traditions, for example *Struwwelpeter* in the 1850's fed into a German narrative of law and order. *The Little Engine that Could* in the 1930's accrued into an American narrative of self-reliance and can-do spirit.

On the other hand, because narrative both "formulates and objectifies a constituted reality" (Feldman 1987:135), it can make people "(mis) recognize" its constructed nature. Feldman writes: "Through its power to encode and clarify one stipulated version rather than another, [language] has the power to entrench one version rather than another. In addition, since language embodies conventional cultural categories, it can impose culturally shared (and shareable) meanings on its constructions" (p.135). The very features that enable the storyteller to draw people into the story can make people hostage to that story's one perspective on events and its way of categorizing them. As Bruner has argued, the power of one mode of thought (the narrative or well-wrought story) needs to be accompanied by the power of the other (the paradigmatic or well-formed logical argument) (Bruner 1986:12).

This is particularly necessary given the accrual power of narrative into larger national narratives that give symbolic unity to a national community. We shall return in Chapter 8 to the search for unifying national stories at a time when globalization and worldwide migrations have complexified traditional understandings of history and are confronting nation-states with the need to invent a new shareable common narrative (Feldman 2001; Freadman 2014). As Freadman noted:

> If we understand by culture the way intergenerational memories pervade present conversations, if we gloss "worldview" as resulting from narratives, and identity as the answer to the question "What story or stories am I a part of?", then traditions of representation must be brought into clear focus. (Freadman 2014:383)

While the *Struwwelpeter* mode of representation of German cultural values has been superseded today by a European narrative of "Unity in diversity," in many countries today national narratives are in search of self (Brooks 2017a, 2018; Delbanco 2018). In the United States, George Packer identified four rival American narratives:

- the libertarian narrative that free individuals are responsible for their own fate (see *The Little Engine that Could*) "The libertarian idea in its current shape regards Americans as consumers, entrepreneurs, workers, taxpayers – indeed everything except citizens" (Brooks 2017a).

- the Silicon Valley narrative of a globalized America, "an exhilarating ideology of flattening hierarchies, disrupting systems, discarding old elites and empowering individuals" (Brooks 2017a) (see *The cat in the hat*).
- the multicultural America narrative, that sees Americans as members of different racial, ethnic, gendered groups seeking to be included in the national identity (see *Last Stop on Market Street*)
- the Trump's America First Narrative that strives to go back to national identity free of "the contamination of others, foreigners, immigrants, Muslims" and standing up to the globalized elite.[10]

Some cultural critics feel that none of these narratives provides an adequate basis for the United States of the twenty-first century. Brooks proposes two other narratives that will be competing for attention in the years to come: a "mercantilist" model of the United States in economic competition with rival powers, and a "talented community" model of the United States leading the world into an open and harmonious information age. These two models are indeed vying for symbolic power right now with the narratives of other nations, whether it is the Chinese "One Belt, One Road" or the European "Unity in Diversity." But mostly he is calling for a return to common human myths "which offer templates of moral progress" and can fill the moral and spiritual void that he feels has invaded our lives today. Reflecting on the amounts of trauma experienced today around the world, he writes: "Trauma is a moral and spiritual issue as much as a psychological or chemical one. Wherever there is trauma, there has been betrayal, an abuse of authority, a moral injury" (Brooks 2018), in other words, a symbolic injury, not just a physical one. We return to these ethical aspects of symbolic power in the Conclusion.

SUGGESTIONS FOR FURTHER READING

The field of narrative inquiry is a tremendously rich field of research into the symbolic world that constitutes human culture and the power of language to construct social reality. Bruner (1990) explores what he calls "narrative thinking" and the way it shapes our conception of ourselves and of the social world in which we live. For the value of narrative in language education, canonical readings include Bruner (1986, 1990, 2001), Ricoeur (1980), Mishler (2006) and White (1980). The edited volume by Brockmeier and Carbaugh (2001) offers a particularly illuminating use of narrative in the construction of identity and culture. Bruno Bettelheim (1975) is a classic study of the beneficial use of fairytales in children's education.

PART II
The Power of Symbolic Action

4 "I Do Things with Words, Therefore I Am"

"WILL ANYONE RID ME OF THIS MEDDLESOME PRIEST?"

On June 8, 2017 the *New York Times* reported on a U.S. Senate hearing at which James Comey, the former FBI director, testified on a controversial incident that took place in the Oval Office at the White House on February 14 of that year. After a cabinet meeting, the President of the United States took Comey aside and, referring to the FBI's investigation of Michael Flynn, his former national security adviser, regarding possible collusion with Russia, he told him: "I hope you can let this go. I hope you can see your way clear to letting this go, to letting Flynn go. He is a good guy. I hope you can let this go." Comey continued his investigation of Flynn and on May 9, Comey was fired. One month later, he was called to testify before the Senate Judiciary Committee in a potential investigation as to whether Donald Trump had committed obstruction of justice by asking the FBI director to drop the case.[1] Here is the report by *The New York Times*.

New York Times, 8 June 2017

> **Trump's Meddlesome Priest**
> By now many people will have googled the words "meddlesome priest."
> The phrase was uttered by James Comey, the former F.B.I. director,
> during his testimony on Thursday before the Senate Judiciary
> Committee. When he was asked if he took President Trump's "hope"
> that he would drop the Flynn-Russia investigation "as a directive," Mr.
> Comey responded, "Yes, yes. It rings in my ears as kind of 'Will no one
> rid me of this meddlesome priest?'"
>
> These are the words that King Henry II of England allegedly cried out
> in 1170, frustrated by the political opposition of Thomas Becket,
> archbishop of Canterbury. Four royal knights immediately rushed off
> to Canterbury and murdered the meddlesome priest.
>
> Unlike many contemporary references to medieval history, this one
> is apt. Mr. Comey's point was that a desire expressed by a powerful
> leader is tantamount to an order. When Senator James E. Risch, a

Republican, noted that the president had merely "hoped for an outcome," Mr. Comey replied, "I mean, this is the president of the United States, with me alone, saying 'I hope this.' I took it as, this is what he wants me to do." (Lipton 2017)

This event encapsulates elements of the symbolic power struggle inherent in any communicative situation but particularly when the stakes are as high as here: on the one hand Trump's effort to mobilize Comey's complicity by using a speech act that tests Comey's loyalty; on the other hand, Comey's suspicion that, despite the legitimacy of Trump's utterance (after all, "this is the President of the United States"), his speech act might be illegitimate ("with me alone"). It is that suspicion that drove him to make a written record of the conversation as soon as he had left the room. Given the circumstances and the powerful status of the speaker as well as the indirect nature of the speech act, that provides the speaker with plausible deniability if an illegal action is subsequently committed in his name, such an utterance was legitimately interpreted by Comey as an order, but not every senator in the room agreed, as the following transcript shows in greater detail.

New York Times 8 June 2017. "James Comey's testimony on Capitol Hill." (James Comey, former FBI Director; James Risch, Republican Senator from Idaho).

RISCH: There's 28 words there that are in quotes, and it says, quote, "I hope" – this is the president speaking – "I hope you can see your way clear to letting this go, to letting Flynn go. He is a good guy. I hope you can let this go." Now those are his exact words, is that correct?

COMEY: Correct.

RISCH: And you wrote them here, and you put them in quotes?

COMEY: Correct.

RISCH: Thank you for that. He did not direct you to let it go.

COMEY: Not in his words, no.

RISCH: He did not order you to let it go.

COMEY: Again, those words are not an order.

RISCH: He said, "I hope." Now, like me, you probably did hundreds of cases, maybe thousands of cases charging people with criminal offenses. And, of course, you have knowledge of the thousands of cases out there that – where people have been charged. Do you know of any case where a person has been charged for obstruction of justice or, for that matter, any other criminal offense, where this – they said, or thought, they hoped for an outcome?

COMEY: I don't know well enough to answer. And the reason I keep saying his words is I took it as a direction.

RISCH: Right.

COMEY: I mean, this is the president of the United States, with me alone, saying, "I hope" this. I took it as, this is what he wants me to do.

COMEY: Now I – I didn't obey that, but that's the way I took it.
RISCH: You – you may have taken it as a direction, but that's not what he said.
COMEY: Correct. I – that's why. . .
RISCH: He said – he said, "I hope."
COMEY: Those are exact words, correct.
RISCH: OK, do you (ph) – you don't know of anyone that's ever been charged for hoping something. Is that a fair statement?
COMEY: I don't, as I sit here.
RISCH: Yeah. Thank you.

(*Politico Staff* 2017)

4.1 *"I DO THINGS WITH WORDS, THEREFORE I AM"*

The power struggle going on between James Comey and Senator Risch circles around an interpretation focused on the *text* of Trump's utterance vs. an interpretation that focuses on the *context* in which the words were uttered. Risch insists on giving the words "I hope" a literal reading, as expressing hope for a certain outcome; Comey considers the totality of the situation: the identity of the speaker, the circumstances, the insistent repetition, and he infers the intention of the person who utters the words. In view of this context, he says, such a speech act could only be understood as an order, and his subsequent firing should be understood as retaliation for the fact that, as he said, he "didn't obey" that order.[2] The literal reading by Risch clashes with the circumstantial reading by Comey. Both, however, adopt a structuralist reading of Trump's utterance, that is, they focus on the linguistic structures used by the speaker, rather than on the institutional constraints on the speech act performed or on the larger political conditions, that is, the very conditions of possibility of such an exchange. Such considerations would provide a reading that went beyond the linguistic or pragmatic structures of the exchange and into post-structuralist considerations of historical timescales and identity play, and they would not be considered appropriate for a Senate hearing. As we shall see in Chapter 6, one of the main ways of obfuscating the making of meaning and of imposing a different symbolic reality on one's interlocutor(s) is to ignore the context of enunciation and change the definition of the speech act under interpretation. For example, insisting that "I hope" uttered by a president is nothing more than an expression of opinion and not the issuance of an order. Similarly, when asked an inconvenient question under oath, one of the avoidance tactics is to start splitting semantic hairs.[3]

In the remainder of this chapter, I want to examine language as symbolic action from well-known structuralist perspectives in pragmatics and sociolinguistics and supplement them with post-structuralist perspectives, in order to explore where symbolic power comes into the picture. I review first what we know about communicative practice from a structuralist perspective: speech acts and face-work, the economy of linguistic exchanges and the power of institutions. I then review approaches that go beyond linguistic and institutional structures and consider more complex, changing and conflictual aspects of the total context in which communicative practices unfold. In each case, I show how these approaches benefit from a theory of symbolic power that can account for the intensity of many of the communication exchanges we experience today (see Introduction).

4.2   THE PERFORMATIVE STRUCTURE OF COMMUNICATIVE PRACTICE

The controversy raised by Trump's words and their intended meaning shows the power of language not only to represent things but to do things with words, that is, to perform speech acts. It also shows how ambiguous such acts can be – in this case "I hope" can be understood as either expressing a desire or giving an order. As we shall see later in this chapter the power struggle that plays itself out here is not just about the linguistic form of Trump's utterance "I hope that" instead of "I order you to" but about the speaker's intent and the conditions that made it possible for him to expect that it would have the desired effect on the hearer.

Austin's Performatives

We know from John Austin's classic *How to do things with words* (1962) and John Searle's work on speech acts (1969) that utterances not only say things about the world, but do things, such as "state," warn," "order," "request," "apologize" and so on. According to Austin, any utterance is also a "performative," because it performs what it says. Some performatives do what they say *in saying it*, such as the boss saying "You're fired!" and you are thereby fired, or the priest saying "I hereby pronounce you husband and wife" and you are thereby married, or the citizen placing an X on a ballot paper and he/she has thereby voted. Even "stating" performs a statement merely by virtue of saying something. Other performatives such as promises, orders or requests do things through their effects, such as a teacher saying to a student "Could you close the door?" and the student gets up and closes the door.

Austin identifies three aspects of performatives: they have a linguistic form that is conventionally understood as appropriate by the speech community (locutionary form); they perform a speech act – promising, commanding, requesting (illocutionary force); and they have effects on the actions, thoughts or beliefs of hearers, for example by warning someone that it is raining, the hearer might grab an umbrella (perlocutionary effect). In order for a performative to work, that is, to be felicitous, it has to have the conventionally recognizable locutionary form; the speaker and the hearer must be able and entitled to respectively perform the act and give the expected response; the circumstances must be appropriate; and the speaker must be sincere in his/her intention to perform the act. Speech acts can be direct or indirect: the more direct they are ("close the door!"), the more unambiguous but the more impolite they can be. The more indirect they are (e.g., "it's cold in here"), the more polite they are because they conceal the illocutionary power of the speech act, and put less pressure on the hearer to comply, but they are then more ambiguous, and a contrarian hearer may answer: "Yes, you're right, it is cold in here" and remain seated.

Austin adds two more features that are going to be important for our interpretation of "I hope you can let this go." A speech act can be infelicitous in two ways. Either "the procedure which we purport to invoke is disallowed or is botched and our act [e.g., ordering] is void or without effect" (Austin 1962:16) – for instance, if Comey had misheard, or misunderstood the President because he spoke too softly or Comey took it as a joke. In that case, the infelicity is called a "misfire." Or the speech act was "professed" or "hollow"; it was achieved but "not implemented or not consummated" – for instance, if the President was speaking as an actor on stage or quoting someone else or ventriloquating Henry II or speaking in soliloquy while looking out of the window. In that case the act was an "abuse," a "parasitic" use of language, called by Austin an "etiolation of language" (p.22). Hurled speech, discussed in Chapter 2, in which the addressee is a third party within earshot, could be seen, according to Austin, as an abuse of language in which the addressee is left uncertain. Henry II's exclamation in front of his knights: "Will no one rid me of this meddlesome priest?" does not specify any specific addressee of the speech act. Similarly, Trump's statement "I hope you can let this go" splits the hearer into two potential addressees: James Comey as the director of the FBI, and James Comey as a loyal servant of the President, taken aside as a co-conspirator. The "you" of the utterance seemed to address the loyal servant, but Comey chose to hear it as addressed to the FBI director and was shocked.[4]

Austin hastens to say that the distinction between misfires and abuses is not a hard and fast distinction, especially with regard to indirect speech acts that are meant to maintain a certain ambiguity precisely in order to remain non-committal. So how do interlocutors disambiguate such speech acts and know how to respond? Social actors, like discourse analysts, cannot only look at the words pronounced. "In order to explain what can go wrong with statements we cannot just concentrate on the proposition involved [. . .] we have to consider the total speech act in the total speech situation" (Austin 1962:52). Which is exactly what James Comey attempts to do by evoking the circumstances that led him to his interpretation of Trump's speech act as an indirect command. He explains this in answer to Senator Mark Warner, a Democrat from Virginia.

WARNER: What was it about that meeting that led you to determine that you needed to start putting down a written record?
COMEY: A combination of things. I think the circumstances, the subject matter, and the person I was interacting with. Circumstances, first. I was alone with the President of the United States, or the President-elect, soon to be President. The subject matter. I was talking about – matters that touch on the FBI's core responsibility, and that relate to the President-elect personally. And then the nature of the person. I was honestly concerned he might lie about the nature of our meeting so I thought it important to document. That combination of things I had never experienced before, but had led me to believe I got to write it down and write it down in a very detailed way.

If, as Austin writes, only the total speech act in the total speech situation can enable us to appreciate the difference between "statements and performative utterances," then a narrowly literal interpretation of Trump's "I hope you can let this go" is not appropriate. We have to factor in the exercise of symbolic power.[5]

But we still have to ask: What did Trump intend to say? Was his utterance sincere? Which perlocutionary effect did he intend for his words to have?

Searle's Speech Acts

In his classic monograph *Expression and meaning* (1979) and again in his book *Intentionality* (1983), John Searle argued that when we consider speaker's intentions and whether they are sincere or not, we need to differentiate between two categories of speech acts. On the one hand, expressives (expressions of joy, sadness, belief, desire) and assertives (statements, descriptions, assertions) intend to represent a state of affairs in the world. Their intention is to make that intentional state clear to the hearer. On the other hand, commissives (promises, vows, pledges, etc.) and directives (orders, commands, requests, etc.) intend to act upon the world and change it. Their intention is to make people act as an effect of that speech act. This distinction leads Searle to dissociate the "representing intention" from the "communication intention." Did Trump only intend to represent his state of hope and have Comey recognize it as such? In other words was it a declarative rather than an order, as Senator Risch seems to suggest? But a declaration, according to Searle, expresses both a belief and a desire: "A man who sincerely declares the meeting adjourned must want to adjourn the meeting and must believe that the meeting is thereby adjourned" (p.172). In that case Comey was right in interpreting Trump's intention not just as a representing intention, but as a communication intention with a perlocutionary effect on his actions, not just his thoughts or his empathy.[6]

Speech act theory introduces an element of symbolic power into the use of language inasmuch as it takes into account human intentions and the consequences of speakers' choice of words in the construction of perceptions and beliefs. To explore further the source of that power and the modalities of its exercise, I examine two other facets of the exchange between Trump and Comey, by drawing on Erving Goffman's notion of participation framework and Brown and Levinson's notion of politeness.

Goffman's Participation Frameworks

We saw that, in the production and reception of speech acts, speakers and hearers can position themselves and others in different ways. By taking Comey aside after having several times in the past inquired about his loyalty, Trump was talking to him not as the director of the FBI, but as a vassal owing fealty to a king, in what Comey called a "patronage relationship," that Comey refused to enter into.

WARNER: [the President's] constant requests [for loyalty], despite you explaining your independence, he said "I need loyalty, I expect loyalty." Have you ever had any of those kinds of requests before from anyone else you've worked for in the government?

COMEY: No, and that made me uneasy at that point. I'm the director of the FBI. The reason that Congress created a 10-year term is so that the director is not feeling as if they're serving at – with political loyalty owed to any particular person. The statue of justice has a blindfold on. You're not supposed to peek out to see whether your patron was pleased with what you're doing. That's why I became FBI director to be in that position. That's why I was uneasy. (Politico 2017)

Goffman shows that speakers can adopt a variety of participant roles that assume various degrees of individual responsibility for their words. In our case, Trump could speak either as "principal," that is, as "someone whose position is established by the words that are spoken, someone who is [institutionally] committed to what the words say" (Goffman 1981:144); or he could speak as "author," that is, as "someone who has selected the sentiments that are being expressed and the words in which they are encoded" (ibidem); or he could speak as "animator," that is, as someone "active in the role of utterance production" (ibidem), but whose words are not necessarily his; they might be from a teleprompter, or he is quoting himself saying these words in the past either in real life or on reality TV. Here, in the Oval Office, Trump was speaking like a private patron, not like the President of a Republic. He was thus not the principal, as one would have expected in this setting, but the author of the words he uttered. However, because he would later deny having attempted to obstruct justice, one could imagine him claiming that he was merely animating words in order to test Comey's loyalty.

Hearers too, can play various participant roles. When Trump said: "I hope you can see your way clear to letting this go, to letting Flynn go. He is a good guy." Comey responded: "I agree he is a good guy," thus animating Trump's words, if not his intent, and thereby saving face. But again, when Comey got fired and subsequently his memos were leaked to the press, Trump tweeted: "James Comey better hope that there are no 'tapes' of our conversation before he starts leaking to the press!"

The tweet was a veiled allusion to the tapes that led to Nixon's impeachment, even though it was proven that there never had been any tapes made of the conversation between Trump and Comey and therefore the tweet was an empty threat, that is, yet another abusive speech act.

Brown and Levinson's Facework

According to Brown and Levinson (1978), every human interaction has to satisfy two contradictory needs or wants (see also Goffman 1967; Tannen 1993; Scollon and Scollon 2001, chapter 3). On the one hand, speakers need to give each other the good feeling that they are worthy of each other's attention, respect and recognition. They do that by saving both their own and the other's positive face through compliments, references to the other's utterances, inquiries, displays of interest. On the other hand, speakers must respect each other's negative face, that is, their need for freedom from interference from others. They do that by refraining from asking too personal questions, from making too direct requests that sound like commands and in general from intervening in others' decisions. Politeness is the name of this achievement of a balance between positive and negative face wants. Because it requires balancing the contradictory demands of power and solidarity, distance and closeness (Tannen 1993), politeness strategies have also been named "independence" and "involvement" strategies (Scollon et al. 2012), that is, they strive to preserve someone's need not to be obligated to anyone, but at the same time the need to be closely involved with others. Every verbal exchange requires this facework that involves symbolic forms of power inasmuch as it determines what one will say to whom, and what one will refrain from saying for fear of committing a face-threatening act.

In the case at hand, by ushering all the other members of his cabinet out of the room and taking Comey aside once they were alone, the President set the stage for a delicate facework that would require him to issue an order without giving the impression that he was doing so, in order to be able to save face later by denying it. In so doing, he also saved Comey's face, as Comey could always say that the President never gave him an order, he only expressed a hope and that was the reason he did not obey it. As Brown and Levinson argue, in verbal exchanges it is of utmost importance to save not only one's own face, but also that of one's interlocutor if one wishes the relationship to continue. If Trump had issued a direct order, not only would he have been legally liable of obstruction of justice, but he would have directly attacked the professional integrity of the director of the FBI. As it is, the exchange remained courteous and a bold on-record face threat was avoided. But was it really?

Brown and Levinson stake out three sociological variables in the assessment of the seriousness of a face-threatening act (FTA):

(i) the social distance (D) of speaker and hearer (symmetric relation)
(ii) the relative "power" (P) of speaker and hearer (asymmetric relation)
(iii) the absolute ranking (R) of impositions in the particular culture (p.74).

They hasten to note that these are not sociologists' ratings of *actual* power, distance and degrees of imposition, but only "actors' assumptions of such ratings, assumed to be mutually assumed" (Brown and Levinson 1978:75–76). P, D, and R are namely highly context-dependent. Thus, "a bank manager might be given a high rating on 'power' and a lowly worker a low one, but when the worker pulls a gun, or sits on a jury trying the manager, or represents his union, the power may be reversed" (p.78). There are many situational sources of power that may contribute to or override stable social valuations, depending on the circumstances or the nature of the speech act. For instance, "when a new President is elected, his old friends may still be friends, but they are unlikely to retain the old equality" (p.79). Similarly, regarding the degree of imposition, the request for permission to smoke outside is less of an imposition (R−) than asking for permission to smoke inside the house (R+).

In the case at hand, while the perception by Comey of the high P, D and R of the request made it an extreme FTA from the President of the United States, Donald Trump, acting as a chummy godfather, perceived the request quite differently, namely as a request for a personal favor. The deliberately vague language, "I hope you can see your way clear to letting this go," sounds like an opening in a business deal. For the director of the FBI, the President's FTA was so severe that he had to write it down afterward in a memo to take the full measure of the face threat. The release of this memo by the media was perceived in turn by the President as such a FTA against him that James Comey was fired two months later in the most humiliating and face-threatening way possible, namely through an announcement on television during the evening news. That's how symbolic warfare looks like (see Chapter 6).

4.3   INTERACTION RITUALS AND SYMBOLIC POWER

In all the research discussed in Section 4.2, symbolic power plays a major role. Its source is to be found in the perceptions, thoughts and beliefs of others and in the recognition by others of one's own legitimacy. Its exercise requires constant attention paid by speakers and hearers, writers and readers to the representing intentions and the communicative intentions of speakers, the illocutionary force and the perlocutionary effects of their speech acts, the work involved in saving their own and others' face, and of assessing the threat of FTAs. What any communicative use of language requires is careful attention not only to one's psychological self, but to one's symbolic self and its standing vis-à-vis others. Erving Goffman writes:

The term face may be defined as the positive social value a person effectively claims for himself by the line others assume he has taken during a particular contact. Face is an image of self, delineated in terms of approved social attributes – albeit an image that others may share, as when a person makes a good showing for his profession or religion by making a good showing for himself [. . .] *One's face is a sacred thing, and the expressive order required to sustain it is therefore a ritual one.* (1967:19, my emphasis)

As we have seen in the previous chapters, such processes as saving face, managing feelings of shame, guilt or awe, threatening someone's face, and caring about one's image vis-à-vis others, are not individual psychological processes. They touch on a deep conception of the self as a sacred entity – a notion that many scholars have traced back to a primitively religious, quasi-magical vision of the world that divided it into sacred and profane realms, taboo and ordinary objects and behaviors. A person's symbolic integrity is one such sacred taboo; taboo violations include not only incest and homicide and public displays of brute force, but also more subtle, ordinary symbolic attacks on a person's dignity such as intimidation, obfuscation, the humiliation of others in one's presence, or even the failure to reciprocate favors or gifts. All these actions do symbolic violence to a person's symbolic self, that is, the sense one has of oneself, one's integrity and self-respect, as seen through one's eyes and through the eyes of others. As Deacon describes it:

The self that is the source of one's experience of intentionality, the self that is judged by itself as well as by others for its moral choice, the self that worries about its impending departure from the world, this self is a symbolic self [. . .] This self is indeed not bounded within a mind or body, and derives its existence from outside from other minds and other times [. . .] This symbolic aspect of self is the source of our internal experience of free will and agency. (Deacon 1997:452–453)

As studied by Sigmund Freud in psychoanalysis, such conceptions of the sacred are still very much with us today.

Taboo is a very primitive prohibition imposed from without (by an authority) and directed against the strongest desires of man. The desire to violate it continues in the unconscious [. . .]The magic power attributed to taboo goes back to its ability to lead man into temptation [. . .] The expiation for the violation of a taboo through a renunciation proves that a renunciation is at the basis of the observance of the taboo. (Freud 1946:48)

To illustrate this I reinterpret a famous anecdote recounted by Goffman in *Forms of Talk* (1981). An exchange between President Nixon and Helen Thomas, senior UPI journalist, in the Oval Office, is used by

Goffman to illustrate his theory of footing, or "alignment we take up to ourselves and the others present as expressed in the way we manage the production or reception of an utterance," that is, the way we frame an event (Goffman 1981:125). Goffman shows how the President, by making a derogatory remark on Thomas' pants outfit and making her do a pirouette before him, changes footing from acting presidential to acting like a male chauvinist. But Cameron (1997) has shown how the derogatory locker room talk of straight men about gay men is less an attack on the latter, than part of an effort by the former to assert their own masculinity. One could say that Nixon was not so much wanting to put down Helen Thomas as he was keen on wanting to make reporters and camera men *laugh at her expense* and thereby *display before the media* his power to make her do a pirouette. Nixon's behavior here is a pure display of symbolic violence, namely the ability to construct a symbolic reality that elevates him and lowers her *in the eyes and perceptions of others*.

The reporter writes:

> Nixon asked Miss Thomas how her husband, Douglas Cornell, likes her wearing pants outfits.
> "He doesn't mind," she replied.
> "Do they cost less than gowns?"
> "No," said Miss Thomas.
> "Then change", commanded the President with a wide grin as other reporters and cameramen roared with laughter. (Goffman 1981:125)

By making the people around him laugh, he is on the one hand "expiating" his violation of Helen Thomas' integrity as a highly respected journalist by making it look like it was just a joke; but on the other hand he is increasing the violation by adding to his own insulting directive ("Then change") the face-crushing, humiliating laughter of public opinion, as represented by the press.[7]

Interaction rituals are suffused with power struggles, but they are not usually referred to as such, in part because interpersonal relationships have been studied from a psychological, not from a symbolic perspective. Thus we talk of "putdowns," "microaggressions," "prejudiced attitudes and comments against others" as individual acts that are reprehensible but not exactly life-threatening, except when these comments prompt others to translate words into action and actually kill people. We have difficulty talking about social death through shaming, shunning, stigmatizing, ridiculing, humiliating/mortifying – all depersonalizing or even desacralizing practices that can be a prelude to physical death as we saw in the fable of the Wolf and the Lamb, or that can be personally as devastating as physical death as we saw in the *Struwwelpeter* stories. In Section 4.4, we examine the relationship of interaction rituals and institutional power in the work of the French sociologist Pierre Bourdieu, who was very much influenced by Erving Goffman.

4.4 THE ECONOMY OF SYMBOLIC EXCHANGES AND THE POWER OF INSTITUTIONS

Pierre Bourdieu develops Goffman's investigation of the symbolic aspects of interaction rituals by exploring further the nature of the power they exercise. We have already seen in the Introduction how symbolic power is, for Bourdieu, "that invisible power which can be exercised only with the complicity of those who do not want to know that they are subject to it, or even that they themselves exercise it" (Bourdieu 1991:164). This is nowhere more apparent than in communication, that is, in linguistic exchanges, where the relations between speakers or their respective groups actualize relations of symbolic power through such speech acts as naming, categorizing and classifying, through facework such as shaming or praising, and through the participation frameworks they adopt. While some might think that the exercise of power is reserved for politicians and corporate executives, and that power does not enter into daily exchanges among friends and acquaintances, Bourdieu shows how subtle social differences like accent, conversation style and register get translated into symbolic differences, that is, perceptions of different amounts of linguistic, economic, cultural or educational capital.

Examples abound. The ability of a husband to ask his wife at the dinner table: "Is there any ketchup, Vera?", expecting his wife to jump up and get the ketchup (Cameron 1998), or of men to interrupt women and dominate family conversations (Lakoff 1975; Fishman 1978; DeFrancisco 1991), or of native speakers to correct non-native speakers on email (Liddicoat 2016), or of senior scholars to monopolize the floor at scholarly meetings, or of Anglos to talk down to members of other ethnic groups (Hua and Wei 2016) – are all blatant examples of the exercise of symbolic power in everyday life.

In these symbolic exchanges, what gives individuals the power to manipulate others is the power of institutionalized cognitive and metapragmatic models of behavior that people have internalized in their habitus (see Chapter 1), and the belief in the legitimacy of institutional differences based on gender, native speakership, seniority, expertise or ethnicity. But what does Bourdieu mean by institution? J. B. Thompson gives a useful definition in his Introduction to Bourdieu's 1991 *Language and symbolic power* :

> An institution is not necessarily a particular organization – this or that family or factory, for instance – but is any relatively durable set of social relations which *endows* individuals with power, status and resources of various kinds. (p.8, emphasis in the original)

Thus, for example, a husband who feels entitled to ask his wife to get him the ketchup is backed by an "instituted," that is, commonly agreed upon, belief in the superiority of men over women that is anchored historically in societal structures and social relations, including family relations. Thus we can speak of male or native speaker privilege, seniority or white power as being "institutions," that is, models of social relations that are taken for granted and recognized by everyone in a particular society at a particular time. Men, native speakers, senior citizens and Westerners draw their authority from such beliefs in contexts in which those beliefs are dominant.[8]

As Bourdieu makes abundantly clear, human-made institutions transform biological and natural differences (sex, age, knowledge, ability, ethnicity) into hierarchical and moral differences that people then take as "natural." In all these instances, symbolic power is not necessarily exercised with the intention of dominating others, but its effect is perceived and registered as such. Hanks summarizes Bourdieu's views as follows:

> Symbolic systems [like language] arise from and reinforce power differences. By engaging in linguistic practice, *and quite apart from their intentions or aims*, actors are complicit with the pervasive power relations in which their language is embedded. [. . .] Assumed, habituated, and schematized in the habitus, systems of difference appear self-evident. (Hanks 2005:77, my emphasis)

As we have seen in Chapter 2, while success in school might seem to be due to individual ability and inborn talent, in fact it depends on the opportunities afforded by such institutionalized social relations as they are found in educational settings that legitimize certain students more than others. This is where Bourdieu takes Austin to task for thinking about speech acts in purely linguistic terms. "To think about speech acts in this way is to forget that the authority which utterances have is an authority bestowed upon language by factors external to it" (Thompson, in Bourdieu 1991:9). For instance, the authority for a husband to proffer an indirect speech act such as :"Is there any ketchup?" comes from the institutional power with which he is endowed, even though such power is intended to be (mis)recognized as a natural endowment of the individual issuing the speech act.

Bourdieu's uncritical reliance on institutions as guarantors of legitimacy is more difficult to uphold at a time like ours when social relations have become more fluid than they used to be, and faith in traditional institutions such as governments, families and schools are being undermined by populist presidents, mass media and social media.[9] So who guarantees the validity of speech acts and the moral basis for taboo prohibition?

4.5   COMMUNICATIVE PRACTICE AS SYMBOLIC POWER STRUGGLE

While structuralist theories of communication have been critiqued by sociologists like Bourdieu for locating power in the individual speaker rather than in the authority of institutions, they have also been critiqued by feminist thinkers like Judith Butler and Chris Weedon. In *Excitable speech* (1997), Butler, drawing on Foucault and Derrida, argues that by focusing on the power of social convention and the intentionality of the speaker, both Austin and Searle fail to take into account the temporal dimension of speech acts. In particular, they do not give due attention to the time-lag between the illocutionary act and its perlocutionary effect. The reason why an insult is so hurtful, she says, is because it reactivates, that is, it reiterates prior traumas triggered by the same locutionary form of the utterance in the past. The meaning of that utterance has sedimented through time and now has a disorienting effect on the addressee by evoking the past hurtful context. But, she adds, this time-lag also offers an opportunity to reframe the injurious speech act by historicizing it and opening up what she calls "the political promise of the performative" (see also Chapter 9). In this respect, she disagrees with Bourdieu regarding the possibility of social action.

> it is the breaking of the utterance from prior, established contexts that constitutes the 'force' of the utterance (141) [...] Bourdieu fails to grasp the logic of iterability that governs the possibility of social transformation. It is clearly possible to speak with authority without being authorized to speak (157) [...] Agency emerges from the margins of power (156). (Butler 1997)

Butler here echoes another feminist linguist, Chris Weedon, who also takes up a Foucauldian stance when she writes:

> Discourse is a structuring principle of society, in social institutions, modes of thought and individual subjectivity. [...] Meanings do not exist prior to their articulation in language and language is not an

abstract system, but is always socially and historically located in discourses. Discourses represent political interests and in consequence are constantly vying for status and power. The site of this battle for power is the subjectivity of the individual and it is a battle in which the individual is an active but not sovereign protagonist (40) [...] To speak is to assume a subject position within discourse and to be *subjected* to the power and regulation of the discourse (116). (Weedon 1997, emphasis in the original)

In the case that has served as an illustration to this chapter, we could say that by writing down verbatim his conversation with President Trump in the form of memos that he then agreed to have released to the public, James Comey "spoke with authority without being authorized to speak," but that he was subjected to the power of the current dominant political discourse in the White House. That he was subsequently fired illustrates the post-modern paradox discussed by both Butler and Weedon that, as speakers, we are free to say whatever we want, but that we are constrained by larger discursive forces that limit what we may say, in this case the discourse of the U.S. Constitution that gives a democratically elected President the power to fire the Head of the FBI. In other words, as per Chris Weedon's definition, we have agency but not sovereignty. But, Butler would add, our vulnerability is the very condition for "expanding the domain of linguistic survival" (Butler 1997: 41). By speaking out, James Comey brought about an investigation by a Special Counsel, Robert Mueller III, to look into the President's abuse of power, and ultimately to his impeachment. I shall return to Butler's theory of performativity and consider further the critics of Bourdieu and Foucault in Chapter 9. For now, I want to close these reflections on communicative practice as symbolic power struggle by remembering Dell Hymes and his notion of communicative competence.

Hymes' original notion of communicative competence (Hymes 1972) encompassed a range of competences that have since then been proposed in literature and verbal art (e.g., poetic competence, rhetorical competence, narrative competence), and in interpersonal use of language (e.g., conversational competence, interactional competence, sociolinguistic competence). But these competences do not take into account the symbolic power needed to make them recognized and legitimated as communicative action.

It is interesting to see how broadly Hymes conceived of the notion when he was asked in 1987 to write an entry for one of the *Handbooks of Linguistics and Communication Science*:

Given the focus of much sociolinguistic work on language varieties and styles, and the general argument that the notion of language should be replaced by that of verbal repertoire as theoretical base [. . .] it is not surprising that communicative competence is often identified as command of alternative varieties and styles [. . .] *Use must not be conceived as merely the execution or contextualization of code [. . .],* but [should] include all abilities that enter into interaction [. . .] The conception of action cannot, however, be limited to that of the propositionally-based speech act [. . .] *A change in the world through words* is brought about not only by 'declaratives', but also by choices in devices of politeness. And communication includes all modalities and codes of sight, touch, and smell that enter into the *status and import of acts.* (Hymes 1987:223–224, my emphases)

As this quote shows, Hymes viewed language use not just as way of linguistically encoding actions and events, pragmatically performing speech acts through the appropriate locutionary forms, and observing the rules of facework or politeness, but as a way of bringing about "a change in the world through words." Communicative competence is the constructivist power to "constitute the given" through multiple modalities that add to the status and power of verbal acts (Bourdieu 1991:170). It is part of a more general competence to wield symbolic power that I called "symbolic competence."[10] In this respect, the most important aspect of Hymes' (1986) acronym S-P-E-A-K-I-N-G to describe the communicative situation[11] has to do with the ability to negotiate the social norms (or N) according to which speakers will interact and interpret each other's utterances. Such a negotiation invariably includes the management of symbolic power, especially in the case of intercultural communication.

By his insistence on the power of the individual speaker to negotiate not only the execution of the code according to existing norms of interaction and interpretation but the norms themselves, Hymes contested Jürgen Habermas' notion of communicative competence (Habermas 1970) that Habermas saw as linked to a commitment to the norms of ethical and political dialogue within a democratic society. I return to Hymes' critique of Habermas in the Conclusion and what Hymes proposes instead.

SUGGESTIONS FOR FURTHER READING

When looking at speech act theory from the perspective of symbolic power, it is good to read Austin (1962, 1979) together with his later critics from sociology (Bourdieu 1991:8–9), and cultural studies (Derrida 1977:15ff; Butler 1997:141–163). Culler (1982:110–134) clarifies

Derrida's post-structuralist critique of Austin's speech act theory. For performativity, Butler (1997) is a must. The difference between performance and performativity is discussed in Pennycook (2007, chapter 4) and McNamara (2019, chapter 2). Facework (also called politeness) theory is discussed in a highly technical way in the canonical Brown and Levinson (1978) study and in a more accessible way in Goffman (1967) and Scollon et al. (2012, chapter 3). It should be supplemented by Mao (1994) and Pan (2000) among others, who offer a critique of Western politeness theory from an Asian perspective. For the paradox of power and solidarity in conversational exchanges, Brown and Gilman (1960) is a must read, as is Tannen (1984), as well as Tannen (1993) and the critique of it offered by Cameron (1998). Videos by Gumperz, Jupp and Roberts (1979) and Tannen (2001) are useful to show how symbolic power is negotiated by interlocutors in interaction. For the use of discourse analysis in the study of intercultural communication, the major work is Scollon et al. (2012). The social institution of symbolic power and its relation to the political field is amply discussed in Bourdieu (1991, Parts II and III). Bourdieu (1996) offers a major study of the elite education system in France (*grandes écoles*), the United States (Ivy League schools) and UK (Oxford and Cambridge), that produces a "state nobility" with an unprecedented range of political, intellectual, bureaucratic and economic powers and distinctive titles to justify its privilege.

5   From Symbolic Power to Symbolic Violence

"I LOVE YOU" AS SYMBOLIC VIOLENCE

Consider the following four anecdotes recounted online by four college students, that is, youngsters between 18- and 22-years-old, in response to an invitation to share their experience of their first "I love you."[1]

1) "The first time I said 'I love you' to my most recent girlfriend, I didn't really say it. Not exactly when I wanted to, anyway. She and I had been dating seriously for about a month. One night, when we were out seeing a show together, we found ourselves drunk in the same bathroom stall [...]. We were having a great time together and both feeling what we thought was the magic of being in love (but what might have really been about five cocktails a piece), and we gazed at each other across the scummy toilet and I could tell we both wanted to say 'I love you.' My girlfriend at the time could tell, too, so she blurted out, 'LET'S NOT SAY IT! Not drunk at a dive bar in a dirty bathroom stall!' Phew! She saved the moment. We both cracked up, kissed, and said 'I love you' for the first time later that night in a gloriously clean and comfy bed."

2) "Before he left to study abroad in Europe, I told him I loved him. When he asked what that meant, I said that I cared about him and that he was a big part of my life. He said that he felt the same way, but he wouldn't say the words. It's a scary sentence, I don't blame him – but I was glad I took the plunge and got hurt, rather than having not jumped at all."

3) "One night, on the phone, when we were hanging up, I blurted out, 'I love you.' I hadn't meant to say it – I was just used to saying it to my friends – but after a second of silence, he said it back, upbeat and happy. From that moment on, we were stuck in weeks of telling each other we loved each other, even though we actually saw each other maybe twice. After a month had passed, I finally called him and broke up with him."

4) "I was in college, and told my boyfriend while we laid in bed one night that I loved him. He said, 'Um, thanks.' It was mortifying. But we talked about it, and he said it when he was ready to say it."

Who would have thought that such a candid, disinterested speech act as a declaration of love could be so fraught with symbolic uncertainties: Is my timing right? Am I imposing too much on him? How will my "I love you" be received? What if my love is not shared? What if her "I love you" is not sincere? In each of these cases, an explicit expression of love is perceived as problematic because it might not match the setting or the circumstances (#1), or because it imposes on the receiver the scary obligation to reciprocate in some form for what the utterer perceives as a gift (#2), or because the "I love you" may lack sincerity and therefore be an abuse of language (#3), or because the timing was not right (#4). In each case, the two interlocutors understand the phrase "I love you" as more than just a declarative, but rather as an expressive/confessional speech act with enormous risks to face. The expectations of the speaker are that the act will be (1) reciprocated with an equivalent speech act, (2) that the response will be as sincere as the original utterance and (3) that this reciprocity will forge a special bond between the two individuals. It is this invisible obligation to reciprocate that prompts Bourdieu to talk about the symbolic *violence* that may be done unto another person through language. While being able to utter the words "I love you" within the required felicity conditions is a sign of symbolic power, such an utterance requires also an awareness of the symbolic violence that these words may exert on others.

While theories of communicative competence have focused mainly on the symbolic power to do things with words, that is, to manipulate the social context in a here-and-now situation by acting on interlocutors and by saving one's own and others' face, a theory of language as symbolic violence draws attention to the way language manipulates the temporal context of human encounters by acting on people's past social memories, rituals and conventions, and on their social expectations for the future. Foregrounding this temporal dimension brings into focus the perlocutionary effect of utterances and the potential of symbolic power to turn into symbolic violence by acting on people's feelings of shame, indebtedness or gratitude, loyalty and rationality. This chapter discusses the nature of symbolic violence and its various temporal dimensions in our private and our institutional lives.

5.1 WHAT IS SYMBOLIC VIOLENCE? BOURDIEU AND FOUCAULT

We have seen in the Introduction that symbolic power is the "power to construct [social] reality" (Bourdieu 1991:166) by creating and using symbols that give meaning to the social world. It is an invisible power that is misrecognized as natural, disinterested and legitimate. "[S]ymbolic power requires, as a condition of its success, that those subjected to it believe in the legitimacy of power and the legitimacy of those who wield it" (Thompson 1991:23). We have seen that this belief requires not just the passive acceptance but the *active complicity* of those who are subjected to it. Because symbolic power makes those subjected to it believe it is legitimate, Bourdieu sometimes calls such power "symbolic violence" because it does violence to people's perceptions and beliefs. Thus, symbolic violence is the power not only to construct reality, but to impose on others a definition of the social world that is best suited to one's interests (see in Chapter 2, "The Wolf and the Lamb").

In his *Outline of a Theory of Practice* (1977a), Bourdieu showed that, as social agents struggle for power, they display various forms of "capital." A person might have social capital (family or networking connections), academic capital (the right degrees from the right schools), linguistic capital (multilingualism or a facility with words), economic or cultural capital (financial wealth or knowledge of cuisine or music). All forms of capital can, depending on the value that is given to them in their respective context, become symbolic capital (markers of prestige) that can be used to impress others, gain favors or further their own interests. In certain contexts, cultural capital is more valued than economic capital, in others academic capital is key to success. These are all forms of "wealth" that we bring to the "social marketplace."

In addition, and more importantly, we all possess and live within what Bourdieu called a habitus. In the words of Bourdieu's editor, J. B. Thompson, "the habitus is a set of *dispositions* which incline agents to act and react in certain ways [. . .] These dispositions are acquired through a gradual process of *inculcation* in which early childhood experiences are particularly important" (Thompson 1991:12; see *Struwwelpeter* and other stories in Chapter 3). "The dispositions produced thereby are also *structured* in the sense that they unavoidably reflect the social conditions within which they were acquired [. . .] Structured dispositions are also *durable*: they are ingrained in the body in such a way that they endure through the life history of the individual [. . .] Finally the dispositions are *generative* and *transposable* in the sense that they are capable of generating a multiplicity of practices in fields other than those in which they were originally acquired" (p.12–13). Thus, for example, if you have learned early on to reciprocate for gifts received, this inculcated knowledge will generate other behaviors, such as sending thank you notes or returning invitations, that will be transposable to other situations throughout your life.

Bourdieu acknowledges the existence of primary, secondary and even tertiary habitus, as when someone develops one habitus in the family, acquires a different habitus at school and yet a third when emigrating to another country or marrying someone from another culture. Such migrations can even lead to a *"habitus clivé"* (split habitus), as in the case of Pierre Bourdieu himself, who grew up in a working-class family in a small rural town in the Béarn and moved to Paris to pursue a prestigious academic career. Most importantly, the habitus is finely attuned to the field in which it operates. "As a durably installed set of dispositions, the habitus tends to generate practices and perceptions, works and appreciations, which concur with the conditions of existence of which the habitus is itself the product" (p.13).

A habitus is an intuitive feel for the social game, that includes the exercise of both individual symbolic power (e.g., when and how to return a gift, how to save face, how to make yourself believed, respected, legitimate), and institutional power (e.g., how to enforce family rules at home, how to impose disciplinary mechanisms in school or how to manipulate the educational system to serve your interests). Both forms of power may include various degrees of symbolic violence. David Brooks offers the following interpretation of Bourdieu's theory of symbolic violence for American readers:

> Every day, Bourdieu argued, we take our stores of social capital and our habitus and we compete in the symbolic marketplace. We vie as individuals and as members of our class for prestige, distinction and, above all, the power of consecration – the power to define for society what is right, what is "natural," what is "best." The symbolic marketplace is like the commercial marketplace; it's a billion small bids for distinction, prestige, attention and superiority. Every minute or hour, in ways we're not even conscious of, we as individuals and members of our class are competing for dominance and respect. We seek to topple those who have higher standing than we have and we seek to wall off those who are down below. Or, we seek to take one form of capital, say linguistic ability, and convert it into another kind of capital, a good job. Most groups conceal their naked power grabs under a veil of intellectual or aesthetic purity. Bourdieu used the phrase "symbolic violence" to suggest how vicious this competition can

get, and he didn't even live long enough to get a load of Twitter and other social media. (Brooks 2017b)

Brooks' characterization of Bourdieu's theory of symbolic power as violence is not wrong, but it emphasizes the nefarious aspects of a symbolic power struggle that is intrinsic to the workings of a free society based on individual entrepreneurship and competitiveness and omits the benefits that such a "pursuit of happiness" entails, for example.[4]

Bourdieu distinguishes two forms of symbolic violence: individual and institutional. And he adds: "All the symbolic strategies through which agents aim to impose their vision of the divisions of the social world and of their position in that world can be located between these two extremes" (Bourdieu 1991:239). In fact, individual and institutional forms of symbolic violence are sometimes difficult to disentangle in the actions of social agents who are themselves not just independent individuals, but members of groups or institutions whose power they tend to reproduce.[5]

Individual Violence

Individual symbolic violence is exerted by social agents who pursue their self-interest (face, honor, reputation, pride, social, cultural or symbolic capital) by placating, complimenting, flattering others, or, on the contrary, by intimidating, insulting or humiliating others (Bourdieu 1991:51). This is the subtle symbolic violence that underlies the whole economy of politeness discussed in Chapter 4, and of the cultural etiquette expected of socialized native speakers – the pragmatic do's and don'ts acquired in childhood that ensure the smooth functioning of social life. Symbolic violence here is the correlate of the symbolic power exerted by individual speakers, writers, bloggers when they use language not just to represent the world but to act upon others and to fulfill their need to be respected, admired, believed. The degree of "violence" of such speech acts has to be seen on a continuum depending on their degree of felicity and on the three dimensions of face discussed in the previous chapter – power (P), distance (D) and degree of imposition (R). For example, the symbolic violence exerted by the cat in the hat in Chapter 3 is mitigated by the fact that his speech acts were made in jest and that his shameful behavior was part of a world of play and fantasy. By contrast, the symbolic violence exerted by adults in the *Struwwelpeter* stories through shaming and humiliating others was made to instill in children a much greater degree of fear, even though it was based on face-threatening tactics that were similar to those used by the cat in the hat.

Institutional Violence

The symbolic violence exerted by individual agents is enhanced when these social agents act as spokespersons for larger institutions, such as the Community or the School, or in our day, the Corporation, the Market, or the Entertainment Industry, or even, as we shall see in Chapter 8, digital media giants like Google or Facebook. Institutionalized violence is exerted then by social agents such as marketing strategists, media columnists or school teachers whose symbolic act of imposition is justified because it is backed by the consensus of the community, and because it is performed by a delegated agent of a legitimate institution. Such violence is experienced by individuals as disciplinary practice in families, as peer pressure in the community and as the brainwashing of marketing ads, but also as the necessary and beneficial management of the production and transmission of knowledge at academic institutions (Foucault 1977/1995; see also Section 5.3). For, the violent dimension of symbolic power needs to be seen as natural, necessary and legitimate and to conceal its fundamental paradoxes. For example, peer pressure forges bonds of solidarity but can foster and even encourage conformism; family pressure preserves tradition but can keep you tied to your past; school pressure opens and builds your mind but socializes you into your proper place in the social structure; Facebook meets your need for friendship but it uses your personal data to enrich Facebook's bottom line.

5.2 THE PARADOXES OF SYMBOLIC VIOLENCE

The paradoxical nature of symbolic power that we discussed in the Introduction is re-enacted in its manifestations as symbolic violence. For example, politeness strategies (see Chapter 4) such as attempts by the mayor of a small town to downplay his institutional power by addressing his constituents in the local dialect even though he is fluent in the prestige variety of the capital, may intend to show them respect, but he might be seen as condescending or inauthentic if he is no longer one of them – what Bourdieu calls "strategy of condescension" (Bourdieu 1991:68–69). The euphemisms we use to save face: "let's do lunch sometime" when you don't really intend the see the person again; or "Oh how interesting!" when you really mean "How boring!", or "That's a challenge" when you mean "That's a problem"; or calling a handicapped person "physically challenged" – are all meant to show tactfulness but they might be viewed as hypocritical political correctness. "Bragging" and "bullying" might be viewed by some as intolerable self-promotion, by others as "telling it like it is." Telling lies might be heard by some as not telling the truth and by others as providing "alternative facts" or just innocent hyperbole. Depending on the context, what Bourdieu calls "interest in disinterestedness," that is, the ability to conceal your interest (in money, power or prestige) "beneath a veil of aesthetic purity" (Thompson 1991:16), might be viewed as admirable or as arrogant.

These paradoxes only show that symbolic violence presupposes an accurate assessment of the context and a correct anticipation of how what you do or say will be received. Politeness or tact are not absolute qualities. Instead, they are, as Thompson says, "nothing other than the capacity of a speaker to assess market conditions accurately and produce linguistic expressions which are appropriate to them, that is, expressions which are suitably euphemized" (p.20). Thus the symbolic power used by teachers, preachers, politicians, fundraisers, marketing strategists and social media platforms exerts more or less violence, depending on how it is received within a given context of situation.[6]

5.3   THE PERLOCUTIONARY EFFECT

By acting on memories, perceptions and anticipations of the responses of others (e.g., responses to compliments, insults and declarations of love), speech acts elicit perlocutionary effects that may do violence to their recipients. Symbolic violence builds into the speech act a temporal dynamic that links the prior needs and interests of the speaker with the projected reaction of the hearer and in turn with the wash-back effect of this reaction on the speaker. The utterance "I love you" made by, for example, a woman to a man carries with it the hope/expectation that he will acknowledge having, or will be moved into having, the same feeling as she and thus will fulfill her need for a romantic relationship. "I love you" is thus a request for reciprocity and a wager on an uncertain outcome. This uncertainty is what makes the utterance so risky and the speaker so vulnerable to a loss of face, but at the same time it is what makes it possible for her to reflect on her desire and to become conscious of her role as a social actor.

As social actors try to impose on others a certain view of reality and to make it stick – whether it is a language teacher wanting to make her learners view the world from another perspective or an immigrant trying to learn the host country's language and become "one of them" – the words they use evoke prior words in prior contexts on various timescales (Blommaert 2010, chapter 2). The perlocutionary effect of the various speech acts through which we address and are addressed by others sediments over time in our habitus, inscribes itself in our body as on a memory pad and becomes second nature (Bourdieu 2000, chapter 4). While we respond to current situations in the present, our body responds simultaneously to various events experienced in the past and imagined in the future. It thus accounts for the power of insults (see Chapter 4), and the effect of condensation symbols, brands and logos (e.g., "the wall" in Chapter 1).

Thus we have to view the perlocutionary effect as part of a whole symbolic ecology that goes beyond the effect of one speech act on the one person to whom it is addressed. Perlocutionary effects interpellate prior feelings of shame, fear, guilt, indebtedness/gratitude, loyalty, legitimacy and rationality. Through words and beyond words, they engage our sense of self and our role in social contexts. When someone uses offensive language about someone else in our presence, we feel not only hurt and shamed, because we are made complicit in the offense, but also ashamed for the offender because he or she violates norms of proper behavior. Similarly, when someone lies to us or to someone else in our presence and we know it to be a lie, we feel not just duped but embarrassed for the liar, because of what we have been socialized into believing is "the truth." In fact, we are caught between the desire to preserve our dignity as rational human beings and call out the lie for what it is, and our need to not take it seriously and go along with it in order to reach some greater good, such as peace in the family or in the workplace, but such appeasement tactics can backfire, as we shall see in Chapter 6.

5.4   AN EXAMPLE OF INDIVIDUAL VIOLENCE: THE RECIPROCITY IMPERATIVE

In his canonical essay *The gift* (1950/1990), the French anthropologist Marcel Mauss, who studied gift-giving practices in Samoa and New Zealand/Polynesia, traces back the reciprocity imperative to ancient beliefs in the sanctity of the person. Each time you give someone an object that has belonged to you or that you specifically chose as a gift, you are giving a little bit of yourself, and as long as the receiver has this gift, he/she has a hold over you. Thus, in order to make you whole again, the receiver is obligated to return the gift or to make a counter-gift roughly equivalent in value. As Mauss writes:

> Even when the gift has been abandoned by the giver, it still possesses something of him. Through it the holder has a hold over the beneficiary just as, being its owner, it has a hold over the thief if you give this gift to a third person. The thing received is not inactive. (Mauss 1990:15)

Similarly, timing is a crucial dimension of gift-giving: making a counter-gift too early after having received the gift gives the impression of wanting to annul the gift, too late conveys an impression of ingratitude or indifference. It is furthermore considered impolite to pass on the gift received to a third party, as it invalidates the generosity of the gift-giver. By passing on a gift received to a third person without acknowledging the first giver, one is in essence erasing the original owner from memory and usurping ownership of the object. But not sharing the gift with a co-present third party might be seen as selfish or exclusionary, hence the social dilemmas with which we are all familiar.[7]

The Economy of Symbolic Goods

Bourdieu explains this economy of symbolic goods under five maxims.

1) To prevent a counter-gift to be a mere swapping, there has to be a time-lag between the gift and the counter-gift.
2) The giver must be given to experience the gift as a gift without reciprocity and to experience the countergift as gratuitous and not determined by the initial gift.
3) The counter-gift should not be the exact equivalent of the gift or else the exchange of gift is destroyed. Both have to dissimulate the truth of the exchange.
4) In the economy of symbolic exchanges, there is a taboo on making things explicit (e.g., the price of things).
5) Silence about the truth of the exchange is a shared silence. It has to look as if there is no calculated action. And indeed the habitus knows unconsciously how to behave, without any calculating intention (Bourdieu 1998, chapter 5).

A symbolic faux pas thus becomes a moral issue. In the foreword to Mauss' essay, Mary Douglas explains this social morality of the gift system.

> Each gift is part of a system of reciprocity in which the honour of giver and recipient are engaged. It is a total system in that every item of

status or of spiritual or material possession is implicated for everyone in the whole community. The system is quite simple; just the rule that every gift has to be returned in some specified way sets up a perpetual cycle of exchanges within and between generations. In some cases the specified return is of equal value, producing a stable system of statuses; in others it must exceed the value of the earlier gift, producing an escalating contest for honour. The whole society can be described by the catalogue of transfers that map all the obligations between its members. The cycling gift system is the society. (Douglas 1990:viii-ix)

Following Mauss, Bourdieu views the transaction of gift-giving and gift-receiving as a typical exercise in symbolic violence that binds the gift-receiver in a loop of reciprocity:

By giving a gift – especially a generous one that cannot be met by a counter-gift of comparable quality – the giver creates a lasting obligation and binds the recipient in a relation of personal indebtedness. Giving is also a way of possessing: it is a way of binding another while shrouding the bond in a gesture of generosity. (Thompson 1991:24)

The nature of gift exchange threatens the negative face of the receiver because the expectation or obligation of reciprocity that is implicit in the transaction threatens the independence of the receiver as it binds him/her to the expectancies of the sender. But at the same time, it reinforces the receiver's positive face and the bonds of solidarity between the members of the community. Ron and Suzanne Scollon have therefore renamed negative and positive facework as "strategies of independence" and "strategies of involvement" (Scollon and Scollon 2001:50; see also Tannen 1993).

Many politeness rituals of everyday life are based on this notion of gift and counter-gift. In the anecdotes that opened this chapter, the utterance "I love you" was intended and understood not just as a declarative ("I hereby love you"), or an expression of feeling ("I am in love"), but as a gift that expected some sort of equivalent counter-gift. Imagine the various ways "I love you" can be used manipulatively, for example, to perpetuate a relationship that may not be worth maintaining, to exert control over an individual through indebtedness, to guilt an opponent, to make somebody develop love towards you, to justify one's actions, and so on. All of these instances use "I love you" with the conscious or unconscious effect of exerting symbolic violence. Hence the frantic efforts by the receiver to neutralize the degree of imposition, for example in #2 through a periphrase "I feel the same way," in #3 through an awkward silence, and in #4 through an embarrassed: "Hm... thanks." It is this desire to reduce the degree of imposition of

"I love you" that might explain the frequent innocuous use of the phrase by mothers as a way of closing a telephone conversation with their children who are trained to respond "I love you too."[8]

Less momentous utterances such as compliments can equally be instances of symbolic violence and threats to one's negative face. Why would "I love your scarf" be a face-threatening act? In many cultures, any personal compliment runs the risk of being perceived as coming too close, as being indiscreet, as lacking tact, especially when said by strangers in public places.[9] One way to reduce the threat is to downplay the illocutionary force of the speech act and pretend that it is not a gift, but a declaration of fact. The answer might then be: "My scarf? I like it too," or "Oh, my scarf? Yeah, I bought it half price at the sale down the street." With globalization and the spread of English as a global language, the pragmatics of such speech acts have become more complex. At a recent conference in Beijing, I overheard a conversation in Chinese between two women, one of whom suddenly said to the other in English, "Thank you!" When asked what she was thanking for, she responded that her friend had just paid her a compliment. But why say "thank you" in English if they were speaking Chinese? "Well, she responded, in China we don't make as many compliments as you in the United States but when we do we certainly can't thank someone for their compliment, that would sound too pretentious. However, we know that nowadays you are expected to say *thank you*. So we say it in English, like that we have said it without really saying it."

People have difficulty accepting that even if they didn't *intend* to bully, hurt or otherwise do violence to a friend, a colleague, a family member or a student, they can still be *perceived* as doing precisely that and be resented for that behavior. Take the case of two friends, one of whom has just had a bad experience (she has been ill or has failed an exam) or a good experience (she has won an award or gotten a new job). If the friend does not ask her about it, or makes minimum reference to it, she might be perceived as lacking in empathy or interest, and her silence might be received as a form of symbolic violence. Sometimes this violence is due to different cultural expectations. In some cultures it might be expected to show empathy or interest by asking questions, in others, questions might be perceived as nosy and inconsiderate. In some cultures it is expected that you show gratitude by saying "thank you" for a service rendered, but that same "thank you" in other cultures would be seen as stuffy and humiliating because it would be too formal.

The concept of symbolic violence can explain many mundane verbal behaviors in everyday life. We considered in the last chapter the dynamic between President Trump and the director of the FBI, James Comey. Trump's utterance "I hope you can let this go" was a clear instance of symbolic violence, that expected James Comey to reciprocate a "gift" of chumminess on the part of the president through a counter-gift of equal chumminess as a sign of "loyalty."

Gift-Giving Rituals in Everyday Life

Such rituals of reciprocity are thus part and parcel of everyday life. In our everyday transactions, in American English we expect compliments to be reciprocated with "Thank you," "Hi how *are* you?" to be reciprocated with "Fine, how are *you*?", the rendering of favors or services to be reciprocated at some point in the future. Invitations to dinner are expected to be returned in some form at some point, or at least to be reciprocated with a bottle of wine or an offer to bring some food ("What can I bring?"). In all walks of life, networking is a social ritual based on the "I-rub-your-back-you-rub-mine" reciprocity principle. Students have been socialized into this ritual, as evidenced by the following journal entry of four students in the *Language and power* course on which this book is based. The students were 22 years old, the first three majoring in electrical engineering and computer science, the fourth in political science.

1) Chinese male student: "My father gave me a Fitbit Chare II for my birthday, some time back. This gift came at a time in something of a dry spell, when we rarely exchanged gifts. Understanding that it would be poor manners to accept such a gift without giving anything in return – when Christmas rolled around, I ordered a carton of German *Scho-Ka-Kola* dark chocolate, shipped in from Finland, as a gift for my father. This would be a textbook example of symbolic power. My father exercised it by giving me the Fitbit – with the implicit, unspoken expectation of a return gift. I recognized this expectation as *legitimate*: and consequently (knowing that he lived in Germany for 7 years), repaid my hidden debt by buying him the German chocolate. In this clash of symbolic swords, we came out even."

2) Korean female student: "I personally do not think I have been given a gift that would fall under symbolic violence, but my parents' overall investments in me do influence me to be obedient: because they have given me so much and I have given them so little (and have not yet been able to), I should do what they say. Since they pay for my tuition, they have the ability to speak their mind about how I spend my college time."

3) Argentinian male student: "I experienced the giving of a gift as symbolic violence when I gave chocolates to my high-school teachers for Christmas; on the outside, I appeared to be a polite and caring student, which I was, but my act also elicited an unsaid claim that I would come back to collect my debt by asking for a letter of recommendation later on in the school year. While this was not explicitly stated, it was rare that I was turned down by a teacher when I had laid the seeds for such a favor through gifts early on. The teachers I gave gifts to did, as Bourdieu notes, have a habitus for this act: of course, many of the veteran teachers had encountered the same situation before, and of course, those students had come back to ask for letters of recommendation. But the disposition which they found most favorable for them over the years was just to smile, thank the student, and take the gift. They even had templates for letters of recommendation prepared, so concrete was their inclination to take these series of actions."

4) French female student: "I experienced such a symbolic violence when a friend of mine came to my birthday party when I was in elementary school with an immense *pièce montée*, which is a very fancy cake mostly eaten for big occasions such as weddings. I was a bit uncomfortable. With hindsight, I would say that she did that because her family had something of an inferiority complex with regards to my family's cultural capital – maybe I was unintentionally exercising symbolic violence on her too –, and was trying to balance it with a display of symbolic capital, showing that they had both the economic capital to pay for this cake, but also the social relations that enabled them to find someone to cook it. She was my friend, so I think this situation matches Bourdieu's description of a 'gentle' violence that is not recognized as such and concealed "beneath the veil of an enchanted relation."

One could think that the authors of such testimonies come from cultures who still honor gift-giving obligations and who still recognize the obligation to reciprocate for gifts received. One could argue that nowadays many youngsters no longer write thank-you notes to their grandmother nor feel obligated in any way to return gifts from family and friends. But that would be to misunderstand the priorities of today's teenagers and young adults. As the third testimony shows, youngsters nowadays are more attentive to what will enhance their chances of success on the job market or in their profession than to the politeness rules of the older generation. In the saturated market of late capitalism, symbolic capital, networking and social connections are more important than ever, even if they are more transactional attempts to secure a job, a promotion or a contract. And that means knowing how to manage the violence inherent in the exercise of institutional symbolic power, including the political arena where much of domestic and foreign policy decisions are based on a form of reciprocity called "diplomacy."[10]

5.5   AN EXAMPLE OF INSTITUTIONAL VIOLENCE: THE EDUCATIONAL SYSTEM

The reciprocity principle discussed earlier in this chapter on the individual level is meant to regulate the bonds of gratitude, that is, dependency, within a community through invisible ties of expectations. It is also the principle that in the form of laws, norms or social conventions regulates the life of institutions and of the expectations they impose on their members. Let's consider here a prime example provided by Michel Foucault in his popular study of educational institutions, *Discipline and Punish* (1995). We discussed in Chapter 2 the opening scene that describes the public execution of Damiens who had attempted to kill King Louis XV and the way his execution was orchestrated as the visible retaliation for his crime. Indeed, the retaliation had to be as horrendous as the crime; not, it is important to note, in order to deter the populace from committing the crime in the future, but in order to reinstate the cosmic symbolic order of things that had prevailed for centuries before the French Revolution.

With the Enlightenment, according to Foucault's narrative, such a physical violence became intolerable. Rather than edifying the people, it started to disgust them. With the change of ideas ushered in by the eighteenth-century reformers and philosophers, and with the rise of a utilitarian-minded bourgeoisie after the French Revolution, people started looking for economically more effective modes of punishment. Retaliation gave way to more rational and equitable forms of reciprocity for crimes committed. The absolute physical violence of the King was first replaced by the cost-effective use of the guillotine, followed in the nineteenth century by prisons as rehabilitation sites where panoptic surveillance was put in place to have offenders and delinquents learn self-control and self-discipline. For Foucault, the move from physical violence to physical detention and reeducation became the rational social contract common to institutions like prisons, hospital wards and schools. If you commit a crime that violates the norms of society, society will reciprocate by reeducating you into its norms and you will reciprocate by "paying your dues" to the society you have offended. Foucault argued that schools, as educational institutions, are structured in such a way that they manage the multiplicity of students not through physical coercion, but through self-disciplinary mechanisms. This self-discipline is a form of symbolic violence that is invisible, perceived as natural and legitimate, and maintained with the complicity of all.

The Power to Impose Meaning

It is this disciplinary regime that Pierre Bourdieu and Jean-Claude Passeron describe in their book *Reproduction in education, society and culture* and on which they base their theory of symbolic violence. In the initial chapter "Foundations of a theory of symbolic violence," Bourdieu and Passeron write:

> Every [institutional] power to exert symbolic violence, i.e., every power which manages to *impose meanings* and to impose them as legitimate by concealing the power relations which are the basis of its force, adds its own specifically symbolic force to those power relations. (Bourdieu and Passeron 1990:4, my emphasis)

Note the way the authors define symbolic violence: not just as the "power to construct reality" – a definition that might sound innocuous enough for educators eager to foster their students' creativity and resourcefulness – but the power to "impose meanings." At a time when applied linguists and literacy scholars encourage teachers to teach "reading for meaning" (Swaffar et al. 1991) or to "expand meaning-making potentials" in modern language education (Kearney 2016) or to promote individual agency in "meaning design" (Kern 2015:37), it is good to remember that meaning is not just there for the taking: it always emerges out of someone's needs and interests, and the desire to impose that meaning on others. The making and imposition of meaning is the source of endless symbolic struggles within and between institutions and their members.

This is particularly true of educational institutions in which nothing less is at stake than the meaning young learners will give to their lives and the society they live in. As Bourdieu and Passeron remark: "All pedagogic action is objectively symbolic violence insofar as it is the imposition of a cultural arbitrary by an arbitrary power" (p.5). As we saw in the Introduction and Chapter 1, Saussure and Bourdieu define "arbitrary" slightly differently. For the linguist, the arbitrariness of the linguistic sign is due to its independence from any individual intention and its dependence on social convention, whereas for the sociologist the arbitrariness of pedagogic action is due to its independence from natural law and its dependence on institutional and cultural convention.

> The selection of meanings which objectively defines a group's or a class's structure as a symbolic system is *arbitrary* insofar as the structure and functions of that culture cannot be deduced from any universal principle, whether physical, biological or spiritual, not being linked to any sort of internal relation to "the nature of things" or any "human nature." (Bourdieu and Passeron 1990: 8)

The knowledge and skills that are taught at educational institutions are not the only ones that could be taught. They have been deliberately selected to meet the needs of various stakeholders: the job market, the market of symbolic cultural goods, well-educated parents from the middle class who fund the schools through their taxes or who impose their middle-class values on the way subjects are taught (see Heath 1983; Bourdieu 1996). Furthermore, the ever-tighter link between educational institutions and the job market ensures that the most coveted knowledge and skills are those in demand by the current high-paying jobs, not necessarily those that would correspond to a student's particular talents. The meanings that schoolchildren and college students are encouraged to make are meanings that will match the interests of the middle-class members at their respective educational institutions.

> The pedagogic action [. . .] is the one which most fully, though always indirectly, corresponds to the objective interests (material, symbolic, and pedagogic) of the dominant groups or classes, both by its mode of imposition and by its delimitation of what and on whom it imposes. (Bourdieu and Passeron 1990:7)

The Power to Exert Symbolic Violence

Like gift-giving, "pedagogic authority itself is a power to exert symbolic violence" (Bourdieu and Passeron 1990:11). Bourdieu and Passeron argue that even in an open society like the United States, the importance given to titles (e.g., Professor X, Dr Y), institutional affiliations (e.g., PhD from prestigious University X, Chair of Y), rankings and grade point averages helps reproduce a disciplinary system which is seemingly based on natural merit but is in fact the result of a systematic differentiation through what Bourdieu calls "social magic" (Bourdieu 1991:119). Social magic is the power of the institution to create difference where there was none (at equal academic achievements) or by exploiting pre-existing differences, like the biological differences between the sexes or the differences in family background (legacy admissions), age or ethnicity, for admitting some students and rejecting others in the name of "diversity" – a radical all-or-nothing decision that might affect an individual's whole life trajectory.

As educational institutions are made to compete for the best students and the best researchers in a global economy, social magic and the obsession with competitiveness are transforming rational modes of evaluation of student performance into a measurement fetishism, where grades and rankings become more important than quality of knowledge, the persuasive prose of a school application becomes instrumentalized in the pursuit of a favorable admission decision, language becomes commodified to fit the current buzzwords in a neoliberal economy (e.g., Gray and Block 2012; Holborow 2012; Schmenk et al. 2019). In the same manner as a gift-system, used not just to reciprocate for a gift received, but to display your superior wealth, "escalates the contest for honor" (see Section 5.2), in the same manner a grading system, used not just to evaluate a student's individual achievement but to gain an edge over others, escalates the competition for symbolic capital. In short, symbolic power turns into symbolic violence, expressed by such phrases as "showing off," "bragging," or "interest in disinterestedness."[11]

5.6 AN EXAMPLE OF COMMUNICATIVE VIOLENCE: CONVERSATIONAL INEQUALITIES

Individual and institutional violence manifest themselves in the seemingly most innocuous verbal activity of everyday life: talk and conversation. The important domain of sociolinguistic research on interaction rituals and forms of talk (Goffman 1981), the systematic turn-taking in conversation (Sacks et al. 1974), the philosophical exploration of the logic of conversation and its cooperative principle (Grice 1975), as well as the studies of conversational style (Tannen 1984), talking power (Lakoff 1990; Cameron 1998, 2000) and conflict talk (Grimshaw 1990) all include the negotiation of symbolic power and hence the potential exercise of symbolic violence.[12] There is no verbal exchange that does not in some form or other involve the management of turns and topics, and the negotiation of subject positions, and that does not do violence to each interlocutor's sense of self and other, whether the interlocutors speak or remain silent, engage or don't engage one another, follow up or not on each other's contributions. Because symbolic violence has to do with the social psychological power of suggestion, it is also, as I noted earlier, largely independent of the speakers' intentions to exert such violence: A can feel that she has been slighted by B simply because B interrupted her, or didn't listen properly, or didn't respond appropriately or didn't let her talk, or didn't show interest, and B can feel that A has done violence unto her for the very same reasons.

Turns, Topics and Tasks

The field of conversation analysis, which has illuminated the turns at talk, the conversational topics and tasks of speakers and hearers in conversation (e.g., Liddicoat 2011), has been supplemented by analyses of the symbolic power at work in such conversations: the turn-taking asymmetricalities, the unequal management of topics, the inferencing deficits, misguided assumption of consensus and bad faith arguments in conflict talk are all ways of exerting symbolic violence (see, e.g., Zhu Hua and Kramsch 2016). You often don't notice that an utterance does violence to its recipients before you see its perlocutionary effect. For example, on a jogging path in California a white American male addressed a Korean-looking woman with "Nice weather today, eh?" and after a few seconds "Where do you come from?". The woman felt aggressed; it sounded as if the man was putting her American identity into question. She responded in kind "I'm from San Diego, how about you?" She had saved face, but her irony was lost on the male jogger (Zhu Hua and Li Wei 2016).[13]

The Instructional Communicative Situation

The language classroom has often been viewed as "bare-bones pedagogy [...] A place where content means almost nothing and power, desire, provocation almost everything" (Kaplan 1993:128–129). The beginner's class in particular has been seen as a privileged space where adult learners become little children again and have to learn how not to be ashamed of making mistakes and even of making themselves ridiculous. Indeed, symbolic violence is not too strong a word for what happens day by day in language classrooms. The native speaker teacher has immediate and uncontested power over the non-native speakers, but the non-native teacher has the symbolic power granted him/her by the institution. No one likes to admit that the learners are competing with one another and with the teacher in this crucible where loss of face, threats to self-esteem and identity abound. But the legitimacy of the teacher is also on the line at every grammatical or spelling mistake, every piece of wrong information or unconventional accent. The fact that with today's technology a teacher's utterances can immediately be checked by any student in the class against the Internet and any unknown lexical item can be found on Google Translate adds to the precarity of the teaching situation. The increasingly multicultural composition of language classes further increases the uncertain power position of the instructor and the trust that needs to be established between teacher and learners for learning to take place. Whether teachers want it or not, they have to juggle the various levels of symbolic power granted to them by the academic institution, but they also have to meet the expectations of the students, the school and the general public as to what meaning to give to their students' language learning experience. For social, cultural and political reasons, such a meaning has been shown to be conflictual and the source of much anguish (Kramsch and Zhang 2018).[14]

At the end of this chapter on symbolic violence, it is good to remember that this term, coined by Pierre Bourdieu with regard to gift-giving practices, does not mean coercing someone to do something against their will. Indeed, for Bourdieu, symbolic power always entails symbolic violence *but it never does that without the agreement of the people involved.* Thus, the word "violence" indexes both psychological pressure and the intensity of this pressure, but it always implies acquiescence on the part of those on whom it is exerted. One could argue that, in the example of the encounter between the two joggers mentioned in the previous section, the Korean-looking woman rejected the symbolic violence done unto her by pushing back; but Bourdieu would point out that, although she had understood perfectly well why the man posed the question (to foreground her ethnicity), she still complied with his request for information by responding, albeit with sarcasm, thus acquiescing to the ambiguous power relations in the United States between white and non-white Americans. This explains how Bourdieu could see evidence of symbolic violence in the most well-intended gift, the most noble educational endeavor and the most friendly conversational turn-at-talk. Rather than a violation of another person's autonomy, such violence has to be understood as the powerful expectation of reciprocity inherent in any act of communication. Ultimately it is this reciprocity principle that constitutes us as social actors in the exciting but risky game of life, love and language. In the next chapter, we consider how this power has been used not just to make friends and influence people, but to transform symbolic violence into outright symbolic warfare.

SUGGESTIONS FOR FURTHER READING

The paramount importance of context in any discussion of language as symbolic power makes Hanks (1996) and Duranti and Goodwin (1992) essential readings for this chapter. The reciprocity principle and the power/solidarity paradox are amply demonstrated in the whole of Robin Lakoff's and DeborahTannen's work (e.g., Lakoff 1990; Tannen 1990). Symbolic violence has been studied in particular regarding discrimination on the basis of gender and sexuality (Fishman 1978; Cameron 1998), ethnic discrimination (Philips 1972), and discrimination against immigrants (Gumperz et al. 1979). The critique by Bourdieu and Foucault of the French educational system is echoed by critical voices in English literacy education (see Wortham 2006; Albright and Luke 2008; Kramsch 2008). For conflict talk, Grimshaw (1990) offers a set of studies of the disputes among adults and children in conversation.

6 When Symbolic Violence Turns into Symbolic Warfare

"FIRE AND FURY LIKE THE WORLD HAS NEVER SEEN"

On August 8, 2017, the *New York Times* published the following report:

> President Trump threatened on Tuesday to unleash "fire and fury" against North Korea if it endangered the United States, as tensions with the isolated and impoverished nuclear-armed state escalated into perhaps the most serious foreign policy challenge yet of his administration.
>
> In chilling language that evoked the horror of a nuclear exchange, Mr. Trump sought to deter North Korea from any actions that would put Americans at risk. But it was not clear what specifically would cross his line. Administration officials have said that a pre-emptive military strike, while a last resort, is among the options they have made available to the president.
>
> "North Korea best not make any more threats to the United States," Mr. Trump told reporters at his golf club in Bedminster, N.J., where he is spending much of the month on a working vacation. "They will be met with fire and fury like the world has never seen." Referring to North Korea's volatile leader, Kim Jong-un, Mr. Trump said, "He has been very threatening beyond a normal state, and as I said, they will be met with fire and fury, and frankly power the likes of which this world has never seen before." [1]

This "chilling" threat uttered at a cabinet meeting in front of the cameras scared the pundits and the world at large in its reference to a possible nuclear Armageddon, especially on the anniversary of the bombings of Hiroshima and Nagasaki in August 1945. But it was also a puzzling speech act, as it seemed to threaten to respond to Kim Jong Un's own threats with the total annihilation of his country. And yet Trump's repetition and amplification of his original statement "they will be met with fire and fury like the world has never seen" into "they will be met with fire and fury, and frankly power the like of which this world has never seen before" gave it a theatrical tone or, as Austin would say, a "parasitic" flavor that diminished the felicity of the threat as such and cast doubt on the speaker's intentions. The expression "fire and fury" was particularly puzzling as a biblical or literary metaphor (or as the name of a videogame) to make North Korea believe he was ready to push the nuclear button, but at the same time he was disclaiming his intention to do so by using vague and stilted language (e.g., "the likes of which"). So, was it an exercise in symbolic violence, a business-like opening move, a declaration of war or just an episode of Reality TV? Because the fire-and-fury strategy is part of an arsenal of other strategies of coercion, deception and intimidation by the current president of the United States, this incident can serve as an entry point to examine more closely what happens when symbolic violence turns into symbolic (and potentially physical) warfare, and to consider how to resist it.[2]

6.1   WHAT IS SYMBOLIC WARFARE?

Over the months and years of Trump's presidency, a multi-facetted verbal profile of the commander-in-chief has emerged. One of those facets has been characterized as that of a mobster or con man. If one recalls the old mafia boss Don Vito Corleone (Marlon Brando) in Francis Ford Coppola's 1972 film *The Godfather*, it is easy to recognize the features of such discourse. It is intended to keep people guessing about the boss's intentions and what he meant to say. Trump's personal lawyer Michael Cohen testified explicitly before Congress on what he called "Trump's use of coded discourse," that is, indirect speech acts, veiled performatives, allusive pronouncements and, in general, vague language that keeps his subordinates guessing and gives him the deniable plausibility that we saw used by monarchs like Henry II in Chapter 4.

In addition to being deliberately vague about his present intentions, Trump manipulates the listeners' expectations for the future. He cultivates among his addressees a climate of uncertainty and unpredictability typical of what Bourdieu calls "absolute power." This is the persona that Trump wanted to present on TV to Kim Jong-Un and that puzzled his audience. Bourdieu describes this as the power to control the public distribution of time:

> Temporal power is a power to perpetuate or transform the distributions of the various forms of capital by maintaining or transforming the principles of redistribution [...] Absolute power is the

> power to make oneself unpredictable and deny other people any
> reasonable anticipation, to place them in total uncertainty by offering
> no scope to their capacity to predict [...] The all-powerful is he who
> does not wait but who makes others wait. (Bourdieu 2000:228)

The use of vague utterances from people in positions of authority –
"We'll see what happens" or "I have not made up my mind yet, but
you will know pretty soon" or "Don't call me, I'll call you" – and
the vague statement "fire-and-fury-like-the-world-has-never-seen" –
controls the time and the rate of fulfilment of people's expectations,
keeps people in suspense and worrying about the future. As Bourdieu
describes it, temporal power delays without destroying hope,
adjourns without totally disappointing, turns down without turning
off and keeps people motivated without driving them to despair.
Total unpredictability creates a context favoring every form of
manipulation of aspirations (such as rumors or empty threats). The
total flouting of anticipation engenders fatalism or cynicism (such as
terrorism).

Yet another facet of Trump's discourse is that it keeps hidden, not
only its illocutionary force and its control over time, but also its control
over truth and reality. We have seen in the discussion of the two
incidents that opened Chapters 1 and 4 how the pundits and the social
actors involved were disoriented and even "terrorized" by the president's use of hyperbole and untruths, and how they feared the veiled
warnings and unfounded threats that were hurled indirectly through
daily tweets. Trump's abuse of symbolic power and his manipulation of
illocutionary space, perlocutionary time and sense of reality are typical
of the weaponization of symbolic violence that Brooks has called *symbolic warfare* (Brooks 2017b).[3]

There is a fine line between symbolic violence and the verbal abuse
characteristic of symbolic warfare. While the first is inherent in all
human interactions and is, as we have seen, the very condition of our
social existence, the second is wielded by individuals intent on exploiting social norms and expectations for their benefit *at the expense of
others*. Symbolic violence and symbolic warfare are thus on a continuum depending on the degree to which an individual's speech
conforms to or deliberately subverts the agreed norms of interaction
and interpretation of the group. At a time of general discontent about
the way globalization has favored some and left many struggling for
survival, and in an era when digital media have given a voice to this
discontent and amplified it, populism is on the rise and the traffic in
symbolic goods quickly turns into symbolic warfare.

6.2 SYMBOLIC WARFARE AND POPULISM

Much has been written and said about what makes populist politicians attractive to voters: economic disenfranchisement, cult of authoritarian personalities, xenophobia/racism/anti-immigrant sentiments, fear of globalization, right-wing extremism and 24/7 media (see Charaudeau 2011; Klein 2017; Woodward 2018; Sclafani 2018; Poniewozik 2019a; and others). To these factors, Bourdieu adds one more that fits into his argument about symbolic violence. Intrinsic to symbolic violence, he says, is a certain "symbolic alchemy" (*alchimie symbolique*), a truly magical force that binds people together because it responds to deep collective beliefs and expectations (Bourdieu 1998:99). Drawing on the double meaning of the French term *reconnaissance*, which means both recognition/acknowledgement and gratitude, Bourdieu argues that the receivers of a gift (e.g., the election of a populist president they voted for) are bound not only by a transactional acknowledgment of indebtedness and the understanding that they must return the gift in the form of loyalty (see Chapter 5), but by a deep feeling of gratitude that can turn into affection and even love.

> One of the effects of symbolic violence is the transfiguration of relations of domination and submission into affective relations, the transformation of power into charisma or into the charm likely to trigger affective enchantment [. . .] The acknowledgement (*reconnaissance*) of a debt turns into gratitude (*reconnaissance*), a durable *feeling* toward the author of the generous act, which can extend to affection or love. (Bourdieu 1994:187, my translation)[4]

Populist politicians and their supporters are bound to one another by mutual bonds of indebtedness and affection according to the motto: "As long as you don't let me down, I won't let you down." Supporters feel grateful that their candidate has given them the attention they crave; the candidate is grateful to his or her voters for their unwavering attention and support. Both are able to wield the symbolic power of words, tweets and the 24/7 coverage of mass media to accumulate a symbolic capital that is both cognitive and affective. Bourdieu explains the magical force of this symbolic capital as follows:

> Symbolic capital is any ordinary property (physical strength, wealth, warlike valor etc.) – which, perceived by social agents endowed with the categories of perception and appreciation permitting them to perceive, know and recognize it, becomes symbolically efficient, like a veritable *magical power*: a property which, because it responds to socially constituted "collective expectations" and beliefs, exercises a

> sort of action from a distance, without physical contact. An order is
> given and obeyed: it is a quasi-magical act. (Bourdieu 1998:102)

To illustrate this quasi-magical power I would like to explore further
the case of populist President Donald Trump, who has been characterized as a master of symbolic warfare precisely because of the symbolic
ties of allegiance and loyalty, affection, gratitude and fear that he
masterfully manipulates.

6.3   A CASE STUDY OF SYMBOLIC WARFARE: DONALD TRUMP

Populists' political success has been viewed as due in part to the
growing class consciousness of the economically disadvantaged
members of society who feel not only materially, but also symbolically,
disregarded and disrespected. As we shall see in Chapter 7, the hunger
for attention and recognition through social media and other forms of
self-assertion is evidence of this growing importance of the symbolic
over the material in all walks of life. It also explains Donald Trump's
fixation on receiving from "the elite" the symbolic recognition he
craves and that has always eluded him, despite his enormous wealth
and his political position as the "leader of the free world." His reputation as an entertainer and a billionaire may have earned him a certain
amount of social and economic capital in the media and the business
world, but it has not earned him the same amount of cultural and
symbolic capital he seeks in the cultural world. His familiarity with the
world of television and the media have made him a master in the use of
symbolic violence to pursue his interests. We have already discussed
Trump's use of symbols to build a highly contested "wall" on the
southwestern border of the United States (Chapter 1) and his manipulation of the indeterminacy of speech acts to give orders with plausible
deniability (Chapter 4). In the following, I consider how symbolic
warfare has become the driving principle of his politics.

Manipulation of Language

The incident with "The Wall" which opened Chapter 1 is a good
example of the potentially abusive aspects of Trump's discourse.[5] Since
the advent of his presidency, Donald Trump has been identified by the
press as a "pathological liar." Indeed, his reasons for building a wall on
the southern border of the United States were based on his false claims
that "hordes of men, women and children" were illegally "invading"

the country, and that drugs were being illegally "smuggled" into the country at "unprotected" points of the border. In reality, most illegal residents were legal visitors who had overstayed their visas, and drugs were being smuggled in mostly at legal ports of entry. The promises Trump made during his campaign were based on distorted facts or "alternative truths" that riled up his base and got him elected, but they also showed how addicted he is to public applause and how aggressive he is at crushing his rivals, all the while he is soliciting pity and compassion by portraying himself as the victim of the press, the media and the Washington elite that are, he claims, out to get him.

The symbolic violence he exerts is difficult to respond to because of its ambiguousness and its bait-and-switch nature. First, his claims are ambiguous. Not only do his lies have to be responded to by constant fact-checking by the press, but he does not allow himself to be pinned down by any "evidence" and he claims to rely only on his intuition. Because after all he is the President, many politicians choose to hold back rather than stand up to him. Second, he has mastered an "art of the deal" that is more bait-and-switch than outright negotiation, as the following incident shows.

On December 11, 2018, the Speaker of the House of Representatives Nancy Pelosi and the Senate Minority Leader Chuck Schumer, both Democrats, are called by the president to a televised interview in the Oval Office to discuss the possible closing of the government if the Congress refuses to give him the money he requested to build the wall.[6] The President spends the first 10 minutes expressing his administration's need for a wall, but remembers suddenly that his advisers have recommended he use the term "border security" instead to assuage his democratic interlocutors.

TRUMP: The wall is a very important thing to us. I might put it a different way. Border security is extremely important and we have to take care of border security.

After 15 minutes during which Pelosi and Schumer try to convince Trump not to shut down the government if he doesn't get his wall, Trump baits them into accepting the building of "border security":

TRUMP: We need border security. I think we all agree that we need border security, is that right?
SCHUMER: Yes, we do. We do.
TRUMP: Good, good. (to the cameras) See? We get along! (To all present) Thank you everybody.

At this point the interview seems to have come to an end, even though the term "border security" remains ambiguous. After a few questions from the reporters to that effect, the president repeats the term "border security" five times but then abruptly switches back to calling his project "building the wall," which is what he wanted to do all along.

TRUMP: (to the cameras) You know what, we need border security. That's what we're going to be talking about, border security. If we don't have border security, we'll shut down the government. This country needs border security. The wall is a part of border security. Let's have a talk. We're going to get the wall built, and we've done a lot of wall already. We're going to talk about the wall.

Trump's cavalier manipulation of the referential meaning of words and his deceptive use of a consensual "we," that masquerades alternatively for "I," "my Administration," or "my Republican supporters" and only feigns to include his current Democratic interlocutors in the room (or forces them to rally behind the "we") – all clearly show the president's *modus operandi*.[7] Critics have called it "bullying." We could call it symbolic violence or even symbolic warfare. As we shall see, the media play a major role in transforming the one into the other.

Manipulation of the Television Camera

From his morning chats with the cameramen on the White House lawn to the cabinet meetings to which he invites the TV cameras to his bouts of anger when he is photographed from the wrong angle, Donald Trump is a product of television and of Reality TV in particular; so any analysis of Trump discourse has to factor in the presence of the cameramen who constitute his "real" audience. Here is one example. Jimmy Kimmel, comedian and television host, who had often criticized the presidential candidate Donald Trump, interviewed him on December 17, 2015, two weeks after a deadly shooting by Islamic extremists in San Bernardino, California. Kimmel takes Trump to task on his call to ban all immigrants from Muslim countries from entering the United States, until, he said, "our country's representatives can figure out what's going on."

JK. "Isn't it un-American and wrong to discriminate people based on their religion?"
(*TV audience applause*)
DT (*switching eye gaze back and forth between JK and camera/TV audience*)

1) (*to JK*) But, Jimmy, the <u>problem</u> (0.2)
2) (*to camera*) I mean, look, I'm for it (=I'm with JK) but look (0.3) we have people coming into our country (0.1)
3) (*to JK*) that are looking to do <u>tremendous</u> harm

You look at the t- look at Paris
Look what happened in Paris

4) *(to camera)* I mean, these people,

5) *(to JK)* they did not come from Sweden, <u>okay?</u>
   Look at what happened in Paris
   Look at what happened last week in California
   With –

6) *(to camera)* with you know 14 people dead
   Other people going to die
   they're so badly injured

7) (to JK) We have a real problem
   There is a <u>tremendous</u> hatred out there
   And what <u>I</u> wanna do is find out

8) (to camera) what is

9) *(to JK)* you you can't solve a problem until you find out what's
   the root cause and <u>I</u> wanna find out

10) (to camera) what is

11) *(to JK)* <u>the problem</u>, what's going on

12) *(to camera)* and <it's temporary> *(accelerated)*
    I've had SO many people call me and

13) *(to JK)* say thank you

14) *(to camera)* now if you remember when I did that a week ago it was
    bedlam. All of a sudden (0.2)

15) *(to JK)* and you watched last night

16) *(to camera)* and you see people talking they said: "Well Trump has
    a point"

17) *(to JK)* we have to get down to the problem

18) *(to camera)* The people that are friends of mine that
    called they said: "Donald, you have done us a tremendous
    service

19) *(to JK)* because we do have a problem

20) *(to camera)* and we have to find out what is the =

    JK *(interrupts)* = they may have been
       prank calls *(audience laughter)* those may have been prank calls

As Trump shifts his gaze 20 times from Kimmel to the camera (and the small TV audience behind it) and back to Kimmel, he adapts his discourse accordingly. In turns 1–11 he focuses on "the problem," in turns 12–18 he diverts the topic onto the public applause of his decision, in 19–20 he returns to "the problem."

In response to Kimmel's original question, Trump immediately reframes the issue from *discrimination-against-Muslims* to *we-have-a-problem* with various constituent parts: comparison with Paris and California; non-white people come to our country, looking to do tremendous harm; there is tremendous hatred "out there"; we need to search for root causes to solve this problem. His discourse is addressed alternatively to Kimmel and the camera, however it gets differently distributed between the two.

Addressing Jimmy Kimmel, Trump repeats again and again (six times) the word "problem" making it collocate with "tremendous harm," "tremendous hatred," "solving the problem," "searching for root causes" – as if to erase in the minds of the listeners any memory of the inconvenient topic proposed at the outset by the interviewer ("religious discrimination is un-American"). Such a strategy sounds logical, rational, even scientific. Problem-solving is, after all, a well-attested American virtue. By contrast, when he turns to the camera (and the millions of his supporters), his discourse becomes less technical, it's all about "people" coming into our country, 14 "people" dead, other "people" going to die, "people" thanking him, together with vernacular phrasings such as "it was bedlam," "it's temporary." This is the plain folks' way of talking that appeals to his base – a populist way of speaking that seeks to rile up "the people" with emotional, fear-raising words against those "other people" who come from "out there." This kind of discourse links immigration policies to "people" from non-white countries entering the United States with the intention of bringing harm and hatred to this country.

With Kimmel, Trump speaks as if the immigration ban he proposed was an exploratory measure to find out "what's going on." By contrast, when addressing the camera and his supporters he seems to already know that "these people are coming to our country looking to do tremendous harm." Such reasoning is meant to justify his proposed ban on immigration from Muslim countries; it is based on the premise "We have a problem," then proceeds through repetition to persuade the listeners that the nature of the problem is not the gun lobby, international terrorism or domestic extremism, but non-white people (not from Sweden) invading our (white) country. Meanwhile, Kimmel's original question remains unanswered.

6.4 TRUMPIAN NEWSPEAK

The way that symbolic violence has taken hold of the discourse in the White House itself is the topic of Bob Woodward's 2018 book *Fear in the*

Trump White House. Woodward, Pulitzer-prize winning journalist, well known for his coverage (with Carl Bernstein) of the 1974 Watergate scandal, identifies several strategies used by the president to enhance his symbolic capital and diminish that of others. These can be seen as manifestations of extreme discursive dysfunction, in part due to Donald Trump's personal communicative style, in part due to his long-time association with TV and the media, including social media (see Chapters 7 and 8). They all command blind allegiance and support through a heightened sense of insecurity and fear. Woodward documents the following major strategies used by the president.

Using Disparagement and Ridicule

Trump has become known for the graphic and profoundly insulting epithets that he regularly affixes on his opponents and on anyone he despises, for example, "Little Rocket Man" for Kim Jong-Un, "Crooked Hillary" for Hillary Clinton, "Sloppy Steve" for Steve Bannon or "The Failing *New York Times*." He has publicly called members of the FBI "scum." He has called Jeff Sessions, the Attorney General he himself appointed, "an idiot" and "a traitor" in front of cabinet members in the Oval Office. He has made fun of his Southern accent ("This guy is mentally retarded. He's this dumb southerner" (Woodward 2018:216). And he has memorably called some African nations "shithole countries" (pp.320–321). This public shaming online or in front of the cameras has been decried by some as inciting violence and as providing an encouragement for the increase in shooting deaths around the country.[8]

Verbal violence has also included the ridiculing of foreign accents or of any political statement that displeases him, like that of his then national security adviser, General H. R. McMaster. As Woodward writes:

> In a searing insult to McMaster, Trump did an imitation of his national security adviser. The president puffed up his chest and started noticeably exaggerated breathing. He said in loud staccato, "I know the president of Iraq. He's a good man, sir! I know he has our best interest at heart." Returning to his normal voice, Trump said, "That guy's just full of shit. I met this guy. McMaster doesn't know what he's talking about." Trump had met the Iraqi prime minister, Haider al-Abadi, at the White House in March 2017. (p.314)

Manipulating the Interactional Context

In addition to invectivity, Trump uses principles of symbolic warfare to get his way. Here are some of the most frequent observed by Woodward during his visits to the White House, expressed in the form of behavioral principles:

– Make bystanders complicit in the verbal abuse
– Never confront people directly but disparage/discredit them indirectly in public
– Turn everyone against everyone else
– Don't hesitate to turn against those who are closest to you
– Put people in double binds
– Use the psychological warfare you use in business
– Use distracting tactics and change the topic
– Accuse others of dishonesties that are in fact your own
– Deny, deny, deny anything that is said about you
– Redefine lexical terms to suit your narrative
– Be unpredictable
– Reframe the terms of the conversation
– Focus at all times on your mediatic image
– Use Twitter as a one-way megaphone

6.5   TWITTER POLITICS

Like many other populist presidents, Donald Trump has continued to use Twitter when he became president, not only as a mode of communication but as a political instrument of symbolic warfare.[9] In addition to watching Fox News daily for several hours, the president spends 60 percent of his time sending up to 100 tweets a day to his 60 million Twitter followers.[10] His "Twitter diplomacy" has offered him an independent channel of communication to the American electorate and the ability to govern by tweet independently of official democratic institutions: Congress, the Justice Department and the Media. He has used Twitter to go after rivals, issue threats, accusations, chidings and demands, and in general to "divide and conquer." Unlike postings on Facebook, tweets don't necessarily expect a response.[11] They rally public opinion behind you, but they can also easily make a third party lose face, as when Trump hurled veiled accusations, threats or warnings against President Xi of China, thus indirectly humiliating and rallying world opinion against China.

By promoting direct demagogy and an alternative form of government, Twitter politics has contributed to creating a parallel state that is at war against what Steve Bannon and Donald Trump called the "deep state" of official institutions. This parallel state has been seen as replacing society by interest groups, citizenship by white supremacy and laws by norms that benefit the moneyed elite. Trumpist discourse:

deep state, the press as enemy of the people, fake news, is eerily reminiscent of Stalinist times.

By circumventing the regular channels of communication, Twitter has also been used to undermine the cooperation expected by participants in face-to-face exchanges. By inserting tweets addressed to a third party (or hurled speech, see Chapter 2) unbeknown to the participants in an ongoing exchange, tweeting bystanders can disrupt the economy of symbolic exchanges described by Goffman (see Chapter 4) and damage the mutual trust and recognition of the conventional participation frameworks.[12]

6.6   RESISTING SYMBOLIC WARFARE

Resisting this kind of verbal abuse is not easy. In a devastating *New York Times* article, former FBI director James Comey described how respectable and professionally respected civil servants like Attorney General William Barr could become coopted into serving the needs of the president rather than serving the Constitution to which they have pledged allegiance. Comey details how people of professional integrity but with insufficient inner strength get roped into becoming complicit in lies, deceptions and the construction of an alternate reality of which they become hostage. "It takes character to avoid the damage," he writes, "because Mr. Trump *eats your soul* in small bites" (my emphasis). How can this happen? Comey writes:

> It starts with your sitting silent while he lies, both in public and private, making you complicit by your silence [. . .] because he's the president and he rarely stops talking. As a result, Mr. Trump pulls all of those present into a silent circle of assent.
>
> Speaking rapid-fire with no spot for others to jump into the conversation, Mr. Trump makes everyone a co-conspirator in his preferred set of facts, or delusions. I have felt it – this president building with his words a web of alternative reality and busily wrapping it around all of us in the room.
>
> [. . .] Next comes Mr. Trump attacking institutions and values you hold dear. Yet you are silent. Because, after all, what are you supposed to say? He's the president of the United States.
>
> You feel this happening. It bothers you, at least to some extent. But his outrageous conduct convinces you that you simply must stay, to preserve and protect the people, institutions and values you hold dear [. . .] Of course, to stay, you must be seen as on his team, so you make further compromises. You use his language, praise his leadership, tout his commitment to values.
>
> And then you are lost. He has eaten your soul.[13]

Over the course of history, writers, linguists and historians have tried to grapple with pathologies of discourse that generally accompany abuses of political and physical power. George Orwell's novel *1984* (Orwell 2017) showed how language can be distorted into Newspeak to mean the opposite of what it usually means for purposes of political brainwashing or indoctrination. Victor Klemperer documented the abuses of the German language through the *Lingua Tertii Imperii* (the language of the Third Reich) (Klemperer 2000). More recently, sociolinguists like Deborah Cameron (2000), Block et al. (2012) and David Block (2018, 2019), applied linguists like Barbara Schmenk et al. (2019) and critical discourse analysts like Norman Fairclough (2014) and Ruth Wodak (2015) have analyzed the nefarious effects of neoliberal jargon, fast capitalistic Newspeak, sloganization and ideological misinformation on discourse practices in everyday life. And in Chapter 8 I will discuss further the current disinformation campaigns that crowd the digital spaces of social media. Resistance to symbolic warfare takes various forms, from avoidance tactics, to remaining silent and biding time, to securing a written record of the conversation, to reframing the issue, to publicly denouncing injurious speech and explicitly talking back. As an example, I cite here another passage from the exchange between Trump, Nancy Pelosi and Chuck Schumer discussed in Section 6.3. The president, faced with the two Democrats' opposition to his wall, turns to the cameras and in a condescending form of hurled speech he puts down "Nancy," implying that because she had not yet been confirmed as the new speaker of the House, she is in a politically precarious situation.

TRUMP: Look, we have to have the wall. This isn't a question; this is a national emergency (. . .) (*turning to the cameras*) I also know that, you know, Nancy's in a situation where it's not easy for her to talk right now, and I fully understand that. [We're going to have a good discussion

PELOSI: [Mr. President

TRUMP: and we're going to see what happens. [But we have to have border security

PELOSI: [Mr. President, please don't characterize the strength that I bring to this meeting as the leader of the House Democrats who just won a big victory.

In this extract, Pelosi immediately fights back, asserting her power as the second, equal branch of government, that has just won a Democrat majority in the House of Representatives – as Trump continues to speak over her (brackets indicate overlap). She zeroes in not on the content of Trump's utterance but on his speech act – his condescending characterization of her, thus avoiding being heard as putting into question the president's political legitimacy, while forcefully reinstating the symmetrical balance of power between her and the president – and, by way of consequence, the legitimacy of her own political power as the Speaker of the House. Symbolic warfare in conversation is particularly difficult to resist in asymmetrical exchanges where the turn-taking and the management of topics are conducted under conditions of extreme conversational inequality and in front of camera spotlights.

In this and other exchanges, Donald Trump seems to be behaving like a private citizen and not like the president of the United States as he flouts all the social and political expectations associated with his position. But if he can afford to do so and still retain the support of his followers, that is because he gets his legitimacy from somewhere else; not from the Constitution, nor from Wall Street, but from the Entertainment Industry. As the television critic James Poniewozik wrote recently: "The institution of the office is not changing Donald Trump, because he is already in the sway of another institution. He is governed not by the truisms of past politics but by the imperative of Reality TV: Never de-escalate and never turn the volume down [. . .] He's half-man, half-TV, with a camera for an eye that is constantly focused on itself. The red light is pulsing, 24/7, and it does not appear to have an off switch" (Poniewozik 2019b).[14]

It is deeply unsettling to realize that the Donald Trump who sits in the Oval Office might be nothing but a persona from "The Apprentice,"[15] but it enables us to see the exercise of symbolic violence in a different light. Indeed, Woodward writes, "during Trump's first six months in the White House, few understood how much media he consumed. It was scary. Trump didn't show up for work until 11:00 in the morning. Many times he watched six to eight hours of television in a day" (Woodward 2018: 299).[16] If Trump the politician is in part the product of television, the media and the digital channels of communication available on social media, then we have to take a new approach to studying the relation of language and symbolic power – one that Bourdieu, Foucault and Goffman could not imagine; one that puts into question our traditional ways of looking at language and language use. Indeed, any analysis of symbolic violence and its abuses must be supplemented by a study of the symbolic power of the media to create the symbolic realities that we live by today. It is to this that we will turn in the third part of this book.

SUGGESTIONS FOR FURTHER READING

In the last three years, American linguists have written on Donald Trump's odd use of everyday language in his public statements and at political rallies. Hunston (2017) zeroes in on his unconventional populist way of talking; Robin Lakoff (2017) calls him a post-truth "hollow man"; McWhorter (2018) gives a sarcastic description of Trumptalk and Trumptweets as "unmonitored language" – a new kind of officialese. Cultural critics point to the dangerous nature of his rhetoric: Packer (2019) compares Trump's populist rhetoric and the Nazi rhetoric of the Third Reich as vividly described by Victor Klemperer (2000). Those interested in the way language and politics intersect in the making and breaking of nations will do well to read Yurchak (2006) on the language of late socialism in the last two decades of the Soviet Union, as well as Young (1991) on totalitarian language in Orwell's Newspeak. Several studies on the symbolic warfare waged by the White House against Trump's opponents reveal also the relentless power struggles inside the Trump administration – the most prominent one to date being Wolff 's (2018) explosive bestseller and its sequel Wolff (2019). Oren and Solomon (2014) are a dramatic reminder of the dangerous perlocutionary effects of ritual incantations of ambiguous phrases for political purposes.

PART III
The Power to Create Symbolic Reality

7 "I Am Seen and Talked About, Therefore I Am"

HARAMBE: THE GORILLA, THE MARTYR, THE MEME

The following incident, written in spring 2018 by Michael Bronstein, a 22-year-old college student at the University of California, is a good example of the kind of symbolic reality we will be dealing with in this chapter.

On the morning of May 28, 2016, an event happened unlike any other. It was a Saturday, a nice sunny day in Cincinnati, Ohio. Families of all kinds were out and about the streets and in parks enjoying the day. One family in particular, the Gregg Family, chose to spend their day at the Zoo. The Gregg Family had four children, the youngest of which being Isaiah Gregg who was four years old. Isaiah was a fine boy, he loved all kinds of things in life, like cars, action figures, and animals, but Isaiah especially loved gorillas. When Isaiah's parents found out that the Zoo had a gorilla exhibit, they knew they had to take their son there. When the family reached the gorilla pit, they began taking pictures together and filming the area. Isaiah, however, loved to climb, and while his parents were busy, Isaiah managed to climb over the barrier and fell into the gorilla pit. Fortunately, Isaiah didn't get hurt in his fall but the moment he hit the ground, bystanders began screaming. There was a boy in the gorilla pit, who knows what could happen. Isaiah's mother started yelling "don't worry mommy's here." However, the scene soon got so intense that security was called and was told that a boy had fallen into the gorilla pit.

Not too long after Isaiah had fallen, a gorilla by the name of Harambe had taken notice that there was a boy in his home. Harambe approached the boy and sensed that the boy was scared. Harambe, mind you, had been known as a nice gorilla who had never caused much of a fight with any of the security in his enclosure, which is what made the next scene so controversial and strange. Harambe lifted the child and made sure the boy was alright before he began dragging Isaiah across the water and splashing him. People opened their phones and began filming and showed the boy being violently dragged but the boy didn't seem to be screaming in pain. Alerted to the scene, the Zoo keepers, worried that Harambe was hurting the child, shot him in the head with a rifle. . .and Harambe fell to the ground.

135

Questions then began rising up as the tragedy became circled by news media across the country and the world. Why was the family not watching out for their child? Why did Harambe drag the child across the water? And why did the keepers kill the gorilla? People were outraged and confused. Harambe, born in captivity, had been in the Cincinnati zoo for some 17 years and had made his mark on the city for being a friendly and kind gorilla who was always putting a show for all who saw him. No one blamed the family, but as news circled around and around, the internet took notice and soon enough Harambe memes were hitting the web. One meme featured a gorilla with angel wings floating in heaven. Other memes came out in droves as people found new ways to "honor" the gorilla by laughing at his death. Memes started circulating showing that Harambe did not only die for the child, he also died for our sins, for our memes, for socialism, for communism, that Harambe had died for a purpose beyond himself. The memes that circulated became so viral that the story of Harambe was taken out of context, and the idea of a gorilla dying for a cause took hold. Harambe had become such a massive phenomenon that at the University of California Berkeley, the school's Facebook meme page organized an event titled "Candlelight Vigil to honor Harambe", where people showed up and thought about "their gorilla". The most extreme fallout came during the 2016 election, when websites began claiming that between 11,000 to 15,000 people had written in on their ballot the name Harambe as the next president of the United States.[1]

7.1   FROM LOCAL NEWS TO MEDIATIC EVENT TO MEME

The student narrator here tells three stories. The first reports an event that the narrator read in the news. Families visiting the Cincinnati Zoo walk over to the gorilla compound, a four-year old-falls into the pit, the mother yells" "Don't worry mommy's here!" as she looks at her child through the frame of her smartphone. Harambe, a friendly gorilla, approaches the boy, starts playing with him and drags him across the pool. Alerted by the scene, and afraid the child is being harmed, a zookeeper draws his weapon and shoots Harambe in the head. These are the actual facts.

The second story describes how the participants not only experience their visit to the Cincinnati Zoo, but film it and film themselves experiencing it so that they can later share it online with families and friends. While this is happening, the 4-year-old is actually experiencing the zoo physically by climbing over the fence and falling into the gorilla pit. As Harambe starts dragging the boy across the pool, the narrator again focuses on the people opening their smartphones and filming the scene of a gorilla playing with a 4-year-old child. Indeed, a seemingly harmless scene captured on film. Suddenly the movie turns violent as a guard rushes to the scene, draws his rifle and shoots the gorilla in the head. This story goes beyond the reality as the participants experienced it. It tells a reality that has already spawned a spectacle of itself and a narrative fit for home video or for public television. That narrative retrospectively generates fear as a way of justifying the brutal murder of the gorilla. The filmed spectacle recorded on cell-phone cameras replaces the event itself. The narrative is now *interpreted* for the benefit of spectators who were absent from the scene: actions are evaluated, if not excused; actors' intentions are made clear; causes and effects are made explicit.[2]

Shortly after the actual event, a third story begins, one to which the narrator and other social media users contribute by *constructing* it online through various postings and expanding it through various off-line activities. Social media witness a highly emotional outpouring of grief for the innocent 400-pound gorilla shot dead just after his seventeenth birthday. The physical violence done to the animal has now morphed into the symbolic violence of digital forms. Internet memes, that is, multimodal signs in which images and texts are combined and (re)posted with different meanings, are some of these favorite forms, but so are slogans, jokes, stories, parodies and cartoons. They all go viral, building on the mix of outrage, compassion and fatalism that the gorilla's death has elicited in the news media. Some of the Harambe memes that were posted in the year following the incident included:

- A photograph of a crouching brown-haired Harambe squarely facing the viewer with a stern look, right arm resting on his right knee, descending from a pale blue heaven in a halo of white clouds, bathed in the rays of a celestial light, like Christ resurrected and transfigured appearing to his apostles. A flight of steps leads towards the viewers, presumably encouraging them to receive Harambe or join him in heaven.
- Four photographs of the same gorilla in various macho poses under the caption "Sexiest man alive."
- Cartoon of a gorilla sitting in a cage with a little boy on his lap. The gorilla is handing the boy a peeled banana. Caption: "The photo CNN doesn't want you to see."
- A human hand holding a plastic bottle of glue. The label on the bottle says: "Incredibly strong GORILLA wood glue. Dries natural color. Made in USA" and features the head and the upper body of a gorilla. Caption: "They call it gorilla glue because Harambe was metaphorically the glue that held this nation together."

– Three black-and-white photos of the faces of Mahatma Gandhi, John F. Kennedy and Harambe, side by side, above the caption: "10 top political assassinations of the 20th century." [3]

Through Facebook, Instagram, Twitter and other social media, these memes construct an alternative symbolic universe in which Internet users can build alternative identities and avatars. Memes have the side effect of creating an insiders' community of like-minded Internet users and reinforcing their shared sense of humor and sophistication. In his report, the student, Michael Bronstein, equates memes' weird form of humor to the Theater of the Absurd that flourished in the fifties following the end of World War II and the start of the nuclear age. At the time, he writes, the dark humor of a Vladimir and Estragon in Beckett's *Waiting for Godot* (1953), or Meursault's numb response to events in Camus' *L'étranger* (1946) were a reflection of the disorienting and distressing political times. Similarly today, the student argues, the Harambe memes proliferate online, creating a goofy alternative reality that provides disoriented and cynical youth alike with a common Mythology of the Absurd that they can fill with their subjective pain, anger and cynicism over current political realities. Harambe the martyr has entered the lives of many college teenagers and become a new (albeit entertainment) reality that is now part of their lives.

Within a year Harambe the beloved ape became, as news editor Hathaway puts it, "a singular, iconic internet meme the likes of which we may never see again" (Hathaway 2017). Indeed, we need to keep in mind the historic context of the incident to understand its significance.

> The tragic story of Harambe's death was a perfect outrage magnet that arrived in the midst of an interminable election cycle. In May 2016, America was ready to talk about anything but Donald Trump and Hillary Clinton for a change. And in Harambe, we had a moral dilemma with an innocent victim and no good solution. Once the boy was in the gorilla's pen, there could be no happy ending, but Harambe's sad death had us searching for one anyway. We questioned the boy's parents, we questioned the zoo's procedures, and we questioned the existence of zoos in general. There was no way to restore Harambe's physical existence, so the internet decided he would live on in another way: as a previously unseen combination of jokey meme and venerated deity. Pledging allegiance to Harambe, and performatively mourning him, became a kind of game. Dropping his name online was an in-joke that could mark someone as part of the meme community [...] Nearly every part of the internet engaged with Harambe. For some, making Harambe memes was a way of coping with the real sadness of his death. For others it was an opportunity for trolling, a way to get a rise out of the genuine mourners. Whenever an

event strikes an emotional chord with the public, the dark underbelly of the internet is there to exploit it. No horrible tragedy is exempt from mockery. You can blame this pattern on a teenage lack of empathy, and that would be partly correct. Making memes about touchy subjects like "the ape who died" also provides a sense of community for teenage edgelords, a way to "ironically" express emotions they probably wouldn't admit they feel. (Hathaway 2017)

The Harambe memes included parody song lyrics, shocking sexual images and irreverent cartoons. But one thing that made Harambe memes special was that they did not become brands, they were not commercialized and exploited for marketing. In fact, some made fun of marketing brands. With Donald Trump's election looming, internet memes became slowly enlisted by Trump supporters for their "internet propaganda war." Hathaway concludes: "In that context, the apolitical, broadly appealing Harambe meme looks like an artifact from a more innocent time. Today's memes tend to be politicized, carrying a pro- or anti-Trump bent, which means they have little chance of becoming everything to everyone, as Harambe was" (Hathaway 2017).

I would like to use the transformation of Harambe into different avatars – Harambe the friendly gorilla, the martyr, the meme – to reflect on the way the incident in the Cincinnati Zoo was constructed by the various participants at the time and by an undergraduate student in a term paper two years later. And how this construction of reality has been theorized by scholars in sociology, cultural studies and applied linguistics. In this chapter, I discuss the more theoretical aspects of the creation of reality through the new digital technologies and how they have ushered in a different way of conceiving of language as symbolic power. In the next chapter I will consider the social and cultural changes brought about by the digital revolution.

7.2 FROM A MODERNIST TO A LATE MODERNIST READING VIA EXISTENTIALISM AND SOCIAL CONSTRUCTIVISM

There are several ways of reading the story recounted earlier in this chapter, depending on which news media reported the story, whether or not one witnessed the scene, and on one's interests, age, social background or political views. In the following, I distinguish between a modernist and a late modernist interpretation of the events.

How Parents and Friends Read the Incident

As was reported the next day in the press,[4] the silverback gorilla was dragging the child in the pool when the child started screaming, the parents cried for help and the zoo's security team made the difficult decision to kill the gorilla, rather than tranquilize him, for fear that he would react violently and harm the child. The reactions from the public were swift. Some criticized the zoo for responding with what they felt was excessive force. Many blamed the boy's mother for failing to look after her son. Some even suggested that the boy's parents should be held criminally responsible for the incident. Petitions on the Internet sprang up, including one called "Justice for Harambe," which demanded that "proper legal action be taken in this matter and responsible parties be held accountable if the investigation was to find that there was negligence involved." That petition attained over 10,000 signatures in a few days and received well over half a million signatures before it finally closed.

This kind of reporting focuses on the facts and their interpretation by witnesses and newspaper readers, many of whom called for remedial steps, problem-solving measures and even legal action. This is, in a sense, a modernist response that draws from the modern faith in the fairness of security guards and the rationality of the justice system as well as from the belief in such moral virtues as responsibility, accountability and good parenting.

How College Students Read the Incident

While many readers were outraged at the facts as they were reported in the press, college students like Bronstein interpreted the event in a more philosophical way. Drawing on some of the existentialist thinkers they had read in college, they started making Harambe into a mythic figure (see Chapter 1) and they asked: What does the creation of the Harambe myth have in common with French existentialists like Camus or Beckett? To be sure, the subversive, offensive, iconoclastic beatification of a gorilla can evoke some of the more absurd scenes in *The Myth of Sisyphus* (1955) or *Waiting for Godot* (2012). They have in common a certain black humor, an acceptance of one's destiny, and a certain despair at ever being able to give meaning to a world apparently without meaning.[5] But the 2010s in the United States are not the 1940s and 1950s in Europe. Existentialism during and after World War II in France was based on anguished questions about the meaning of existence, the possibility of free will, the nature of hope and the future of humanity threatened by mass slaughter, nuclear annihilation and totalitarianisms of various sorts. It located freedom not in people's actions and abilities to "change the world," but in their consciousness of their limits and their faith in their ability to construct the meaning of their lives on their own.[6] In doing so, existentialism paved the way for a mode of thinking that would be later called post-structuralist or late modernist, and that channeled the imagination of the creators of memes like the Harambe meme.

Foucault, whose Preface to *The order of things* (1970) the students had read in class, was a major influence on this shift from a focus on facts to a focus on larger discourses that construct our sense of reality. For the students, Harambe's death felt as absurd and incomprehensible as the taxonomy of animals in Borges' famous Chinese encyclopedia, which Foucault discusses in that Preface. In their minds, there had to be another larger discourse that justified such a senseless death. They grasped at late modern theories that suggested that such events are socially constructed, for example through the invention of the smartphone, the cultural obsession with selfies and American child-rearing practices. The incident was also constructed by the public and the press as a potential legal issue. Their outrage at Harambe's death was not due only to a sympathy for an innocent gorilla, but to the students' ability to place the event within a larger historical framework of growing surveillance and securitization, and of the increasing power of digital technologies to record and document every instant of our lives (see Section 7.3). The second meme already mentioned about Harambe's gender drew on yet another discourse, this time a late modern feminist discourse, that posits that biological sex itself is not 'natural' but is always filtered through social preconceptions about gender and through the discourse we use to characterize our sexuality.[7] Applying this discourse to a gorilla, of course, replaced one absurdity by another.

Thus, through the micro-lens of the Harambe story, we can see larger philosophical ways of interpreting events. They go beyond the facts (or social structures of knowledge) and relate them to larger discourses of a post-structuralist or late modern kind – in the case at hand, the discourse of security, legal accountability and parenting, but also the discourses of truth, justice and mediatic reality.

In applied linguistics research, post-structuralist and late modern theories of discourse are often conflated but they have different roots.[8] Post-structuralism is a linguistic effort by scholars in the social sciences to overcome the linguistic and social determinism that often accompanies structuralist theories of language and draws attention to sociolinguistic ideology and inequality (McNamara 2012). Late modernism is a social and cultural effort by scholars in cultural studies and critical theory to account for feminist, gender related, post-colonial, and globalized realities (Cameron 2005; Kramsch 2012a). Both post-structuralists and late modernists agree that "language neither reflects nor expresses meaning, *but constructs it*. The temporary fixing of meaning is never a neutral act; it involves both interests and questions of power" (Weedon 1997:171, my emphasis). Meaning, as we saw in Chapter 2, is therefore always a site of struggle over which and whose meaning will obtain. Part of the cathartic aspect of the Harambe memes lies precisely in their creators' power to construct sense out of a seemingly senseless act. It enables them to create a memory of the event and thus an historical record by embedding it into the larger context of violence experienced by users of social media. I return to this form of "documediality" in Section 7.8, but for now I want to hold on to the constructivist view of meaning offered by the Harambe fans to highlight one more facet of what has been called "late modern" thinking.[9]

The uncertainty, posited by late modern theory, regarding truth, knowledge, meaning and subjectivity, and its focus on the social construction of reality has led some to accuse late modern thinkers of moral relativism and academic elitism. After all, they would say, whether the gorilla intended it or not, the boy's life was potentially in danger and the guard took the only morally justifiable action; the victimization discourse intoned by the students is an elitist discourse that ignores the harsh reality of the event. While Harambe the gorilla was real, they might argue, Harambe the meme is "just" a figment of the imagination and not to be taken seriously. These arguments have been made frequently, and the philosopher Ian Hacking has addressed them head on in his provocative book *The social construction of what?* (Hacking 1999a).

Taking several concrete examples to distinguish physical reality from the discourses that construct it, Hacking shows convincingly that while a rock is a rock – an uncontrovertible material reality irrespective of the discourse that surrounds it, what counts as "a rock" is subject to scientific and popular discourses and their metaphors. The perception of what constitutes a rock versus a stone or a pebble is as "real" as the object itself (see also Latour 1999). Similarly, while the physical mistreatment of children is a real criminal practice, the coining of the term "child abuse" at a conference in 1961 in Denver enabled the crystallization of a whole symbolic field around this new concept and the construction of a specific social and political discourse that became as real as the physical practice itself (Hacking 1999b). In the case at hand, we could say that the shooting of the gorilla was physically real, but that the Harambe discourse is psychologically, emotionally and symbolically no less real.

This symbolic reality has complex moral implications. Who is responsible for Harambe's fate: the guard? the parents? iPhones? social media? A late modern stance transforms "responsibility" into what Bakhtin would call "answerability" (see Chapter 9), a much more nuanced notion that takes into account the conditions of possibility created by a complex combination of factors: permissive parents, smartphone technology, armed zoo keepers and a unique social media culture. In this late modern dispensation, the social actors in the event (gorilla, child, guard, parents, on-lookers, tweeters, bloggers, as well as smartphones, weapons and computers) each have agency in their material existence, but not sovereignty over the discourse that brought them into socio-symbolic and political existence. What the student was "answering" to in his depiction of the events was the larger transformation of society that made such events possible – the transformation from the modern "disciplinary society" described by Foucault (1995) to the late modern "spectacle society" depicted by Debord (1983) and even to the "expository society" discussed more recently by Harcourt (2015).

7.3   FROM THE DISCIPLINARY SOCIETY TO THE SPECTACLE SOCIETY

In Chapter 2 we saw how Foucault extended his analysis of the modes of public punishment in the Middle Ages and Renaissance to a more invisible mode of disciplining and surveillance characteristic of the Modern Age. He titled the first chapter of *Discipline and punish* (1995) "The spectacle of the scaffold," thus underscoring one of the major principles of pre-modern monarchical sovereignty, namely, the absolute power of the King to crush his opponent *in the presence of the King's subjects*. The public execution of one man given "in spectacle" to multitudes of witnesses was reversed by Jeremy Bentham's invention of the panopticon – a mechanism whereby one guard located in a central tower was able to discipline a multitude of inmates who would end up disciplining themselves for fear of punishment. Foucault was intrigued by this epistemic change in the basis of the legitimacy of power and knowledge. If the king needed the complicity of his subjects to establish his legitimate claim to absolute power (see Chapter 2), more democratic forms of government in the modern age need scientific forms of management, measurement and evaluation to legitimize their favorite form of punishment – imprisonment. In Foucault's view, the spectacle of the scaffold was replaced by the spectacle of graphs and statistical charts that disciplined the population in more insidious but no less powerful ways.

We have seen in Chapter 5 how Pierre Bourdieu described the symbolic violence exercised by the French public education system in the name of the republican values of *liberté* and *égalité*. Foucault too saw the disciplinary power of the educational system but interpreted it through Bentham's panopticon, which is, he argued, at once an architectural feature, a normalizing form of judgment, and a generalized form of truth production through examinations that prompt those being watched to discipline themselves (Harcourt 2015:86).

Such a disciplinary mechanism can be easily mapped onto the architecture of college campuses in the United States, that on the one hand enable the transmission of knowledge in a peaceful, secure, organized setting; and on the other hand serve the needs of a neoliberal society built on competitivity, itself based on rational forms of measurement, normalization, hierarchization, comparison and exclusion.[10] On this last point, Foucault, like Bourdieu, was particularly interested in the power of modern tests and exams, that reverse the ancient one-on-one master–apprentice relationship into the panoptic power of an educational institution that manages multiplicity through invisible forms of social engineering.[11]

> The examination transformed the economy of visibility into the exercise of power. Traditionally, power was what was seen, what was shown and what was manifested [. . .] Disciplinary power, on the other hand, is exercised through its invisibility; at the same time it imposes on those whom it subjects a principle of compulsory visibility. (Foucault 1995:187)

Later Foucault became interested in the security aspects brought about by this compulsory visibility.[12] Playing on the double meaning of the French term *sécurité*, which means "safety" as well as "police," Foucault shows that while disciplinary power seeks control of individual movement and behavior, securitarian power seeks to manage large populations to make them feel both safe and policed in a neoliberal economy. As Harcourt explains:

> Security differs markedly from surveillance. Discipline is centripetal: it focuses on every instance of minor disorder and seeks to eradicate even the smallest occurrence. Security, by contrast, is centrifugal: it is tolerant of minor deviations and seeks to optimize, to minimize or maximize, rather than to eliminate. (Harcourt 2015:93)

We are today a disciplinary society that relentlessly monitors our credit cards, our driving behavior, our educational achievements, and requires us to account for ourselves in all aspects of our lives. But in our neoliberal, entrepreneurial and consumer society, securitarian power seeks to "manage and control large flows of populations in order to maximize the number of visitors, to optimize consumption, to attract more advertising and to facilitate spending" (p.94). In the case of Disneyland, this kind of power is what Harcourt calls "securitarian logics":

> First, the effective management of large numbers of people; second, the control of their movements to increase their spending and to police their behaviors; third, the predictability of the experience; and finally, the computability, the calculability, the quantification, the measurability of each queue, each amusement ride, every game. (p.95)

Debord's Spectacle Society

Foucault's use of the spectacle metaphor in the opening chapter of *Discipline and Punish* had no doubt been inspired by a contemporary of his, Guy Debord, who around that time was arguing that through television and its publicity ads we have become a "society of the spectacle" – a society of consumers linked together socially through the mediation of images (Debord 1983). TV viewers or "spectators," says Debord, are heavily conditioned to recognize themselves in the images offered to them 24/7, but the more they identify with those images, he says, the less they understand their own desires.[13] This spectacle society has three characteristics: identification, a-historicity and the erasure of truth.

Identification. Under that term, Debord characterizes several ways of identifying with material goods: fetishism of consumer products, promise of abundance, focus on the quantitative; fabrication of pseudo-needs; importance of stars, who embody the appearance of a life with which spectators can identify and which they strive to imitate.

A-historicity. In a spectacle society, the reality of time has been replaced by the publicity of time. Real time has been eliminated: under constant "bombardments of publicity," ageing has become disallowed. "This social absence of death is identical to the social absence of life" (Debord 1983:158, section 160). Pseudo-historical "frozen time" is precisely the basic structure of TV consumer ads. TV juxtaposes the images of decontextualized locations as tourist destinations thus guaranteeing their symbolic equivalence and touting their irenic character. While TV does show conflict and violence happening around the world, one conflict becomes the sensationalized equivalent of any other conflict on the small screen of one's living room television set.

Erasure of truth. The spectacle in the "spectacle society" is also "the erasure of the limits of the true and the false through the elimination of all lived truth under the *real presence* of the false, ensured by the [systematic] organization of appearance" (p.207, section 219). What Debord calls "spectacle" is the predominance of appearing over being, and of being visible over having. This mythic dimension of TV reality is accompanied by a narcissistic and addictive dimension that Debord identifies as the major characteristic of a spectacle society.[14] It becomes irrelevant whether the images we see on the screen are true or not; the main thing is that they be perceived as authentic in the character that the timeless image has constructed and that will be remembered much longer and better than words.

Baudrillard's Hyperreality, Simulacra, Simulation

The rise of a consumer society saturated with television images of consumer products combined with their lack of historicity was forcefully critiqued by another French philosopher Jean Baudrillard in the eighties, at a time when television shows and marketing publicity were only starting to permeate French society. Baudrillard (1983) critiques the structuralist foundation of modernity that saw in Saussure's linguistic sign the stable and reliable foundation of the meaning of our existence (see Chapter 1). With the spread of mass media and the advent of what would be called "the mode of information" (Poster 1990; see Chapter 8) , signs have been severed from their referents.

> In TV ads, floating signifiers are attached to commodities only in the virtuoso communication of the ad [. . .] the ads constitute the viewer in a nonrepresentational, noninstrumental communications mode, one different from reading print [. . .] [for] the ad only works to the extent that it is not understood to be an ad. (pp.62–63)

For Baudrillard the object marketed on TV does not represent a real object in the world nor is it just an instrument of information about this real world. And it does not construct the viewer as someone in need of information. Instead, it constructs an *object of desire* that is "magical, fulfilling, exciting" (Poster, p.63). An object that has become "hyperreal." The TV ad does not follow the linear logic of reading; the spectator/consumer must accept its commercial intention to sell you a product and must create its meaning. That meaning is more than just a reference to a commodity; it becomes the myth of a simulatory, hyperbolic or "hyperreal" lifestyle. For example, the TV ad for Johnson's floor wax ceases to advertise a product for cleaning floors; associated with a prim-looking housewife pushing a wax applicator on her kitchen floor and an on-looking adoring husband standing by, this consumer product acquires a symbolic value that is distinct from its use value. Floor wax here = romance (p.58).

Like Harcourt, Baudrillard was intrigued by American amusement parks, for example, Disneyland; however, he saw in Disneyland not an example of securitization, but a quintessential example of hyperreality. As a private commercial space made possible by state and city governments, Disneyland is under continuous surveillance so that visitors can enjoy the reality of a consumer society without any of the risks of big crowds and long waiting lines. But mostly, as Baudrillard saw it,

> Disneyland is a digest of the American way of life, panegyric to American values, idealized transposition of a contradictory reality [. . .] But Disneyland is there to conceal the fact that it is the "real" country, all of "real" America, which *is* Disneyland [. . .] Disneyland is presented as imaginary in order to make us believe that the rest is real, whereas all of Los Angeles and the America that surrounds it are no longer real, but belong to the hyperreal order and to the order of simulation. (Baudrillard 1983:25, italics in original)

Baudrillard's argument is provocative, for sure, and many Americans did not recognize themselves in his scathing analysis when it was first translated into English. But now that real-life politics and reality TV have merged in the White House (see Chapter 6), it is easier to admit that the simulated situations we see on TV have become simulacra, that is, copies of the real that are more real than reality, and that the hyperreality in which we live no longer differentiates between life on the screen and life in the real world.[15]

7.4 HARCOURT'S EXPOSITORY SOCIETY

More recently, some critics have felt the need to supplement Debord's spectacle society and Baudrillard's hyperreality with another metaphor that better captures the spirit of our digital age. One of them is the sociologist Bernard Harcourt, who writes: "We are not being surveilled today, so much as we are *exposing* or *exhibiting* ourselves knowingly and willingly, with all our love, lust and passion. [...] It seems as if, today, we live in the *expository society*" (Harcourt 2014:11). Harcourt describes our current obsession with being seen, "liked," solicited, popular and in general given social worth and symbolic distinction through the approving gaze of others.

> We expose our most intimate details in play, in love, in desire, in consumption, in a stream of texts, Tweets, emoticons and instagrams, emails, and Snapchats, Facebook posts, links, shares and likes – throughout our digital lives, in our work, for our political convictions, to satisfy our appetites, to become ourselves. (Harcourt 2014:11)

But in fact, this lust for exhibition, confession, and this performance of authenticity is exactly what Foucault argued was the essence of our late modern disciplinary societies. It has three characteristics: visibility, conformity and veridiction, that each contain fundamental contradictions.

Visibility. Visibility online has replaced symbolic status through birth, pedigree, economic wealth or education. Our promiscuities on social media, as compromising as they may be to our privacy, compensate for our humiliations in real life.[16]

Conformity/normativity. We polish our profiles and sculpt our public personae on social media in conformity with norms that are recognizable and therefore legitimate, but in our never-ending quest for symbolic distinction we have to flout those norms. Even populist politicians, who perform the breaking of norms, conform to models of behavior anchored in the collective unconscious of the culture they belong to. Which is why we recognize in their behavior a behavior that Reality TV shows have always valued and that is at once iconoclastic and deeply conservative: disparagement, bullishness, fighting/pushing back, crushing your adversaries, "nothing left to lose," "never say you're sorry," "never look back," "time to turn the page," "move on," "winner takes all," "winning is everything" (Lakoff 2017).[17]

Veridiction. Responding with a certain prescience to the current need to "perform authenticity" rather than be authentic, Michel Foucault coined the concept of "veridiction" or self-policing that a disciplinary society requires (Foucault 2005:229). Veridiction, that is, telling the truth about oneself, forces members of a society to give account of themselves in front of teachers, school boards, recruiting officers, employers and friends through exams, testimonies and other observation and evaluation technologies. It is also the means by which subjects learn to see and govern themselves and others. Today, as Blommaert (2017) points out, such veridiction manifests itself also in the peer compulsion to reveal oneself in social encounters and on social media ("What's-your-name? Where-do-you-come-from? What-do-you-do?"). The use of digital social media encourages not only veridiction, but through its anonymity it also encourages a certain avatar mentality, playfulness, theatricality, showmanship and even con-artistry. Even though many teenagers are ferocious about protecting their privacy, they reveal so much of themselves that no one knows what is true and what is not – they obfuscate through flooding. Digital technology also facilitates outlandish counterfactual ideologies, alternative truths and post-truths that will be discussed in the next chapter.

All three aspects of the expository society contain fundamental paradoxes. Visibility is used both to reveal and to obfuscate; conformity both reinforces and breaks norms of behavior; veridiction requires the display of authenticity but is at the same time a deeply inauthentic performance.

7.5 FROM MEDIALITY TO DOCUMEDIALITY

Looking back, the Harambe incident would have developed quite differently without the technology that enabled the event to be recorded on video, preserved in cyberspace and disseminated on social media as document or meme to thousands of "friends" who gave it their own twist and interpretation. This conjunction of the constructive force of documentality and the communicative and mobilizing power of the web has given rise to a phenomenon that has been called "documediality" (Ferraris and Martino 2018).[18] Documediality is characterized by its virality, both through the speed of reproduction and the exponential multiplication of the source document. It is also characterized by its decontextualized character and its ahistorical, anonymous nature. Memes and other documents found on the web "float on the web out of time, determining temporal loops that give the impression of a repetition of the news due to its numerous occurrences [. . .]These [characteristics] undermine the idea of authoritativeness and responsibility, transforming the web into the world of 'they say'" (p.26).

The mythic transformation of Harambe and its ability to rally large numbers of fans both on the web and in real life is explained through the documediality of the web itself and the way in which it creates a complex network of relationships among individuals whom it at once brings together and makes more aware of their individuality. But here again, the word "individual" has changed meaning. It means no longer the autonomous citizen entitled to the pursuit of happiness, endowed with rights and obligations under a nation's constitution. Instead the term denotes what Ferraris and Martino call "a monad," that is, an indivisible unit sealed off from others and impervious to any outside influence.

> Documediality is inherently normative. It has a responsible function; it generates intentionality and even moral anxiety: we are called to 'respond to', respond to an appeal that the web addresses to us, and only to us, and that we cannot ignore. This is a much stronger mobilization, only apparently less invasive, than that of the last century [. . .] This mobilizing system produces self-affirmation [. . .] a transformation of the subjects themselves: the classes, united by a common socio-economical element, transformed into users, united by the spectacle they enjoy individually, become monads: individuals who assert themselves on the web and incessantly produce documents. (p.30)

If such a definition sounds pretty depressing, it is because the monad metaphor doesn't capture the paradox of digital communication. On the one hand social media and its memes interpellate us, they mobilize us to respond, to participate; they affirm our membership in a digital community and uphold the promise of a communal belonging that we are aching for; indeed, they hold up participation as a norm that we are constantly enjoined to embrace. On the other hand, by not providing us with the historicity of an institution and the rules and laws of an organized society, and by offering us instead only transient and ever-changing connections, we are caught in the random, unpredictable trajectories of pinballs in a pinball machine.

7.6   VIRALITY, COMMUNITY, CONVIVIALITY

What Is Conviviality?

It might very well be that we are not using the right language to describe what is going on. If, as Miller argues, we have entered an era "in which networks, rather than (traditional organic) communities, are the central fora for establishing social ties between people" (Miller, cited in Varis and Blommaert 2015:31–32), then we need to review what we mean by community. As Varis and Blommaert argued, the purpose of posting anything on social media is not so much to send informational content whose denotational-textual meaning needs to be decoded and responded to by members of a pre-existing "speech community," but rather it is to participate in phatic activities with a collectivity of individual users. These include: the posting of viral 'likes' and 'shares'; the "self-interpellation" of YouTube videos; the sharing as a form of re-entextualization and re-semiotization of various "texts."[19]

> Re-entextualization refers to the process by means of which a piece of 'text' (a broadly defined semiotic object here) is extracted from its original context-of-use and re-inserted into an entirely different one, involving different participation frameworks, a different kind of textuality – and entire text can be condensed into a quote, for instance – and ultimately also very different meaning outcomes [. . .] Re-semiotization [. . .] refers to the process by means of which every 'repetition' of a sign involves an entirely new set of contextualization conditions and thus results in an entirely 'new' semiotic process, allowing new semiotic modes and resources to be involved in the repetition process. (Varis and Blommaert, p.36)

Viral memes, as multimodal signs or 'texts', are subject to intense resemiotization and to situational adjustments that are likely to produce very different communicative effects, as we shall see in Chapter 8.

> Memes, just like Mark Zuckerberg's status updates, do not need to be *read* in order to be seen and understood as denotationally and informationally meaningful; their use and re-use appear to be governed by the 'phatic' and 'emblematic' functions often seen as of secondary nature in discourse-analytic literature. (p.41)

The purpose of such phatic exchanges is not to reach a deeper understanding of the Other by learning and using his/her language, becoming familiar with his/her culture, asking follow-up questions, managing topics of conversation – all conversational strategies that used to be part of communicative language teaching. Instead, as in the original Harvard facebooks, it is all about fostering relations of sociality and civility that maintain contacts that could become useful some time in the future. Indeed, viral memes force us to reconsider the online social structuring necessary for preventing social, political or moral differences from turning into conflicts, and for constructing a form of sociality that is paradoxically at once sincere and euphemistic, earnest and playful, close and respectfully distant. Such a sociality has been called "conviviality." According to Vaidhyanathan, Facebook encourages conviviality, not community.

> Avoidance of overt neglect and rejection are narrowly connected to avoidance of intimacy and 'transgressive' personal interaction: what needs to be maintained [. . .] is a relationship of conviviality – a level of social intercourse characterized by largely 'phatic' and 'polite' engagement in interaction. Acquaintances are not there to be 'loved', they are there to be 'liked.' (Vaidhyanathan 2019:42)

Conviviality vs. Imagined Community

This notion of conviviality is different from the notion of community, or even "imagined community" proposed by Bonny Norton in 2001 (Barney 2004). Borrowing from Etienne Wenger's "community of practice" and Benedict Anderson's "imagined community," Bonny Norton had proposed that English language learners would do well to strive to belong to a community of English speaking practice and to develop their own imagined English speaking community in contradistinction to the one imposed on them by nation-states. This proposal was based, however, on particular assumptions about the community that learners of English should strive to belong to. As Norton notes, Wenger distinguished three modes of belonging, referred to as engagement, alignment and imagination. While "engagement refers to active involvement in mutual processes of negotiation and meaning" and "alignment addresses the extent to which we coordinate our energies and activities in order to fit within broader structures and contribute to broader enterprises," "imagination addresses the extent to which we create images of the world and see connections through time and space by extrapolating from our experience" (Norton 2001:163). What attracted Norton to Wenger's notion of community of practice through imagination was not so much the fortuitous creation of images and the making of connections, but the "creation of new images of possibility and new ways of understanding one's relation to the world that transcend more immediate acts of engagement" (Norton 2001:163) – in other words, a new mode of belonging that is different from the old national citizenship (see also Norton 1995).

This is where Wenger's (1999) notion of imagination was made to meet Anderson's (1991) notion of imagined community. In his book *Imagined Communities*, the anthropologist Benedict Anderson had discussed the role of technology (printing, map-making etc.) in constructing/categorizing the world in such a way that nation-states became "imagined communities," not through some evil imperialistic design, but through technological developments and inventions and through trade and commerce. The nation became an emotional metaphor for a sense of national belonging that welded a people together after the demise of the monarchy. By contrast, Pavlenko and Norton (2007) conceived of the imagination as the prerogative of the individual against the state as an institution and for a more global community that speaks English. In their article, "Imagined communities, identity and English language learning," they demonstrate "how nation-states may shape the imagination of their citizens and how actual and desired memberships in various imagined communities mediate the learning of – or resistance to – English around the world." In their view, English empowers learners of English to "extend their range of identities and reach out to wider worlds" (p.670). But how are English learners to imagine this global community? This is where conviviality comes in.

Conviviality is a much more transient, expedient, utilitarian mode of association than Wenger's notion of community of practice or Anderson's notion of national community. It fits the multiple, mobile, changing and sometimes conflictual world of social media that offers both closeness and distance, sincerity and showmanship (Barney 2004). It enables immigrants to a national community to both integrate into that community and maintain ties to a global collectivity of other

English speakers around the world through convivial technologies like Facebook. However, as Vaidhyanathan (2019) points out, by encouraging conviviality, Facebook also encourages surveillance. Not state surveillance as described by Foucault, nor corporate surveillance as documented in Gee et al. (1996), but peer surveillance. Based as it is on a business model of consumer addiction, Facebook asks only one question: "How can we consume as much of your time and attention as possible?" But Facebook is Janus-faced. At the same time as it demands our attention, it makes us addicted to peer-feedback and to the way we are seen and talked about. Thus, conviviality can be in competition with the old notion of community.

The development of the new media discussed in this chapter shows how much the conditions for the exercise of symbolic power have changed in the last thirty years. Our power to "construct the given" and create new symbolic realities has been inordinately enhanced by digital technologies. But at the same time, the very algorithms of the Internet have changed what we mean by "the given." Symbolic reality has become the fluctuating frequency of hits and clicks on digital media with paradoxical effects. On the one hand, the new media can bring people together, offer emotional support, and forge more or less durable friendships. On the other hand, they can lead to internet vigilantism with all the accompanying cyberbullying, internet fury and disinformation practices that constitute online abuses of symbolic power.

SUGGESTIONS FOR FURTHER READING

Foucault (1970) offers a dense but superb philosophical and historical backdrop to everything discussed here. The preface and the first two chapters are worth reading before plunging into Foucault (1995) that deals more specifically with panoptic methods of socialization and punishment throughout the ages. For Foucault's ideas about the disciplinary society and the forms of political control or "governmental rationality" that it imposes, see Foucault (1979) and Gordon (1991). Those interested in post-structuralism and late modernism in applied linguistics will find useful discussions in Weedon (1997, especially chapter 5), Cameron (2005), Pennycook (2001, chapters 4 and 5), and McNamara (2012). On surveillance and securitization, see Khan (2014), and the excellent tie-in with Foucault and Gumperz in Rampton (2016). On the pervasive intrusion of "hidden persuaders" in both the surveillance and the marketing industry, see Luntz (2008) and the PBS Frontline video *The Persuaders* (Dretzin et al. 2004).

8   Language as Symbolic Power in the Digital Age

THE FACEBOOK ME

Here is how Jian Gao, a 22-year-old student in the *Language and Power* class on which this book is based, described how Facebook functions.

> When a new user registers on Facebook, he is first prompted to answer a few standard questions, such as his birthday, favorite books, places he has visited and his major life events. Facebook then creates a profile page for the user that connects the dots and weaves them into a story. The user can then add additional posts and photos to continue the storyline and make his profile publicly available to everyone. Through such standard questions and public posts, a living human with blood and bones is compressed into a sequence of 0s and 1s. However, in this condensation process, a considerable amount of information is inevitably lost, and the corresponding profile forms only an incomplete picture of who a person really is. Although they offer unfaithful representations of users, Facebook profiles and posts have been playing an essential role in information collection and identity construction. When new friends connect on Facebook, they usually first browse through each other's profile, from which they develop a certain impression of each other as an individual. The impression-forming process continues as people follow status updates to peak into each other's life. These impressions, informed by Facebook's incomplete – and sometimes even inaccurate – data representations of users, then constitute a power net that primes our expectations of each other and influences our daily interactions with each other. Based on the interactional feedbacks, a person then adjusts his behaviors to fit into others' expectations, matching himself with his data representation and further strengthening the power of Facebook's data-representation system. Each social body thus becomes a shadow of his own data bytes.[1]

This characterization of Facebook highlights several of the features of digital symbolic systems that will be discussed in this chapter. First, Facebook is described not as technology but as a social actor that "prompts us to answer questions," "creates for us a profile page," "connects the dots of our profile and weaves them into a story." In other words, Facebook gives our lives a meaning that we can share with others. Second, Facebook makes us enter an environment with a past, a present and a future: we "browse" through people's profiles, we "update" our own, we meet other Facebook users' "expectations." Third, Facebook is not about truths or facts, but about "impressions," and "status" is conceived as a cross between the scientific meaning of the term (as in "state of things") and its symbolic meaning (as in "symbolic status"). How do symbolic systems like Facebook exert so much power that they can make us into a "shadow of our own data-bytes"?

In this chapter, I discuss the ways in which digital technologies are transforming the political dimensions of language as symbolic power. I consider in particular how the Web and social media have changed the epistemological, social and cultural landscape as well as increased our capacity to create, store, disseminate and impose meaning, and to use the power of institutions to have these meanings accepted as legitimate.

8.1   DIGITAL MEDIA AS SOCIAL SYMBOLIC SYSTEMS

In the last chapter we saw how, under the influence of late modern theories of knowledge, symbolic power has come to be seen not as something that someone possesses and others don't, or that some people use to dominate others, but rather as the very principle of social life. For Foucault, as for all the scholars inspired by him (e.g., Butler, Weedon, Pennycook, Cameron and others), symbolic power is the condition of possibility of knowing anything at all, a way of structuring reality, of classifying, controlling and disciplining knowledge as well as people's bodies and thoughts. As such:

- *It is diffuse*, not owned by anyone in particular, exercised by all on all through the complicity of all.
- *It is self-perpetuating.* The individual becomes the instrument of his/her own discipline because it is in his/her interest to do so.
- *It is relational.* The way it is exercised depends on how social actors are positioned vis-à-vis others as they engage in social activity.
- *It is exercised through discipline,* understood as a decentered, self-regulating mechanism.
- *It likes to remain invisible but all-seeing.* In the same manner as schools, prisons and hospital wards are invisibly monitored by

a web of rules and regulations (see Foucault 1995) built into the system, in the same manner Facebook is invisibly regulated by algorithms that condition the behavior of its users.

– *It seems natural, neutral and beneficial*, yet it binds everyone through bonds that are at once historical, social and cultural.

Given this late modern definition of power, it is easy to see the link between critical theories of knowledge and the new digital technologies based on complex networks and relational frameworks.[3]

The Mode of Information: A Digital Revolution

The critical theories discussed in Chapter 7, in conjunction with the Harambe incident, benefit from being put in relation with the electronic information technologies and the cultural revolution these technologies have ushered in over the last thirty years. The historian and philosopher Mark Poster (1990) looks at electronically mediated communication in light of post-structuralist theories of language, knowledge and the self and their relation to symbolic power. Taking as a point of departure the post-structuralist theme that "subjects are constituted in acts and structures of communication," he argues that the shift from the oral and print to the electronic medium "reconfigures the subject's relation to the world" (p.11).[4] We have entered, he says, an era characterized by what he calls "the mode of information," that is, new forms of social interaction based not only on economics (like Marx's theory of the mode of production) but on linguistic symbols and their discourse orders.[5] This mode of information requires that we "retheorize the relation between action and language, behavior and belief, material reality and culture" (p.5). Note that Poster does not discard the crucial importance of economic material reality in a subject's well-being; rather, he draws our attention to the equally crucial role played by symbolic systems in the constitution of the subject and by the mode of information in shaping our thoughts and imaginations.[6]

The increased speed and scope of electronic communication have transformed quantity into quality, thus making the economic, utilitarian benefit of efficient language transmission into a new social and symbolic phenomenon. Information has become a privileged term in this new culture. In the same manner as in the 1970's, an American child counselor could suggest that I had a "communication problem" with my children (see Chapter 3), my American students at the time insisted that the use of TV ads was merely to "inform" consumers about consumer products. In fact, as we saw in Chapter 7, the mode of information of TV ads did not just inform, it redefined our relation of words to things. It changed the way people like the American counselor and my American students talked about things.

Like the concept of "community" discussed in the last chapter, ordinary referential words like "communication," "information," "choice" have become metaphors loaded with a neoliberal ideology that has taken on an emotional and moral value. (Who could be against more effective communication, better information, more choices?). Images and words on the screen have reconfigured verbal and visual symbols from a direct translation of reality into an "infinite play of mirror reflections and indeterminate exchanges in which the real and the fictional, the true and the false" combine to appeal to viewers' emotions, memories and aspirations and, ultimately, to their pocket-books (Poster 1990:11). Poster argues that electronic communication transforms the representational power of language by shifting to the forefront the self-referential aspect of discourse that was already theorized by Roland Barthes in his analysis of the PANZANI pasta ad (see Chapter 1), and that transforms words and images from referential symbols of reality into instruments of emotional and epistemological manipulation. I shall consider in the Conclusion the implications of this for language learning and teaching, but in this chapter I want to consider various aspects of the digital revolution in some of the platforms it has made available to us, in particular the Google search engine.

The Googlization of Everything

The Google search engine, founded in 1999, is universalist and altruistic in its vision and mission statements. Its vision is "to provide access to the world's information in one click"; its mission is "to organize the world's information and make it universally accessible and useful." This is quite an idealistic agenda.[7]

Indeed, Google does not claim to provide knowledge or information, but claims instead to simply set the procedural framework within which information is collected, ranked, linked and displayed for everyone in the world to access and use. The information itself is provided by the users, who thereby exercise as much symbolic power as Google. This decentralized control also forms the basis of Google's architecture in which knowledge is the sum of its users' knowledge, is shaped and reconfigured by each user's input, is organized and ranked according to the choices of the majority, and is posted on Google's splash page according to the amount and frequency of their clicks. While users give Google the information about the world that Google organizes, ranks, links and displays, Google collects information about them, their goo-gling habits and idiosyncracies, and sells that information to marketing corporations for targeted advertisements.

This, as Vaidhyanathan himself admits in his 2011 book *The Googliza-tion of everything (and why we should worry)*, was from the start a visionary project and one that was linked in the nineties to dreams of universal democracy, global prosperity, and the global spread of mass education. I remember well the euphoria we experienced in the eighties at the prospect of an "unlimited database" accessible to all for free from anywhere in the world. At the time we could not imagine information technology and the World Wide Web being anything else than a huge facilitator of research, scholarship and political participation.

But then came Google, which offered to organize all this bounty and to put the information in the hands not only of libraries and other institutional repositories of knowledge, but of individual citizens and consumers. The commercialization of the Internet that followed shortly thereafter radically changed the nature of the information exchanged, as it introduced an element of competition and symbolic power struggles to manipulate rather than just enlighten others. Elec-tronic communication through the Web and other Google platforms (Gmail, Instagram, YouTube, Wikipedia) started exercising an inordin-ately greater power to shape the way we represent, act upon, create and impose realities than the declarative framework used in the age of print under gatekeepers such as grammars, publishing houses, educa-tional systems and legal institutions. Like print technology, but more quickly, more ubiquitously and more forcefully, Google was shaping the very way we think.[8]

In his chapter "The googlization of us," Vaidhyanathan spells out this Newthink that has been promoted by Google and has now infil-trated much of our thinking about the world. Google's main moral imperative: "Don't be evil" has been translated into such pragmatic values as: "comprehensiveness, precision, speed, inclusion." Global civic responsibility and notions of the public good have been inter-preted as "efficiency, convenience, profitability." Google does have moral values, but they are not what we generally associate with biblical Good and Evil. They are of a pragmatic/transactional kind. Take, for example, Truth. "[For Google] truth is not attached to a thing in the world per se, but to our experiences of that thing and to our conversa-tion about and collective understanding of it. People and peoples can disagree over what is true, and that disagreement is a part of the process of lurching toward truth" (Vaidhyanathan 2011:61). Not every-one in the world would agree that Truth is "lurched toward" by process and consensus! Wouldn't they think that there is something like objective, factual truth? Take another example: Privacy. Google might have a different view of privacy than its users. Users believe that they have preserved their privacy if they have retained some control over what they reveal of themselves. Google, by contrast, doesn't care what you reveal, it is only interested in your patterns of behavior and the choices you made – information that it can then pass along to advertisers. This convergence of moral and economic power has led Vaidhyanathan to talk of Google's "infrastructural imperialism" (p.2).[9]

And indeed, there are in Google's mission statement some controversial elements that have raised concern around the globe, especially in Europe and China. Under its universal reach there is an assumption that knowledge is synonymous with information, that the most important and useful information is the most popular information (and the information that appears on Google's splash page), and that quality of knowledge equals quantity of hits. Google's (like Facebook's) business model can favor certain kinds of knowledge (e.g., effective, useful in solving problems) at the expense of others that fall into oblivion, certain kinds of users (e.g., English speaking, wealthier, younger or better educated), and certain kinds of information (e.g., Western bias). Indeed, the notion of "useful" information mentioned in Google's statement of mission has been questioned as its advantages have to be assessed against the risks of deleterious information such as hate speech and incitements to violence, but also against less instrumental but equally important knowledge such as poetic insights, aesthetic judgments or religious beliefs.

Moreover, the economic incentives in the traffic of knowledge are casting a cloud on our dreams of objective truth. Yes, searches on the Internet can yield truthful information, but precisely because this truth is no longer guaranteed by institutional gatekeepers, the digital medium forces us even more urgently than print to ask: Who is speaking? In answer to what or whom? In which context? From whose perspective? More importantly: Why is this expressed this way? Organized this way? What does this manner of speaking index about its author and his/her worldview? And, most important of all: What is not being said? Ultimately, as much as we create Google, Google creates us: it ranks our knowledge, observes our habits, sells our data to advertisers, who in turn classify, categorize, control us through targeted advertising and electoral manipulation. There are concerns that Google serves the interests of the capitalist class by privileging consumption over inquiry, sampling and shopping over learning, entertaining over critiquing; in other words, that Google's architecture solidifies the knowledge and opinions of the dominant group.

The case of Google shows that real symbolic power comes not from knowledge content but from the manipulation of the very conditions of epistemic possibility. To echo Foucault in his preface to *The order of things* (1970), symbolic power is the power to manipulate the fundamental codes of knowledge in a given culture. In the same way as the French encyclopedists of the eighteenth century appealed to reason to construct, display and transmit knowledge – through rational displays and organization of knowledge in encyclopedias, grammars and dictionaries, through the surveillance and control mechanisms built into an education system based on print literacy, and through rational rewards and punishments built on measurement and evaluation (see Chapter 5), in the twenty-first century Google disciplines us to also think in a certain way. It appeals not just to our reason, but to our emotions, our desires, our fears. For example, scholars have to worry now about whether their work will be visible if it does not appear on the first page of Google's search engine; what will attract readers' attention; how it will affect them because of its informational and emotional impact; what will be cited by others because of its accessibility and convenience; what will be forgotten or disregarded because of a non-google-able title or a non-sexy abstract; what will be punished by a loss of symbolic capital or by social oblivion because of unpopular content.

The procedural power of Google is at work also in social media like Facebook and Twitter, that offer platforms not for researching, but for exchanging information among users. They too wield infinitely more power than just the exchange of information.

8.2   SOCIAL MEDIA AS PLATFORMS FOR THE EXERCISE OF SYMBOLIC POWER

The Nature of Facebook

Facebook, an electronic platform for connecting people, is a world-wide extension of a Harvard college tradition to receive upon graduation a "facebook" containing the mugshots and the biographical profiles of all the students in the same dormitory. The digital Facebook founded by Mark Zuckerberg in 2004 is more ambitious. Its avowed mission is to "give people the power to build community and bring the world closer together." We find the same elements as Google's in Facebook's management of multiplicity – in this case not multiplicity of information, but multiplicity of users, the tracking of their online habits, the predictability of their behaviors based on past behaviors and the computability of their "likes" and "shares." Facebook is both a platform for its user postings and a publisher for its newsfeeds, and thereby it inevitably makes decisions about values. One of its main values is attention-grabbing through curiosity-inducing "clickbait" headlines. Its algorithms favor both non-news content shared by friends and news from "trustworthy" sources, which Facebook engineers interpret as a boost for anything in the category of politics, crime and tragedy. Like Google, Facebook is based on a business model that provides access to "friends" and acquaintances in exchange for personal data that Facebook sells to the marketing industry and opinion polls.

Facebook has received quite a bit of criticism in its handling of hate speech and the weaponizing of information for political gain. Some, like the co-founder of Facebook Chris Hughes, have argued that Facebook has accumulated too much power and must be broken up. "Facebook's business model is built on capturing as much of our attention as possible to encourage people to create and share more information about who they are and who they want to be. We pay for Facebook with our data and our attention, and by either measure it doesn't come cheap."[10] Indeed, the price we pay for using Facebook is our very self-image as shaped by others.

Not only does the social network construct a "truth" of every user, it also facilitates a normative framework for human behaviors and an ideal way of living. The "like" button on Facebook, stylized as a "thumbs up" icon, enables users to easily interact with others' status updates and profess their reactions. Once clicked by a user, the designated content appears in the News Feeds of that user's friends, and the button also displays the number of other users who have liked the content, including a full or partial list of those users. The number of likes and the nature of comments signals to Facebook users what posts and contents are considered appropriate and likeable by the general public, which in turn influences how they behave and portray themselves in social media and in real life. In particular, if a post receives many likes and favorable comments, everyone exposed to the post, including both the original poster and the poster's friends, will want to repeat or imitate the behaviors and mentalities that the post conveys.

Many youngsters like Jian Gao feel addicted to the constant feedback they receive and to the image of themselves they constantly feel compelled to curate in order to live up to expectation.

The Nature of Twitter

Twitter started in 2006 as an online short messaging service restricted to 140 characters per message, similar to text messages on cell phones (Rogers, 2014). It is a micro-blogging platform that allows users to display their messages or tweets to other users who have subscribed to follow that particular user's Twitter stream. The tweets are accessible on the Twitter feed in reverse chronological order as a string of messages that can include pictures or hyperlinks to other content and can be accessed via computers or smartphones. Twitter has developed rapidly and currently allows tweets up to 280 characters. It now boasts some 695 million users all over the world who generate an average of 58 million tweets a day ("Statistic Brain," 2017). Twitter is the current leading micro-blogging platform worldwide to debate news, politics, business and entertainment in 33 different languages.

Twitter, as other social media, presents what Gainous and Wagner describe as an "alternative environment that is multidimensional and largely unique in the history of our political system and by which opinion leaders, politicians, and citizens can engage with each other [. . .] It is a network that lacks an editor or gatekeeper, and is governed by a new set of rules and codes of behavior that are only now being developed" (Gainous and Wagner, 2013:3). Varis and Blommaert (2015) compare the nature of audience design in Twitter and email. Citing Alice Marwick and danah boyd (2010:120), they explain the difference.

> The difference between Twitter and email is that the latter is primarily a directed technology with people pushing content to persons listed in the "to:" field, while tweets are made available for interested individuals to pull on demand. The typical email has an articulated audience, while the typical tweet does not. (Marwick and boyd, cited in Varis and Blommaert 2015:42)

Precisely because its audience is ill-defined and up for grabs by like-minded users, Twitter encourages attention grabbing, sensationalizing, emotional tweets. Jenny Wortham, a *New York Times* journalist writes the following in response to the question "How do you think about life on social media?":

> In the Twitterverse, ideologues have far more power than moderates. They have more followers; their tweets get more traction (studies have shown that emotional tweets pretty much always have more traction); they set the terms of their neighborhood's culture and tone [. . .]. I try to be extremely aware of my urges to contribute to social media and of the way it feels to observe others' highly-curated looking glasses. What do I want to share? What does it mean to parcel out bits of myself for

consumption? What does it mean to consume others' bits? I really love getting insights into the highs and lows of the human experience and, at the same time, am aware that we're being coerced into participating by companies that trade on our emotions and impulses. At social media's best, I'm laughing alongside some of the most interesting and innovative do-it-yourself creators of my time. At its worst, I'm experiencing a desperate longing for a life that is not mine. That's a hard spectrum to travel along on a daily basis. (Wortham 2019)

On Twitter, as on Google, symbolic power shapes and is shaped by its users, who both welcome it and resist it. Twitter has become a major player in present-day populist politics, where it competes with mass media to influence public opinion and thus elections in democratic societies (see Chapter 6 on Twitter politics).[11]

8.3   ALGORITHMIC CONTROL

The Internet, with its decentralized, user constructed and user managed architecture, its deinstitutionalized knowledge, reorganized according to user recommendations and the number and frequency of user hits, provides less of a new communication tool than a new *symbolic environment* – a gateway to an infinity of meanings unconstrained by institutional norms and conventions. It is instructive in this regard to read descriptions of the Internet written in languages other than English by scholars who come from epistemological cultures different from the American culture that gave rise to the Internet in the first place. Let us look, for example, at two French scholars, writing for a French readership.

The philosopher Paul Mathias' little book *Qu'est-ce que l'internet?* [What is the internet] explains to French readers how the Internet draws its symbolic power precisely from the perception by its users that it is legitimate because it is seen as natural, arbitrary and normal, as defined by Bourdieu (see Introduction).

> We only see a usable interface, of which we make only rudimentary technical use and of which we are condemned to misrecognize or rather even *forget* the complexity and the transparency – the *invisibility*! (Mathias 2009:17, my translation, emphasis in original)

Mathias is less sensitive to the efficiency, speed and usefulness of the Internet and more concerned about the Internet's instrumentalization of knowledge and of the semantic galaxy that it creates based not on identifiable authors' intentions but on proximal electronic links between information bites – a challenge to the French humanistic approach to language.

> While we use Google to "search" for meaningful information, Google's algorithms search for syntactic units formed by numerical positions in databases [. . .] Since the algorithms for the organization of information are not qualitative but quantitative, we are bound to receive responses to our search that are adapted to the statistical frequency of the mere *words* we use. (p.41, italics in the original)
>
> Knowledge has become something that we manage, manipulate, transfer, displace, and quantify. It is no longer that with which we identify or in which we could reflect and recognize ourselves [. . .] [We are given] an instrumental relation to networks that we perpetuate without really questioning them. (p.27, my translation)

Coming from a French intellectual culture still steeped in the eighteenth-century belief in the link between human language and human thought, and in the integrity of the individual endowed with reason, Mathias warns against the standardization, conformism and commodification of our thoughts that such a symbolic system subtly promotes.

In *A quoi rêvent les algorithmes? Nos vies à l'heure des big data* [What do algorithms dream of? Our lives in the era of big data] (2015), French sociologist Dominique Cardon further shows concern for what he calls "the algorithmic society" or *la société des calculs*. In his view, we have to understand the power of algorithms if we are to understand how symbolic power is exercised in the digital world.

> Like a kitchen recipe, an algorithm is a series of instructions that make it possible to obtain a result [. . .] It hierarchizes information, guesses what interests us, selects the information we prefer, and strives to assist us in various tasks. We construct these calculators and in turn they construct us. (p.7, my translation)

Thus the admirable way the Internet has of ordering, sequencing, comparing, grouping, ranking, selecting and displaying information is also the way it has of predicting, and ultimately, orienting our choices and behaviors. It suggests that because we bought product X, read article Y, wrote to person Z, we are interested in buying, reading or writing more of the same. By keeping track of our every click, the Internet channels our research, orients our readings, monitors our personal connections. Google's and others' algorithms seek to make internet users prisoners of their past behaviors in order to predict their future behaviors (including their consumer habits). The avowed goal is to better meet their needs and desires, but it also runs the risk of closing them off from other sources and forms of knowledge.[12] This is particularly worrisome for foreign language teachers whose aim it is to acquaint learners with other ways of thinking and knowing by teaching them other ways of speaking and writing.

Such concerns are shared by American scholars as well, but they pertain less to the architecture of the Internet, which embodies values familiar to American culture (e.g., individual choice, majority rule, standardization), than to attempts to spread its benefits beyond the monolingual use of the English language. How can we transcend the curse of the Tower of Babel through the use of Big Data? Machine translation has made great progress since Artificial Intelligence research ceased to search for the syntactic rules governing the translation from one human language to another, and focused its efforts instead on matching patterns found in enormous amounts of "big data." This ambitious enterprise is bearing spectacular results that are immediately relevant to applied linguists and language teachers in the form of Google Translate.

But beyond these efforts at linguistic translation, there are other efforts aimed at facilitating data retrieval across individual languages through the appropriate algorithms. In his article "Supralingualism and the translatability industry," David Gramling describes some of the problematic strategies employed by linguistic engineers to develop algorithms that aim at greater comprehensibility across languages through what he calls "supralingualism."

> Supralingualism is an applied research enterprise that embraces an insatiable and totalizing belief in the value (in all senses) of coordinating translatability among global languages for practical purposes. It presumes the underlying good of doing so – for individuals, firms and investors; for social justice movements; for economic development and political stability; for education, literacy, and knowledge-sharing, and for scientific progress alike [...] We can think of supralingualism as a global transposability grid which various interlocking commercial industries engineer and maintain in order to ensure low-delta meaning-transfer across 60–170 world languages. (Low-delta here means non-prohibitive or diminishing procedural expense and/or delivery time-lag). (Gramling 2019)

Elements of this grid include such strategies as:

1) "commensuration" or making use of the resources of two or more languages to coin hybrid forms that are claimed to be universally understandable such as Fr. *agentivité* [agency] or Ger. *Literalität* [literacy];

2) "literalization" or elimination of non-literal uses of the language;

3) "de-historicization/ decontextualization" or elimination of any meaning that depends on the historical context for its comprehensibility.

Some of this supralingualism is at work in the very language used to describe it as we can see from the statement. The phrase "ensur[ing] low-delta meaning-transfer across 60–170 languages" by means of a "global transposability grid" expresses the delicate work of translation in quite a different way than usually thought of in applied linguistics. The focus here is clearly quantitative, commercial and a matter of information transfer. Indeed, this is an example of a discourse that superimposes itself on plain English and claims to be universally comprehensible. Together with Google and social media, cross-linguistic data retrieval is part of the digital revolution that is upending our traditional views of language and language use. This revolution is accompanied by a revolution in our social and cultural way of life.

8.4   A SOCIAL AND CULTURAL REVOLUTION

Electronically mediated communication, says Mark Poster, changes the relation between the speaking body and the listening body, thus destabilizing the speaking subject. While he admits that electronically mediated information systems have brought as many benefits as telegraph and photography in the nineteenth century, and while we could argue that the Internet has inordinately improved the quality of communication through Skype and voice recognition devices, he reminds us that the mode of information represents not just a digital revolution, but also a deep social and cultural revolution. What is the nature of that revolution?

A Culture of "Connected Individualism"

In *Information please. Culture and politics in the age of digital machines*, Poster writes:

> The condition of globalization of which the Internet is a major component, imposes a new and heightened level of interaction between cultures [. . .] Local beliefs, values, and practices can no longer be held as absolute or as exclusive, at the expense of others. On the other hand, a new opportunity arises for a practical definition and articulation of global, human, or better posthuman culture" (p.9). With globally networked digital communications, one must be

especially careful in taking as an offense the legitimate cultural
practices of another even if they are on one's own soil. (Poster 2006:22)

Fifteen years later, such a statement is bound to sound a little too
idealistic. As we have seen, the symbolic power of the Internet can
work both ways. It can connect us with one another across the globe
and it can imprison us in our own filter bubble among like-minded
"friends" (Zuboff 2019). The populist backlash of the second decade of
the twenty-first-century has shown how the Internet can be used to
divide us and pit us against one another. The debate about whether it
prepares us to be good citizens or good consumers (Kramsch 2020)
raises once again the age-old distinction between the political and the
economic uses of language. Countries like France that, historically,
have had a different adherence to capitalism than, say, the United
States, also have a different attitude to the Internet.

The French sociologist and media scholar Rémy Rieffel's book *Révolution numérique, révolution culturelle?* [Digital revolution, cultural revolution?] (2014) is enlightening in this regard. Rieffel argues that digital
technology has ushered in three different cultural revolutions:

1) a new technological and economic context, in which visibility
   and user recommendations dominate the market of attention;
2) a new relation to others, in which connectivity, sociability and
   inventiveness are prized and where knowledge acquisition
   becomes polyphonic and adaptive;
3) a new relation to information and to *le politique* (see Introduction),
   where citizens' participation online has moved from deliberative
   to participative democracy and where the Web serves to both
   subvert abuses of power and repress attempts to prevent these
   abuses.

Rieffel elaborates on these three revolutions as follows. In the same
manner as post-modernism after May 1968 ushered in a healthy
questioning of the stable, predictable, homogenous world we had
inherited from the pre-World War II generation, the digital technology
of the 1980's and 1990's has brought with it a questioning of the
traditional nature of language as a tool for the development of individual thought and institutional power; the structural certainty of meanings, the integrity of texts, the sanctity of the author and the academic
monopoly over knowledge and information were all aspects of language use that in the age of print were essential components of language as symbolic power. Now in the digital age, meaning can be
created through a variety of semiotic systems with different structures

and codes, texts can be cut and pasted, tweeted and re-tweeted, authorship is multiple and often ill-defined, and institutional authority is undermined by social media.

Inserting itself into all aspects of the old literate culture and re-appropriating its old vocabulary in digital garb (e.g., web*pages*, *text*ings, *icons*, *language*, *documents*), the Internet has replaced an historical culture of faith in institutions and in the value of tradition by a culture of what Rieffel calls "connected individualism" (Rieffel 2014:263), based on relationality, visibility, un-mediated and diversified access to knowledge, and communication for the sake of communication (Castells 2009:64; see also Varis and Blommaert's notion of "conviviality"). While the Internet and social media have clearly fostered contact, connection, collaboration and participation, they have also exacerbated inequality of use, intercultural incomprehension and incompatibility of perspectives on who we are and where we are going.

Rieffel argues that technology must be understood within its political economy. The Internet, in particular, is not responsible per se for democratization or right-wing radicalization; it is imperative to understand the long-term structural interactions between technology, institutions and culture. For example, the use of the new media is quite different in the United States and in France or Germany. In the United States, their use fits into an American culture of television entertainment, marketing ads, competitive individualism, celebrity and success, consumerism and brinkmanship, and a generally low respect for institutions like public media and public education. By contrast, the use of the new media in France and Germany has accommodated itself to a tradition of trust in public education and public media, a foundational respect of the written word (*Académie Française* in France, *Bildung* in Germany), a distrust of the moneyed business world and of conspicuous consumerism, and a fervent ecological mindset. That too should be taken into consideration by applied linguists studying or teaching language in its social context.

The Hunger for Attention or the Inescapable Town Square

More recently, cultural critics have identified a dimension of this "connected individualism" that is particularly relevant for communicatively oriented language educators: the inextinguishable hunger for attention.[13] The philosopher of technology L. M. Sacasas (2019) describes how digital communication and particularly social media are reshaping the social contract of oral and literate communication into a team-mindedness that he calls "performative pugilism," that is, the competitive desire less to exchange information than to bid for attention and affection. Postings become less messages destined to inform than "gestures designed to generate a response" (Brooks 2019). The new social type that emerges in such a communications regime is, Brooks argues, the "troll," who "bids for attention by trying to make others feel bad." "Trolling" is one of the frequent abusive forms of communication that I discuss later in this chapter.

Following up on Walter Ong's (1982) analysis of orality and literacy into the digital age, Sacasas convincingly shows how the passage from orality to literacy gained in reflexivity what it lost in face-to-face oral closeness; it gained in printed documentality what it lost in personal memory. But the passage from literacy to digital media did not lose the benefits of the two previous eras; it refunctionalized them to fit the new era.

> When we type out our statuses, link to articles, post memes or images, we do so as if we were members of literate but pre-digital societies, for we are not present before all those who will encounter our messages. Yet, given the immediacy with which the messages arrive, we are in an important way now much closer to one another. We might say that we have an "audience" whose immediate presence is constituted in time rather than space.
>
> The result is that we combine the weaknesses of each medium while losing their strengths. We are thrust once more into a live, immediate, and active communicative context – the moment regains its heat – but we remain without the non-verbal cues that sustain meaning-making in such contexts. We lose whatever moderating influence the full presence of another human being before us might cast on the passions the moment engendered. This not-altogether-present and not-altogether-absent audience encourages a kind of performative pugilism. The contrast of President Truman writing and not sending his letters with President Trump's use of social media is stark and instructive. (Sacasas 2019: 50–51)

Sacasas concludes by acknowledging that we are in the midst of a broad and profound social transformation brought about by the very technology that is revolutionizing our way of knowing. As such, digital technology itself offers no clear solution to the problem of how to maintain one's dignity as an individual while participating with others in real-life and on social media – and this leaves us vulnerable to discipline, both from others and from ourselves.[14]

These questions return us to a notion broached by Foucault in *Discipline and punish* (1995) and that surfaces again and again when we look at language as symbolic power – namely: How can we protect privacy and encourage participation, guarantee individual autonomy and exercise discipline? We have seen in Chapter 7 how network technology can foster peer monitoring and vigilantism online, and how in the United States norms, not laws, govern a lot of this day-to-day personal privacy (Kaminski 2018). In countries like France and Germany, the state is much more likely to intervene with privacy laws that discipline citizens into compliance through surveillance and penalties, than in the United States, where discipline tends to be used to reeducate citizens through behavior modification and to thus securitize society.

It is no coincidence that the use of the Internet, which was imagined by American scientists and engineers, draws on such a disciplinary principle rather than on a centralized system of penalties and rewards. Those who abuse the system by posting offensive material, rather than being forbidden access to the platform by Facebook for not abiding by its norms, or punished by the state for not respecting its laws, are left to be sanctioned or brought into conformity with expected behaviors by fellow users online.

This indirect, invisible, centrifugal monitoring of all by all, which is characteristic of digital technologies from Google to Facebook and Twitter, has led to another feature of our digital age that I want to focus on in the remainder of this chapter. I have already alluded to the fact that from Google's transactional perspective notions like Privacy and Truth lose their absolute value and become instead dependent on information processing algorithms and on the opinions of the majority of users. We are then only one step away from a phenomenon that has captured the imagination of many under the name "post-truth."

8.5 POST-TRUTH AND OTHER DISINFORMATION IN THE INFORMATION AGE

After seeing a 2,000 percent spike in the usage of the term "post-truth" over 2015, the Oxford English Dictionary chose the term as its 2016 word of the year.[15] OED defines post-truth as language "relating to or denoting circumstances in which objective facts are less influential in shaping public opinion than appeals to emotion and personal belief." The term refers to the proliferation of phenomena like fake news, alternative reality, mis- and disinformation characteristic of today's political landscape.[16] Whether we see the post-truth phenomenon as directly related to post-modern thought of academic origin, as does Maurizio Ferraris (2019), or whether we see it as a parallel event, born of the rise of global media, global modes of communication and the breakdown of national institutions, as Matthew d'Ancona (2017) suggests, there has been a generalized "war on truth" in today's politics that is of concern to social scientists (see Block 2018, chapter 6; McIntyre 2018; Block 2019; and others).[17]

Symbolic violence in the form of manipulation of the truth comes in different forms under various labels:

Hearsay. As we saw in Chapter 2, reference to hearsay can enhance one's legitimacy and damage that of others. Social media can spawn and spread hearsay, ruin our reputation, and otherwise directly attack our social symbolic self (see Section 4.3).

Disinformation. Websites launder varying degrees of misinformation – whether conspiracy theories or polarized slants on the news. But because the primary point is not to spread false information, but to muddle the conversation, make people question what is true, and erode trust, these have been called "disinformation" campaigns. Disinformation is meant to divide people, increase their distrust and undermine their faith in institutions and democracy itself.[18]

Amplification, clickbait, outrage. As we have seen, the algorithms of social media reward content that keeps users engaged, which means posts that stir anger, help it spread and get clicks.

Trolling on the Internet is starting a quarrel online by posting inflammatory or digressive messages with the intent of provoking readers into displaying an emotional response.[19]

"Fake news" is not simply news that is false. It is a claim made against some journalists, accusing them of deliberately falsifying the news to serve their political interests or for mere mediatic display.

Propaganda. A deliberate attempt to promote a particular ideology for political gain. Propaganda is meant to build allegiance, not to communicate information but to get us to "pick a team." Those who spread propaganda do not strive to convince people that they are right, but to demonstrate that they have authority over the truth itself. Because of the new digital forms of communication, propaganda works differently today than it did, say, under fascist regimes: "propaganda works today not by restricting information, but by flooding the field with content, thus sowing confusion and generating epistemic apathy and despair" (Sacasas 2019).

Ultimately, we have to ask: Why are these forms of post-truth important for applied linguists? As will be discussed in Chapter 9, post-truth creates a profound and unsettling mismatch between words and things, between the symbolic and the material world, and between expectations and lived reality; it generates distrust and anxiety. Indeed it disrupts the very axes of time, space and causality that, according to artificial intelligence scientists, form the basis of our humanity.

8.6   ROBOTICS AND SYMBOLIC POWER: A.I. AND GOOGLE TRANSLATE

Finally, in the social and cultural revolution ushered in by the digital age we have to consider the much deeper influence of Artificial Intelligence and Google Translate on language and language use. Cognitive psychologist Gary Marcus and computer scientist Ernest Davis envision a much more ambitious research goal for artificial intelligence than envisioned up to now.[20]

> We need to stop building computer systems that merely get better and better at detecting statistical patterns in data sets – often using an approach known as deep learning – and start building computer systems that from the moment of their assembly innately grasp three basic concepts: time, space and causality. (Marcus and Davis 2019b)

For example, for the moment computers cannot answer the question: "Did George Washington own a computer?" – a question whose answer requires relating two basic facts (when Washington lived, and when the computer was invented) in a single temporal framework. Similarly, to understand what a cheese grater is good for, they argue, the computer has to understand how the shape of an object is related to its function and how an object's physical features correspond to its potential causal effects. Without the concepts of time, space and causality, much of common sense is impossible – nor, one could add, Bourdieu's practical sense that creates a social, cultural and moral habitus.

Humanists might feel tempted to stem research in robotics for fear that robots will supersede humans, but this is not the conclusion that Marcus and Davis draw. In order to conceptualize harm, they argue, rather than train computers to yield only statistical correlations, you have to program them to understand what harm means to a human being subjected to time, space and causality. For example, you have to program them to follow more general instructions such as: "A robot may not injure a human being or, through inaction, allow a human being to come to harm." But what if time, space and causality are precisely the three axes along which humans wield symbolic power over the computer? A philosophical challenge indeed, and one for which we need to consult in Chapter 9 both humanist and post-humanist thinkers.

SUGGESTIONS FOR FURTHER READING

The last fifteen years have seen a plethora of books on the relationship of language and digital technology in the exercise of symbolic power. Apart from Harcourt (2015) and Vaidhyanathan (2011), critical perspectives on the Internet and the World Wide Web are offered by Morville and Rosenfeld (2006) and Morozov (2012). Meyrowitz (1985), Nissenbaum (2009), Rettberg (2014) and Vaidhyanathan (2019) study the impact of digital media on social behavior. In applied linguistics, Jones (2016) gives an informative summary of what we should know about surveillance in the digital age. Jones and Hafner (2012) and Jones et al. (2015) offer excellent introductions to digital literacy. Bucher (2018) and Jones (2019a and b, in press a and b) are the most useful for the teaching of language and literacy by helping us understand the algorithms and socio-technical assemblages that determine our experience of interacting with texts.

9 Engaging with Symbolic Power — Responding to Symbolic Violence

HOW SER CIAPELLETTO BECAME SAINT CIAPELLETTO

From our discussion of the digital revolution and of its social and cultural effects in the use of language as symbolic power (Chapters 7 and 8), it has become clear that we are dealing with a much greater transformation in our use of language than just a change in language technology and literacy practices. Indeed, we are dealing with a complete rethinking of what constitutes the fundamental axes of our human existence – time, space and causality – the very axes that Marcus and Davis advocate building into computers to make them behave in a more human-like way. But these are momentous concepts, associated since Kant with a modernist humanistic philosophy that critical applied linguists like Pennycook are rejecting in favor of a post-humanism better suited to our complex times (Pennycook 2018). How are we to conceive of these three concepts today when studying and teaching languages as a human activity? How can learning another language help us better understand the symbolic complexity of the human condition? And how can it enable us to respond to symbolic violence?

In this chapter, we look for guidance from five thinkers who have specifically addressed these questions. With Judith Butler (1997, 2016), we continue the discussion started in Chapter 4 on the political promise of the performative, and we examine the time dimension of the speech act in responding to symbolic violence. With Michel de Certeau (1984a), we investigate how people gain symbolic power by capitalizing on space in the practices of their everyday lives. We then turn to Mikhail Bakhtin (1981), who developed a theory of the time-space combination (or chronotope) that leads speakers and writers to engage with symbolic power on a dialogic basis. We look at how Pierre Bourdieu (2000) expands on Pascal's theory of causality to support his notion of the embodied habitus and its never-ending quest for symbolic capital. Finally, we consider how Alastair Pennycook (2018) engages with symbolic reality as he redefines all three axes in an era of post-humanist realism. As in the other chapters, we start out with a story that captures the theme of the chapter.

In "The politics of representation," the Bakhtin scholar and translator Michael Holquist tells about Bakhtin's lifelong affection for the first story of Boccaccio's *Decameron*, "How Ser Ciapelletto became Saint Ciapelletto." As Holquist tells it,

> it is a funny – but somewhat eerie – tale about an evil merchant who has lied, cheated, and indiscriminately fornicated all his life. He falls ill and recognizes that he is about to die while visiting a strange town where no one knows him. He calls for a priest in order to make his final confession and, by a series of subtle indirections, convinces the priest he has led a life of the most unexampled virtue. After the evil merchant's death, the priest to whom he confessed tells everyone about his discovery of a secret saint. Soon pilgrimages are made to the merchant's tomb, and, before very long, miracles begin to occur on the site. (Holquist 1981:182)

In light of Bakhtin's experience with censorship and exile, and his taste for carnival, Holquist concludes: "This tale [. . .] serves to remind us that although the politics of representation are vexed, it is still a politics insofar as it is an art of the possible. Paraphrasing Stephen Daedalus, we may say that silence is not mandatory, exile may be overcome, as long as cunning reigns." (Holquist 1981:182). In the interpretation I propose here, this story enacts our ability to wield symbolic power through cunning and a political grasp of the fundamentally symbolic nature of our existence.[1] It shows the workings of symbolic power through the three coordinates that govern human experience – time, space and causality.

Boccaccio's narrative clearly capitalizes on the first coordinate – time – on various levels of simultaneity. On the level of the story, we have: the time of the evil merchant's past life memories as shared with a representative of the Church in the present sacrament of confession; the time elapsed between his death and the spread of the priest's gossip; and the timeless time of miracles and canonization. On the level of the narrative, we have: the time-lag between the publication of the *Decameron* in 1353 and the reading of it by Bakhtin, a Russian language teacher and scholar, several hundred years later;[2] and the time of an American scholar like Holquist, reader and translator of Bakhtin into English, another sixty years later.

The narrative also capitalizes on the second coordinate – space. As in many folktales, the evil merchant, who has spent his life on the road, happens to find himself in a foreign town at the time of his death. The ambiguous words of his confession materialize in the social and geographical space of a Catholic country familiar with beatified visions and pilgrimage sites. Through miraculous cures, Saint Ciapelletto regains control over perceptual space – he makes the blind see, the lame walk. He also rehabilitates his reputation in the social space of the local community and regains control of the world's linguistic/literate space as his story, first told in Italian, gets translated into Russian, then into English and becomes a printed text published by an American university press.

One of the reasons that Bakhtin liked this story was the way it illustrated his understanding of the third coordinate of human existence, namely causality. As I shall discuss later in this chapter, the relation of cause and effect here is anything but linear. Human actions get entangled in a web of coincidences independent of human intentions, human words take on a life of their own, literary verisimilitude trumps factual truth. Artful cunning seems to be in the Decameron the name of the symbolic power game.

9.1 TIME: THE POLITICAL PROMISE OF THE PERFORMATIVE IN BUTLER

We first go back to the conceptualization of the speech act discussed in Chapter 4. We noted that a late modern feminist thinker like Judith Butler focused on the temporal dimension of speech acts, that she felt was missing from Austin and Searle's speech act theory. In her 1997 book *Excitable speech*, written in the wake of the debate surrounding Proposition 229 that allowed gays to serve in the military but only under the "Don't ask, don't tell" ruling, Butler examined the use of hate speech from the perspective of speech act theory. Against the Pentagon's belief that prohibiting homosexual talk solves the problem of gays in the military, Butler rejects the "Don't ask, don't tell" ruling by arguing that talk about homosexuality should not be conflated with homosexual conduct. Homosexual speech should be protected by the Freedom of Speech Amendment and not be regulated by law. Symbolic violence in the form of hate speech directed at homosexuals should be resisted through political activism for gay rights, not prohibited by the state. "The collapse of speech into conduct, and the concomitant occlusion of the gap between them tends to support the case for state intervention," whereas "to insist on the gap between speech and conduct is to lend support for the role of nonjuridical forms of opposition, ways of restaging and re-signifying speech in contexts that exceed those determined by the courts" (Butler 1997:23).

As she analyzes the personal and political effects of performatives, Butler draws on Althusser and Derrida to explain why the First Amendment of the U.S. Constitution on freedom of speech should be upheld and not regulated by the State, despite the symbolic and physical violence that may occur.

We are, says Butler, interpellated by hate speech, as when a policeman hails us on the street: "Hey you there!" and we turn around, acknowledging in that moment both our identity as an addressee and the right of the police to hail us (Althusser 1971). By being addressed, we feel obligated to respond by facing our addressor. In the same manner, a slur or any other derogatory form of address stops us in our tracks, so to speak. Whether the insult targets our race, our ethnicity, our sexual orientation or any other parts of our identity, it has a disorienting effect. While we see ourselves from the inside as complex, changing and multiple, this outsider's characterization of who we are, couched in a term that has a long history of racism, sexism or xenophobia, singles one of our identities and throws us back to other times, other contexts that get reactivated by the insult and causes us pain and suffering. How should we respond? Should there be limits to free speech?

The Time of the Performative

This is where Butler argues that we have to look at the time dimension of performatives. While, as we saw in Chapter 4, the illocutionary force of speech acts comes from the force of social convention, that convention itself is the product of ritualized sedimentation over time in a given speech community. Each utterance draws its legitimacy from the historicity of discourse, that makes it repeatable (iterability) and quotable (citationality). Thus every utterance is always reiterating prior utterances and reactivating past contexts.

> The policeman who hails the person on the street is enabled to make that call through the force of reiterated convention. This is one of the speech acts that police perform, and the temporality of the act exceeds the time of the utterance in question [...] The act works in part because of the citational dimension of the speech act, the historicity of convention that exceeds and enables the moment of its enunciation. (Butler 1997:33)

We will always be vulnerable to verbal injury, says Butler, for that is also what brings us into social existence and constitutes us as social subjects:

> It is by being interpellated within the terms of language that a certain social existence of the body first becomes possible [...] One comes to "exist" by virtue of this fundamental dependency on the address of the Other. One "exists" not only by virtue of being recognized, but, in a prior sense, by being *recognizable*. (p.5)[3]

But, while hate speech seeks to reactivate past stereotypes and current myths (see Chapter 1) about Blacks, Jews, gays, foreigners and various minority groups, we should not confuse the emotional effect of speech acts in the immediate present with a potential political response to such acts, which Butler calls "the political promise" of the performative (p.145). We have, namely, the possibility of seeing ourselves from the outside ("One is constituted by discourse, but at a distance from oneself," p.35) and of breaking with prior contexts, even though we can still be hurt by injurious speech.

Because any speech act is uttered and received on different time-scales by individuals with different biographies, memories and aspirations, "a speech act always says more, or says differently, than it means to say" (p.10). Thus, the effectiveness of the performative does not depend entirely on the intention of the speaker, nor on some kind of "magical" effect on the receiver (p.21). The evil merchant in Boccaccio's story might not have had the intention of being canonized after his death and, seen from the perspective of his illocutionary act, he remains in death the same as he was in life – an impostor, a cheater, a liar. However, seen from the perspective of his act's perlocutionary effects, he redeemed the pain he had caused others by performing miracles and healing people after his death. As we shall see later in this chapter, both Butler and Bourdieu shift the attention to the perlocutionary, but while Bourdieu focuses on a more ecological view of causality, Butler focuses on the opportunity to reposition human agency from the orbit of the illocutionary to that of the perlocutionary. How does this work?

From Linguistic Vulnerability to Linguistic Survival

As discussed in Chapter 4, Butler draws on Derrida (1978) to argue that there is a time gap between the illocutionary force of an utterance and its perlocutionary effect. Furthermore, while speakers are clearly responsible for their speech, they are rarely the originators of that speech. Injurious speech often takes the form of ritual insults that are repeated but not necessarily invented by individual speakers. In other words, we control neither the origins nor the effects of our speech, even though we are held accountable for both. Such an awareness of the historicity of speech opens up the possibility of a response that breaks with previous contexts. "The time of discourse is not the time of the subject" says Butler (1997:31), but "it makes possible the *speaking* time of the subject" (p.28). Even though as speaking subjects we are subjected to orders of discourse over which we have no control, that is, even though we have no sovereignty over language, we do have agency.

This agency manifests itself in two ways: first in the recognition of the "historical density" of speech that carries with it the traces of prior historical contexts of enunciation:

Context is invoked and restaged at the moment of utterance (p.13). The possibility for a speech act to resignify a prior context depends, in part, upon the gap between the originating context or intention by which an utterance is animated and the effects it produces. (p.14)

Second, it manifests itself in the recognition that, except for a very restricted class of declarative speech acts (i.e., "you're fired!"), words do not do what they say. Because of the time-lag between illocutionary act and perlocutionary effect, we are free to break with past context and to resignify it by attaching to it a different perlocutionary effect.

Whereas illocutionary acts proceed by way of conventions, perlocutionary acts proceed by way of consequences and there is always a lapse of time between the two. (p.17)

In the late nineties, such resignification was fought for by the LGBTQ movement for gay rights, which led to the repeal of the "Don't ask, don't tell" ruling and the Supreme Court decision to allow gays to serve in the U.S. military. Butler's insistence on the "possibility of speaking with authority *without* being authorized to speak" (p.157) has been recently on display in the rhetorical resistance to Trump's symbolic warfare (see Chapter 6). Such possibilities of response to symbolic violence contributes, says Butler, to "expanding the domain of linguistic survival." (p.41)[4]

We could represent such an expansion through the following diagram shown in Figure 9.1.

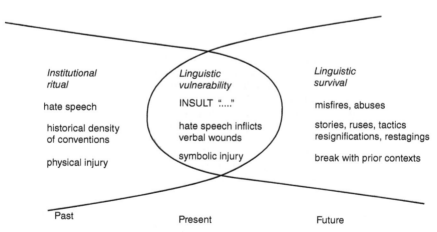

Figure 9.1 Linguistic survival is possible because of the iterability of discourse open to the past as well as to the future

9.2 SPACE: STRATEGIES AND TACTICS IN DE CERTEAU

Around the time that Foucault studied the disciplinary mechanisms of French hospitals and prisons and Bourdieu studied the French educational system (Chapters 2 and 5), their contemporary Michel de Certeau (1925–1986) was studying the small-scale coping strategies of everyday people having to deal with the workings of power in their daily interactions with one another.

Strategies vs. Tactics

In *The practice of everyday life* (1984a), de Certeau distinguishes between strategies and tactics. Strategies, he says, are the practices of people with symbolic power, that is, who hold various amounts of social, cultural, political or symbolic capital (see Chapter 5) and who have both the space and the time to plan ahead. For example, members of a political party in power will have the privilege to decide which issue will be put up for a vote in Parliament; a father who controls the finances of a family or the manager of a corporation will have both a place (house or office) and the time to plan ahead to decide on the best strategy to use to achieve their goals. Strategies make it possible to "transform the uncertainties of history into readable spaces" (p.36) of plans and organizational charts. By contrast, tactics are the practices of those who do not have the ability to plan ahead.

> A tactic is a calculated action determined by the absence of a proper locus [. . .] The space of a tactic is the space of the other. Thus it must play on and with a terrain imposed on it and organized by the law of a foreign power. It does not therefore, have the options of planning general strategy and viewing the adversary as a whole within a distinct, visible, and objectifiable space. It operates in isolated action, blow by blow. It takes advantage of 'opportunities' and depends on them [. . .] What it wins it cannot keep. [. . .] It must seize on the wing the possibilities that offer themselves at any given moment [. . .] It creates surprises in them. It can be where it is least expected. It is a guileful ruse. In short, a tactic is an art of the weak. (p.37)

Of course, as de Certeau notes, tactics can be used by the powerful as part of a strategy to deceive their target. The weaker the forces at the disposal of the strategist, the more the strategist will resort to deception tactics.

Strategies and tactics are a form of response to symbolic violence that can be used both by the powerful and the powerless, but they operate differently for each. Strategies capitalize on proprietary space – mass mediatic coverage, conversational doggedness and dominance, persuasive clout, institutional backing. Tactics capitalize on borrowed space – interstitial opportunities, an outsider's humor, reframing and renaming practices, and social media; but because tactics are, like guerilla warfare, dependent on the circumstances of the moment, they rely on a fundamental belief that in time things will change. We can consider as an example two forms of resistance to the symbolic violence exerted by the Monarchy in eighteenth-century France.

Two Historic Examples

Subversive Strategies in Diderot's Encyclopedia

It is informative to look at earlier strategies to respond to the symbolic violence exerted by the King and the Church in eighteenth-century France. As we have seen with the Fables of La Fontaine in Chapter 2, writers had to be particularly cunning to avoid censorship or public pillory that could send them to the Bastille, like Diderot who was imprisoned for three months in 1749 on account of his atheistic views. Upon coming out of prison, Diderot started on his major project, the Encyclopedia, that the historian Andrew Curran describes in *Diderot: The art of thinking freely* (2019). In this Encyclopedia, says Curran, Diderot challenged virtually all of his century's accepted truths, from the sanctity of the monarchy, to the racial justification of the slave trade, to the norms of human sexuality. His often iconoclastic stands on art, theater, morality, politics and religion come across indirectly through such strategies as feints, irony and satire and through the rational structure chosen for this Encyclopedia.[5]

Encyclopédie, or a Systematic Dictionary of the Sciences, Arts, and Crafts (Dictionnaire raisonné des sciences, des arts et des métiers), edited by Denis Diderot and Jean Le Rond d'Alembert, and published in France between 1751 and 1772, was to incorporate all the world's knowledge in one book accessible to all. Unlike the democratic structure of Google, the many contributors to this *Encyclopédie* "or *Encyclopédistes*" were chosen from the scholarly elite of the time, who had to tread the fine line between political loyalty and scientific integrity. This was a time when Louis XV was at the height of his reign but it was also a time when the forces of the Enlightenment were gaining ground all over Europe. These forces challenged both the power of the Church and the power of the King. Curran writes:

> Far more influential and prominent than the short single-authored works that Diderot had produced up to this point in his life, the *Encyclopédie* was expressly designed to pass on the temptation and method of intellectual freedom to a huge audience in Europe and, to a

lesser extent, in faraway lands like Saint Petersburg and Philadelphia. Its extended and self-important title, which indicated a *systematic* and critical treatment of the era's knowledge *and* its trades, promised something far beyond a normal reference work. Ultimately carried to term through ruse, obfuscation, and sometimes cooperation with the authorities, the *Encyclopédie* (and its various translations, republications, and pirated excerpts and editions) is now considered the supreme achievement of the French Enlightenment: a triumph of secularism, freedom of thought, and eighteenth-century commerce. (Curran 2019:102–103)

Curran brings to light the ruses and obfuscations that the editors deployed to evade the King's censors: voluminous cross-references, lengthy footnotes and a savvy way of using alphabetical order to negate existing hierarchies (e.g., the entry *Catholicism* finding itself under "C" in the same section as *Cuivre* [Copper]!). This enabled them to juxtapose items of knowledge that belonged to two separate conceptual realms, and thus deny the Church the exclusive claim to human knowledge. Indeed, Diderot was intent on secularizing knowledge to a greater extent than his English counterparts, notably Francis Bacon.

At first glance, the Encyclopedia's large map of topics, which ranged from comets to epic poetry, seemed quite inoffensive. Indeed, the *Encyclopédie*'s earliest critic, the Jesuit priest Guillaume-François Berthier, did not quibble with how Diderot had organized the "System"; he simply accused Diderot of stealing this aspect of Bacon's work without proper acknowledgment. Diderot's real transgression, however, was not following the English philosopher more closely. For, while it was true that Diderot freely borrowed the overall structure of his tree of knowledge from Bacon, he had actually made two significant changes to the Englishman's conception of human understanding. First, he had broken down and subverted the traditional hierarchical relationship between liberal arts (painting, architecture, and sculpture) and "mechanical arts" or trades (i.e., manual labor). Second, and more subversively, he had shifted the category of religion squarely under humankind's ability to reason. Whereas Bacon had carefully and sagely preserved a second and separate level of knowledge for theology outside the purview of the three human faculties, Diderot made religion subservient to philosophy, essentially giving his readers the authority to critique the divine. (Curran 2019:115–116)

Curran sums up Diderot's subversive moves against the established wisdoms of his time in the following terms: "This new interdynamic presentation of knowledge and cross-references [. . .] intentionally and blatantly put contradictory articles into dialogue, thereby underscoring the massive incongruities and fissures that existed within the era's knowledge"(p.119). At the time of Diderot's Encyclopedia, the French Revolution was still four decades away, but already official discourse was being undermined by such literate strategies, that spread distrust, scorn and resentment against the symbolic violence exercised by King and Church. This was nowhere more prevalent than in the tactics of the French populace to hollow out the public image of the monarchy through popular songs and jokes.

Resistance Tactics in the Eighteenth-Century "Early Internet"

In the eighteenth century, resistance to symbolic violence was assisted in its development not only by the scientific elite of the time, but by the tactics of the common people who gave voice to their criticism of the monarchy through songs and ribaldries in the Paris taverns. In "Paris, the early internet," the historian Robert Darnton documents how the people managed to evade the King's spies who were standing at the door (Darnton 2000a). By looking at the gossip, the stories and the songs that were exchanged all throughout Paris around 1750, he shows how the people were able to vent their anger at Louis XV's abuse of power, his sexual infidelities and his disdain for the common folk, while avoiding being arrested for blasphemy and sedition. Darnton writes:

> In such an environment, a catchy song could spread like wildfire; and, as it spread, it grew – inevitably, because it acquired new phrasing in the course of oral transmission and because everyone could join in the game of grafting new stanzas onto the old. The new verses were scribbled on scraps of paper and traded in cafés just like the poems and anecdotes diffused by the *nouvellistes*. When the police frisked prisoners in the Bastille, they confiscated large quantities of this material, which can still be inspected in boxes at the *Bibliothèque de l'Arsenal* – tiny bits of paper covered with scribbling and carried about triumphantly, until the fatal moment when a police inspector, armed with *a lettre de cachet*, commanded, "Empty your pockets." A typical scrap of verse, the latest stanzas to "*Qu'une bâtarde de catin*" – one of the most popular songs attacking Mme. de Pompadour, the king, and court – was seized from the upper left vest pocket of Pidansat de Mairobert during his interrogation in the Bastille. (p.30)

Darnton's study of the sources of information in eighteenth-century Paris offer a fascinating example of the tactics used in the construction of a counter-discourse to the dominant and only legitimate political discourse of the time. The tactics used by the poor and the dispossessed took the form of popular ballads, jokes, pamphlets and pictures that got circulated underground in marketplaces, taverns and cafes.

Throughout the eighteenth century, they made fun of the King and the Royal Family in crude and graphic ways. Songs managed to evade the King's police by being decentralized collective creations without any single author. Such tactics were dangerous and jokers could end up in the Bastille, but over the years they undermined the people's respect of the monarchy, degraded its legitimacy, hollowed out the language used to uphold it and prepared the way for the French Revolution of 1789. Such tactics might not work as well in the digital age and in a time of populism, but they remind us that each age develops its own unique ways of responding to and countering symbolic violence in tune with the spirit of the times.

9.3 TIME-SPACE: DIALOGISM AND ADDRESSIVITY IN BAKHTIN

We next turn to Mikhail Bakhtin (1895–1975) whose whole work was a response to the physical and symbolic violence that accompanied the Soviet Revolution and the social and political upheavals that ensued in the 1920's and 1930's. Bakhtin's translator Michael Holquist explains that Bakhtin took part in the twenties in the passionate philosophical debates surrounding Marxism-Leninism, Einstein's theory of relativity and the new conditions of cultural and political life in the young Soviet Union (Holquist 1990). He experienced exile, rejection and bad health, but kept asking fundamental questions about language and existence. Among those was one that lay at the core of the new socialist discourse order: "What is it in language that binds individuals into groups and at the same time enables individuals to exist as selves?" (p.57) or "How can I know if it is I or another who is talking?" (p.13). In other words, how can I retain my integrity as a speaking subject and at the same time respond to the demands of the group that ensures my existence as a social actor?

As Bakhtin tried in his work to draw the philosophical and ethical consequences of the socialist revolution, he developed a theory of what Holquist would later call "dialogism," in which he argued that we are bound to others by links of simultaneity in time but in different spaces.[6] By virtue of being in the world, we are constantly addressed by events that happen elsewhere even if we are not always responsible for them. How can we answer them, that is, how can we be answerable for other human beings with whom we share the same planet? As with all things human, we can only express ourselves by using pre-existing, repeatable words that have been used by others. However, each one of us occupies a unique, unrepeatable subject position that only we can fill. For example, in the Decameron story that opened this chapter, Ser Ciapelletto's confession to the priest was, on the face of it, like any of the many confessions that priest had heard over the years, and yet an unexpected constellation of factors (a dishonest scoundrel, an unprofessional priest, credulous parishioners and the vagaries of the Catholic Church) made it into a unique event with life-changing consequences for many in the community and beyond. Not to forget the unique position of the storyteller himself, who was able to inject the right dose of humor into the account.

The Chronotope

The relationality of events in both language use and human existence in general constitutes Bakhtin's dialogism, that is, the idea that people and events have to be seen both from an insider's and an outsider's perspective to be fully understood and that the two perspectives have to be in dialogue with one another.

> The only way I know of my birth is through accounts I have of it from others; and I shall never know my death, because my 'self' will be alive only so long as I have consciousness – what is called "my" death will not be known by me, but once again only by others. (Holquist, p.37)

I understand my life subjectively, as I live it instant by instant, with elastic memories and aspirations that fit my sense of identity in the present; but only others can see me in the fullness of the place I occupy in history and society. Hence the "dialogue" that necessarily takes place between self and other perspectives, between words and their contexts of enunciation, between the actual and the possible.

It is this belief in the dialogic nature of human existence that led Mikhail Bakhtin to his signature concept of time-space or chronotope. Nourished by Bakhtin's Christian and literary imagination, this concept captures his fundamental insight that we can only understand who we are if we see ourselves *simultaneously* through the unique place and time we occupy *and* through the eyes of others who occupy a different time and place. "We perceive the world through the time/space of the self and through the time/space of the other" (Holquist 1990:35). Like figure and ground, the two are indissociable. Hence the term "chrono-tope," a term that, in Bakhtin's original sense, was meant to denote a category of narrative analysis, that comprised both a plot (or brute chronology) and a story (the telling of it), as well as an evaluation of the narrated events, that is, their value. To take Boccaccio's example again, the chronotope here would be not just the events as they unfold sentence by sentence, but the thematic or generic pattern of a "redemption" or "hagiography" story, held together by the ironic value given by Boccaccio or the moral proposed by Holquist.

Thus on one level, the chronotope is "the intrinsic connectedness of temporal and spatial relationships that are artistically expressed in literature" (Bakhtin 1981:84). But on another level, it is more than that. The chronotope is a general principle of human existence, that offers a broader framework on how to respond to symbolic power.

> all deeds are connected to the deeds of others, so their meanings can never be grasped in themselves or from the point of view of a supra-situational end. In dialogism, 'subject' and 'intention,' are positional or interlocutive terms [. . .] Chronotope is a useful term not only because it brings together time, space, and value, but because it insists on their simultaneity and inseparability. (Holquist 1990:155)

By showing us how the actions of a sinner are related to the gullibility of a country priest and how the evil nature of the first is inseparable from the complicity of the second, and by tying their actions to a miraculous outcome, Boccaccio gives us – tongue in cheek – a graphic illustration of the chronotopes that govern our lives. Bakhtin's philosophy should be seen not as moral relativism (this story does not excuse the evil merchant), but as ethical perspectivism. Before we condemn others, we have to see them from the unique place each of us occupies in time and space. In that sense we are "answerable" to that place and that environment, all the while that we are "responsible" for the authorship of our response (Bakhtin 1990). It is in this sense that we have to understand the notion of "complicity" inherent in symbolic power that has been a recurring theme throughout this book.

Bakhtin's message is thus one of hope. It is true, he would argue, that we are constantly in interaction with others through relations of power and symbolic violence, but these relations extend far beyond what is said in the here-and-now. They encompass what is said and what is not said, what has been or could have been said by others in the past and what could potentially be said by others in the future. It is this dialogue that constructs us and others as speaking subjects and as social actors. "Each time we talk, we literally enact values in our speech through the process of scripting our place and that of our listener in a culturally specific social scenario" (p.63). It should be no surprise that Bakhtin was fond of the Boccaccio story. It illustrates his deep personal belief in the power of language to break the linearity of cause and effect and to contribute to the larger traffic in meaning on which we rely to ensure our existence.[7] As Bakhtin wrote:

> There is neither a first word nor a last word. The contexts of dialogue are without limit. They extend into the deepest past and the most distant future. Even meanings born in dialogues of the remotest past will never be finally grasped once and for all, for they will always be renewed in later dialogue. At any present moment of the dialogue there are great masses of forgotten meanings, but these will be recalled again at a given moment in the dialogue's later course when it will be given new life. For nothing is absolutely dead: every meaning will someday have its homecoming festival. (*Estetika*, p.373 cited in Holquist 1990:39)

Humor and the Carnivalesque

Bakhtin's insistence on the value of "transgredience," that is, the ability to see yourself and others from the outside, is epitomized not only in his work on Rabelais (Bakhtin 1984), but also in the many uses of humor and parody during Soviet times (e.g., Yurchak 2006; Boyer and Yurchak 2010)[8] and in the renewed success of political stand-up comedians and "culture jammers" that are proliferating today.[9] Outsideness, says Bakhtin, enables us to break the Marxist dialectic that relies on one-dimensional Cartesian axes such as Self vs. Other, individual vs. society, and to conceive of our lives as dialogic along several dimensions simultaneously. Outsideness enables social actors to grasp a situation in its total historicity and relationality through multiple chronotopes.[10] For example, Foucault's laughter at reading Borges' description of the fictional Chinese encyclopedia is a perfectly normal response to the symbolic violence such a text does to our rational, sensible understanding of the relationship of words to things. We read this text not from within the fictional universe of this encyclopedia, but from the outside. And this outsideness is what makes us for the first time grasp our own order of things, that we would otherwise take for granted – as natural as the air we breathe. We suddenly realize that we can read and say the words on the page, but we cannot *think* that way.[11] Their chronotope, Bakhtin would say, eludes us as real-life event but is accessible to us as a work of art, and in turn art can change our lives.

Laughter can of course also be a kind of "humor through adversity" or tactic of despair. Martin Luther King, in response to a question by Studs Terkel: "Would you say more about the matter of humor through adversity?," answered:

> I think you've got to have the ability to engage in creative laughter in order to live amid difficulties and tension. A great deal of truth often comes through laughter, and some people have developed the talent to

get this truth over to many people by laughing the truth *in* to them and *out* of them [...] Often people misinterpret the laughter of the Negro. It's a deeper laughter. It's the kind of laughter that molds a creative optimism out of a very pessimistic situation. It is a laughter that kept the Negro slave going amid a very trying and difficult and bewildering situation. (Terkel 1964)

We find a similar combination of insideness/outsideness, closeness/distance in the position adopted by Bourdieu in his last book in which he meditates on the debt he owes the French philosopher and mathematician Blaise Pascal, in particular regarding our third axis – the relation of cause and effects and our sense of the real.

9.4   CAUSALITY: "THE REASON OF EFFECTS" IN BOURDIEU

By calling his last book *Pascalian meditations* (2000), Pierre Bourdieu (1930–2002) explicitly distanced himself from Descartes' *Meditations* (1911), preferring Pascal's perspectival approach to truth and reality to Descartes' rational, objective and scientific thinking. Rejecting Descartes' irreducible separation of mind and body, individual and society, Bourdieu shows that mind and body intimately merge in people's habitus, that both structures and is structured by the social fields in which the habitus develops. As opposed to the liberal and neoliberal views of the autonomous, self-directed and free individual inherited from seventeenth/eighteenth-century Cartesian scholastic philosophies, Bourdieu adopts Pascal's conception of the vulnerable human being trying to find his or her place in the immensity of the universe.

Pascal's Understanding of Causality

In their times of religious persecution and technological innovations, both Descartes (1596–1650) and Pascal (1623–1662) – both philosophers and mathematicians – anguished about the possibility of knowing what makes us human. But they ended up with two different conclusions. Descartes came up with the *cogito ergo sum* [I think therefore I am] as guarantee of humans' superiority over animals, whereas Pascal was much more aware of the "wretchedness" of the human condition. The only advantage I have over plants and animals, he said, is that I know how vulnerable I am. "L'homme n'est qu'un roseau, le plus faible de la nature, mais c'est un roseau pensant" [Man is a reed, the weakest of nature, but it is a thinking reed] (Pascal 1976:149). Bourdieu liked to quote Pascal's famous aphorism:

"par l'espace, l'universe me comprend et m'engloutit comme un point; par la pensée, je le comprends" [By space the universe comprehends and swallows me up like an atom; by thought I comprehend the world]. (Bourdieu 2000:130)

But what does he mean by "thought"? For Pascal who strongly believed in God, even though he was tormented by the impossibility of proving his existence, thought was the consciousness of God's greatness and man's wretchedness. "Man knows that he is wretched. He is therefore wretched, because he is so; but he is really great because he knows it [. . .] The weakness of man is far more evident in those who know it not than in those who know it" (quoted in Bourdieu 2000:131). This awareness of one's vulnerability as the condition for being fully human was echoed by existentialist thinkers after World War II (Chapter 7) and has been picked up today by late modern thinkers like Butler, as we have seen.

Bourdieu explains how he expanded the notion of physical space, which Pascal was concerned about, to what he calls social space, that is,

> the locus of the coexistence of social positions, mutually exclusive points, which, for the occupants, are the basis of points of view. The 'I' that practically comprehends physical space and social space [. . .] is comprehended, in a quite different sense, encompassed, inscribed, implicated in that space. (p.130)

This inscription, says Bourdieu, takes place through the formation of a habitus, a system of dispositions that understands the world not through conscious intellectual comprehension and reasoning, but through a practical sense formed of expectations and anticipations.

> Against the scholastic illusion which tends to see every action as springing from an intentional aim, and against the socially most powerful theories of the day which, like neomarginalist economics, accept that philosophy of action without the slightest questioning, the theory of habitus has the primordial function of stressing that the principle of our actions is more often practical sense than rational calculation. (pp.63–64)

Causality and the Habitus

Pascal's metaphysical anguish as a philosopher in the seventeenth century finds an echo in Bourdieu's anguish as a sociologist from the Béarn coming of age in the highly stratified Parisian society of the mid-twentieth century. Hence his deep understanding of the tensions caused by having a *habitus clivé* or cleft habitus mentioned in Chapter 5, split between different social classes, disciplines, histories and intellectual traditions.

> I have many times pointed to the existence of cleft, tormented habitus bearing in the form of tensions and contradictions the mark of the contradictory conditions of formation of which they are the product. (Bourdieu 2000:64)

Such a cleft habitus is particularly relevant today in our times of extreme geographical mobility, multilingual communities, economic inequalities and global communication technologies that all disorient our capacity to make sense of the past and to anticipate the future.

How does Bourdieu's theory of the habitus lead him to redefine the third axis of our human existence – causality? While in a modern conception, time and space are two dimensions of the context in which we live our lives, and causality (causes and consequences) is the relation between two separate phenomena that occur one after the other in linear time and measurable space, the late modern conception adopted by Bourdieu (and all the thinkers discussed here), sees causality differently. As our habitus is not distinct from the world that produced it, the habitus, as embodied dispositions that enable it to adapt its present and future behavior in accordance with its environment, contains the world as much as the world encompasses it. As Bourdieu says: "The instruments of construction that man uses to know the world are constructed by the world" (p.136).

This means that we should not try and find out the causes of events, but we should instead see events as the effects of larger phenomena that have happened for a reason and it is that reason that we should seek to understand. This is what Pascal called "*la raison des effets*" [the reason of effects] and we can comprehend it because our habitus is itself such an effect whose reason has become socialized into our bodies as "bodily knowledge."[12] For example, insulting terms used to address African Americans have inscribed themselves into the very bodies of Black Americans and should be understood not as the consequence of any individual (insulting) intentionality on the part of the speaker, but as the effect of a much larger historical past. The reason for the pain inflicted by such insults is not to be found in a direct, linear "cause," such as this particular insult or that particular speaker, but in the effects of institutionalized racism and the unerasable history of slavery. With this different understanding of causality, our era acquires a different sense of reality.

For Bourdieu our sense of reality stems from the match between our habitus and its environment. The practical sense developed in time and space and through a correct understanding of the reason of effects is very much linked to the ability to meet social expectations and to anticipate social reactions. What happens today, now that the social world has become global and that digital symbolic systems have pretty much disrupted the three coordinates of our human existence? Are we in a hyperhuman hyperreality or have we entered a post-human world?

9.5   POST-HUMANISM IN PENNYCOOK AND LATOUR

With Alastair Pennycook's post-humanist approach to the question, we are back to "mugs, rocks and tables" and to the question we asked in Chapter 1, "Is a table really a table?" Pennycook encourages us to re-engage with reality: Does reality only exist insofar as humans experience it? Is a table with its flat surface and its four legs an undisputable fact, or is it a social and discursive construction? After examining the various scholars who have picked up recently this age-old question, Pennycook comes to the conclusion: "For Teubert (2013), reality is a discursive construct, while for Sealey (2007), material reality is independent of discourse, [but] neither of these positions helps us understand the *radical indeterminacy* of the sign" (Pennycook 2018:116). As we saw in Chapter 1, this indeterminacy stems from the nature of symbolic representation and the position of the person using the sign. Pennycook reminds us that objects, events, laws or beings are always correlated with the point of view provided by the humans who have access to them, and that if humans are social actors, they are not the only actors; an object like a table, an animal like a cat in the garden, a computer with its algorithms, are also actants. A table is not just a table, it is also the repository of a host of memories, hopes and expectations; a cat in the garden is not a just a visual experience, it indexes other pets and metaphors of pets, such as, for example, *The cat in the hat* (see Chapter 3); and my computer seems to just regurgitate some encyclopedic knowledge but in fact this knowledge is constructed by the human users who contribute to its database, and its algorithms construct the way I in turn organize, remember and understand that information (see Chapter 8).

Pennycook's Assemblages

Pennycook then proposes an alternative way of looking at tables, namely:

> as vibrant objects in temporary assemblages (that include chairs, tablecloths, food, drink, cutlery, conversation), as actants that interpellate us into forms of socialization. It is not just a question of what the human brings to the table but also what the table brings to the human. (Pennycook 2018, p.121)

Drawing on Barad (2007:133), he proposes a way forward in which our "thinking, observing, and theorizing are understood as *practices of engagement* with, and as part of, the world in which we have our being" (p.122, my emphasis). He advocates moving away from viewing tables, computers and symbolic systems as separate from human beings and as merely subservient to humans' desires and interests; he suggests moving instead into seeing humans as "*entangled* and *implicated* in other beings" (p.126, italics in the original). Instead of mastery, control and usefulness, "we need to think in terms of entanglements, assemblages and attunements" (p.136). Thus, in his view, the term "posthumanism" does not "seek to efface humans but rather to reorganize the relationships among humans and other animals and objects to move towards a new settlement that is less anthropocentric" (p.135).

Pandora's Hope

Does this new way of re-engaging with the reality of global, digital communication destroy or enhance our symbolic power? This is a question to which the philosopher of science Bruno Latour returns again and again in his work. In *Pandora's hope* (1999) he draws on the myth of Pandora to make his point. Pandora, a woman "with many gifts" (Gr.pan-dora), is sent by Zeus on earth carrying a jar filled with all kinds of afflictions, wars and diseases. She is to take revenge for Prometheus stealing the fire from the gods by spilling the contents of her "box" on mankind. But Zeus has made sure that one thing is left lying on the bottom of Pandora's box, namely, hope. Pandora's hope, Latour argues, is that humans cease to treat nature as their servant and plants, animals and computers as mere tools to master nature. Instead, they should start realizing that humans and non-humans, rather than being distinct from one another, exist in a symbiotic relationship, both shaping and shaped by one another. Objects, plants, animals and, one could add, symbolic systems like language are made by us as much as we are made by them. In the same manner as a "gun-in-your-hand" is a different object from a gun-on-the-rack, because it becomes an actant in a situation that also includes a human holding the gun, we could say that a word-in-the-dictionary or a-word-on-your-computer-screen is not the same as a word-in-your-mouth, addressed to someone you can see and touch.

Paraphrasing Latour, we could say:

> You are different with words in your mouth; the words are different with you uttering them. You are another subject because you utter these words; the words are another object because they have entered

into a relationship with you. Learning another language would mean not acquiring another tool to communicate with others or to achieve your goals, but engaging with language in such a way that you allow the foreign words to shape your thinking, your emotions, your memories, and to make you into a self you had not even imagined before. It would mean engaging with the historicity of words, their indexicalities and their symbolic power. And engaging thereby with your own symbolic self, made and shaped through the symbols you have created.

In that sense, Pennycook's notion of *entanglement*, that indexes more symbolic power struggle than the simple notion of *engagement*, contains a distinct political promise. It entails namely an increased awareness of the symbolic stakes at hand, of the weight of past human hubris and of the insatiable human desire for symbolic capital. Whether symmetrical entanglements with tables, cats and algorithms are possible might become a moot point if the survival of the human race is at stake. We might have to use old-fashioned humanist thinking to understand what forms of entanglement are necessary for our survival as "posthumans."

More recently, Latour (2017) sees in Pandora's hope a hope for a return to earlier models of knowledge, where the human sciences, the natural sciences and the social sciences were not yet under the dictatorship of facts and skills but offered ecological images of nature that were able to move us morally and aesthetically. In this new political dispensation, his response to the question "*Où atterrir?* [where to land?]" is neither a hyperhumanism nor a post-humanism, but a decidedly terrestrial ecological denizenship of a transdisciplinary and universal scope rather than a local or global reach.[13]

SUGGESTIONS FOR FURTHER READING

Butler et al. (2016) is important to understand Butler's insistence on the indissociable nature of vulnerability and resistance. De Certeau's famous essay "Walking in the City" on seeing Manhattan from the 110th floor of the World Trade Center and his sympathetic critique of Foucault and Bourdieu can be found in de Certeau (1984b). The best introduction to Bakhtin is Holquist (1990) before plunging into Bakhtin (1981 and 1990). A good supplement to Bourdieu's Pascalian critique of Cartesian reason is Bourdieu (1998). Critical perspectives on his work can be found in Calhoun et al. (1993) and Swartz (1997). But to really understand Bourdieu, one has to read chapter 1 in Bourdieu (1990) as well as Bourdieu (2008) on his own personal and intellectual trajectory. The documentary made by Pierre Carles (2001) is a must-see. The video of the famous debate between Noam Chomsky and Michel Foucault in the Netherlands (Mortensen 1971) echoes many of the themes developed in this chapter.

Conclusion

LANGUAGE: THE MEASURE OF OUR SYMBOLIC LIVES

In this book I have wanted to illuminate the pervasive power exercised through language in the real world of politics, workplaces, digital spaces, and everyday life. By focusing on the symbolic dimension of this power, I wanted to link the micro-level of the use of linguistic symbols to the macro-level of the uses and abuses of symbolic power. For this, I had to apply a post-structuralist/post-modernist approach to both the micro- and the macro-levels, and consider the teaching of language as the teaching of discourse and symbolic action right from the start. This has required drawing on: cognitive linguistic theory that links symbolic forms and cognitive categories of the mind; constructivism theory that links symbolic forms and symbolic action; performativity theory that links speech acts and their perlocutionary effects; politeness theory and sociolinguistic manifestations of symbolic power; communication theory and the use of digital symbolic systems like the Internet.

The current political situation in the United States has, I must admit, powerfully affected the way I view the issues discussed in this book. I have had to refrain from letting Donald Trump's abusive use of language dominate the discussion, but there has been a silver lining to his verbal excesses. His norm-defying, truth-bending, thoroughly crushing verbal actions have, like Harold Garfinkel's ethnomethodological experiments, revealed in a negative way the invisible workings of symbolic power as never before. Such a revelation has been both debilitating and encouraging. Besides creating a climate of symbolic uncertainty and anxiety, it has raised the awareness of language users and users of digital systems to the paradoxical effects of language as symbolic action in our daily verbal exchanges.

At this point in our exploration of language as symbolic power, we come to realize that the research on language and language use as I have described it in the first four chapters of this book has radically changed from what it was only fifty years ago. Applied linguists in the 1980's were still studying how language represented the social world through conventionally agreed-upon linguistic signs and idealized cognitive models of thought (Chapter 1); how it managed conversations through systematically regulated turns at talk and cooperative maxims (Chapter 2); how it referred symbolically and indexically to stable realities and ascertainable truths that could be taught and learned in schools (Chapter 3); how it acted upon the world through identifiable speech acts with recognizable intentionalities and how it adapted itself to the social and cultural variations found in everyday life (Chapter 4). Such modern descriptions, which are still found in language learning textbooks around the world, seem now far removed from the postmodern realities of language use in this early twenty-first century.

Indeed, every step of the way, we saw that the idealistic descriptions of linguists mostly ignored the symbolic power struggles in which social actors are engaged.[1] Today, they glare you in the face. Verbal meanings have now been supplemented and in large part replaced by visual images, whose truth can be altered by photoshop and other digital technology. Truth has been replaced by a multiplicity of equivalent opinions; politicians' speeches or debates have become shouting matches or conduits for propaganda. It has always been the case that people don't necessarily mean what they say nor say what they mean, but with social media today's uncertainties of meaning have grown exponentially. And cultural variation has been overlaid by a global internet culture that makes local cultures into consumer products.

C.1   SUMMARY OF THE ARGUMENT

Before I reflect on what this book might contribute to research in applied linguistics and in language education, let me summarize the main themes we can take away from our discussion.

Symbols Mediate Our Relationship to Physical Facts and Material Culture

As we discussed in Chapter 1, the fact that members of the human symbolic species developed the capacity to move from the mere iconic and indexical relations to symbolic relations gave them inordinately more power to act upon the people around them, providing that they used a symbolic system that was agreed upon by their speech community. The pervasive indexicality of language, that is, its ability not only to refer to objects in the world, but to point to other signs in the immediate context or in past and imagined contexts, both on the micro-level of proximate events and on the macro-level of collective discourses, beliefs and ideologies, gives individual speakers, writers and bloggers an enormous power to construct an interpretation of social reality and make it stick. But the weight of history and of collective memory has the power to limit any individual's meaning-making power.[2] Symbolic systems preexist individual social actors, and, irrespective of their intentions or aims, actors are unconsciously subjected to the power of history and the power of society. Thus they are made "complicit with the pervasive power relations in which their language is embedded" (Hanks 2005:77).

The Use of Symbols Enables Us to Construct and Thus Manipulate Social Reality

In the various verbal encounters discussed throughout the book, we have seen that, by the very act of engaging in linguistic practice, social actors construct the worlds they have been socialized into through their habitus. Because the words they use are "embedded in a universe of categorization, selective distinctions and evaluations" (Hanks 2005:77) that preexisted individual speakers, the worlds that speakers construct are in part independent of their individual intentions. Symbolic systems are structured by the history of their use, but their use also structures the way social actors experience the world. Routine language use provides what Hanks calls "ready-made terms in which actors apprehend and present reality, including language itself" (Hanks 2005:77). What the theory of linguistic relativity implies is that not only do our words reflect the cultural and social structures that created them (for e.g., the *tu/vous* distinction reflects the structure of French society at a historical point in time), but they manipulate social reality each time they are uttered. Speakers are complicit in the power relations constructed and perpetuated by language and upheld by the institutions of a given speech community.

Symbolic Forms Have Symbolic Functions That Are Multiple, Changing and Conflictual

As we saw in the Struwwelpeter story of Fidgety Phil (see Chapter 3), a physical behavior such as sitting still at the dinner table can become a symbolic form, namely, "sitting-still-at-the-dinner-table," imbued with momentous symbolic value. This symbolic form can fulfill multiple functions; for instance, it can construct an image of a well-brought up self, provide tangible, objective evidence of a family's bourgeois values, reinforce patriarchal authority and discipline, and serve to bond the family and establish a continuity with ancestral traditions. In turn, one function (e.g., bonding the family into a tight communal unit) can be achieved through other symbolic forms, from a mother's *I-love-you* assertions on the phone, to parental expectations of reciprocity for gifts received, to the monitoring of children through texts or tweets. We know that such symbolic forms can only wield symbolic power if they are (mis)recognized as natural and self-evident and, therefore, legitimate. In other cultures, at other times, sitting still at the table might be given a quite different symbolic value, e.g., alert the family to the needs of fidgety young children and reinforce an anti-authoritarian ideology and a more egalitarian relationship between parents and children.

But such symbolic power can also fulfill contradictory functions, as we saw in Chapter 4 with the paradoxical demands of facework. In the nineteenth century of Heinrich Hoffmann, an illustrated story about sitting still at the dinner table served both to strengthen a society's institutions and organizational values and to entice youngsters to overturn them. It reinforced the institution of kinship within the family but it also revealed the arbitrariness of family rules and the vulnerability of parental authority. The punishments for infractions to those rules as depicted in the *Struwwelpeter* stories were both fear-inducing and entertaining.

Symbolic Power Can Turn into Symbolic Violence

While symbolic power is constitutive of any social relation and cannot be wished away through friendly or generous behavior, it can have both positive and negative effects precisely because of its paradoxical nature. Because we are not isolated monads, but social actors that depend on one another for symbolic survival, we are inevitably entangled or implicated in symbolic power struggles to be heard, recognized, respected by others. As we have seen, it is not enough to speak with correct grammar and vocabulary, we need to use words in such a way that we will be recognized as legitimate speakers. This legitimacy will not come from our words alone, but from the institution we belong to, the rank or the reputation we have in our family, workplace or classroom, our gender or social class, or from our expertise in the topic at hand.

However, the paradox is as follows: We need to gain legitimacy as users of language because without it we cannot survive as social actors. But in order to be recognized as social actors, we need to recognize the legitimacy of others. Invariably such recognition entails a symbolic power struggle, as individual needs and interests collide. One of these paradoxical needs is the need for solidarity with others and thus equal legitimacy, and the need for power over others and thus unequal legitimacy (see Chapter 4).

Social life is made up of such small symbolic power struggles that we take as natural. They can, however, become symbolic violence if, for instance, you are given a present that is so expensive that you can never hope to reciprocate. In that case, the gift-giver has done violence to your sense of self. That violence, as we saw in Chapter 6, can even become symbolic warfare if someone abuses symbolic power to crush your self-esteem and destroy your legitimacy through such symbolic weapons as hurled slurs, insults and other face-threatening acts.[3] We have seen in Chapter 9 how symbolic violence can be responded to by capitalizing on the very axes of our symbolic existence and viewing time, space and causality in a different way.

Language as Symbolic Power Has Been Transformed by the Use of Symbolic Systems like the Internet

The advantage of focusing on symbolic power is that it illuminates many aspects of how we use language in everyday life, how we create and communicate meaning and how we have these meanings legitimized through the power of institutions. The decentered nature of the Internet and the interactional networks in which it engages us have certainly liberated us from the exclusive authority of traditional institutions like our School, our Family, our Church, our Party as we seek to know who we are and what we may believe. They have increased our ability to create knowledge from a variety of sources and to disseminate that knowledge to an infinite number of "connected individuals" like us, backed by the legitimacy granted to Internet users by such new institutions as Google, Facebook and Twitter. In that sense, digital technology has inordinately enhanced our symbolic power. As anthropologist Terrence Deacon remarks:

> If symbols ultimately derive their representational power, not from the individual, but from a particular society at a particular time, then a person's symbolic experience of consciousness is to some extent society-dependent – it is borrowed [. . .] Consciousness of self in this way implicitly includes consciousness of other selves, and other consciousnesses can only be represented through the virtual reference created by symbols. (Deacon 1997:452–453)

By broadening our consciousness of self in others and others in self through the use of words, images, memes, videos, digital technology has enhanced what Deacon calls our "symbolic self" (see Chapter 4).

Our distress is all the greater when we see that the symbolic meanings we have constructed are publicly and systematically contested, belied, attacked in the name of post-truths that defy any reason or logic. What is at stake when we use symbolic systems is the sanctity of our symbolic self, the one we rely on to make meaning rather than fall into insanity, the moral compass of our actions and behaviors, our consciousness of what is real and what is unreal, what is objective truth and what is subjective opinion, what is good and what is bad, and ultimately, what is Self and what is Other. The very existence of our symbolic self is dependent on rationality and consistency of meaning. Constant attacks on our sense of factual reality put into question integrity, that is, our capacity to exercise free will and agency. Thus, the use of symbolic systems like the Internet can lead to feelings of enhanced symbolic power or increased symbolic powerlessness, outrage or resignation. But these can have physical consequences as well – incendiary words online can lead people with guns in their hands to move from symbolic to physical violence.

C.2   IMPLICATIONS FOR APPLIED LINGUISTIC RESEARCH

So what does this mean for us, researchers and educators in applied linguistics? Every language education website claims to offer language instruction for a variety of uses: professional, commercial, recreational, academic, humanistic, economic, civic. All these uses are of interest to a field of research like applied linguistics, whose object of study is avowedly "the theoretical and empirical investigation of real-world problems in which language is a central issue." (Brumfit, as cited in Davies and Elder 2004:3). But who defines the real world? What counts as a problem? Who decides which problems to solve? And who qualifies as an investigator?

In the preceding chapters, I have passed in review some of the major theoretical writings that applied linguists draw on to define the real-world problems in which language is a central issue, as well as some theories on the symbolic power of internet systems and social media.[4] They all address directly or indirectly the issue of symbolic power and symbolic violence, its paradoxical nature, its interpellative nature, its political implications. While it has always been a dimension of symbolic systems, the symbolic power of language has become more visible in recent years due to the explosion of new media, a globalized economy and the ubiquitous access to the Internet, which have exacerbated the competitiveness among various political narratives, the fights for truth and individuals' desire to be seen and heard in the public sphere. Symbolic violence has in some cases turned into symbolic warfare, which, like any symbolic struggle, calls for an ethical response and even some form of political action.

With regard to research methodology, studying language as symbolic power calls for continuing the post-structuralist/post-modernist approach used by scholars such as van Lier (2004), Larsen-Freeman and Cameron (2008), McNamara (2012), Kramsch and Zhang (2018), Pennycook (2002, 2007) and many others who describe real-world problems within an ecological or complexity framework. It also calls for supplementing studies of identity and subjectivity through attention to their social symbolic dimension; supplementing the psycholinguistic by the symbolic in second language acquisition research; theorizing language technologies and problematizing social media as language learning environments; questioning the appropriateness of Google Translate as an environment to teach the indeterminacy of meaning and contextual interpretation; bringing back questions of ethics and politics in all domains of applied linguistics. Finally, viewing language as symbolic power prompts us to question the relation of research and practice in applied linguistics and to investigate the extent to which the solving of real-world problems risks being hijacked by professional experts, yet again devaluing the social symbolic contribution of practitioners in language education.[5]

C.3   IMPLICATIONS FOR COMMUNICATIVE LANGUAGE TEACHING

Language teaching and learning, be it a first, second or foreign language, is a major area of applied linguistics – one that raises all the ethical and political questions of an applied field, in addition to its epistemological and psycholinguistic mandate. As with all academic subjects, language teachers are called upon to transmit to their students the knowledge and skills that they will need to communicate with others once they have left school. But because they are dealing with a symbolic system, not just with a structural code that students learn to encode and decode, language educators have an additional responsibility to teach something about the symbolic power of language as discourse – how it works, how it affects people, how they can harness it to represent themselves and the reality that surrounds them, to act upon it, and to create future possible worlds.

We saw in Chapter 4 how the theory of communicative competence, developed by Dell Hymes in the seventies (Hymes 1972), included an

ethical dimension that would be later overshadowed by a more transactional understanding of communication in a neoliberal economy.
Hymes always saw communicative competence as a "vantage point
for critique and transformation of society" (1987:225). Reflecting on
the contribution that Habermas (1970, 1984) had made on the development of the concept (see Introduction), he notes:

> The virtue is that Habermas, like Grice, adds to knowledge of 'that' and
> 'how' the issue of 'should'. The postulation of commitment to norms
> makes ethics and politics part of a theory. The defect, as with Grice, is
> that the norms are taken as inherent. They rather are not inherent.
> They point to dimensions to which communicative conduct may be
> oriented in more than one way. The necessary questions are: what do
> people believe and do with regard to each [ethics and politics]? (Hymes
> 1987:225)

By insisting on exploring together and negotiating the norms of interaction and interpretation under which we use language, rather than
taking them off the peg so to speak, Hymes is displaying the post-
structuralist/post-modernist stance that I have adopted throughout
the book. Such a negotiation has to deal not just with issues of linguistic accuracy, appropriateness and comprehensibility, but with deeper
issues of beliefs, memories, morality and symbolic power. Hymes
goes on:

> Habermas brings the efforts of many Marxists in this century to come
> to terms with cultural hegemony into direct connection with language
> and communication, but occludes particular existence and concrete
> individuality. His ideal of consensus through unlimited turn taking,
> whatever its difficulties as a theory of truth, is inadequate as a model of
> practical action, if the differential distribution of abilities in actual
> groups is not taken into account. (Hymes 1987:225)

In language classes, "unlimited turn-taking" and "consensus building"
in communicative activities both in face-to-face and online have often
replaced any deeper reflection on the nature of the symbolic system
that is being learned and used. Hymes reminds us that such a reflection
can be painful because it can bring to light deep differences of experience and interpretation.

> If theory must start from ideal communicative intention, Moltmann's
> (1983) self-communicating God has the advantage of explicitly
> including suffering. (Hymes 1987:225)

As a Christian and a Quaker, Hymes draws an analogy to the mystery of
the Trinity, that a Christian theologian like Jürgen Moltmann sees as
three persons in one God: the Father, the Son and the Holy Spirit,

communicating with one another in love and pain.[6] Beyond the Christian references of this quote, Hymes alerts us to the difficult and even painful aspect of intercultural communication, one that is often minimized in electronic communication through the ease with which one can just log out whenever an exchange becomes too difficult. In reality, as Bakhtin would say, "we have no alibi in existence" (Holquist 1990:29). One of the ethical commitments of a field such as applied linguistics is to bring this Bakhtinian truth to the fore.

C.4   SYMBOLIC POWER IN EDUCATIONAL PRACTICE

I promised in the Introduction to examine the implications of a theory of language as symbolic power for language education. Let me hasten to say that I am not proposing to replace any of the well-established practices that language educators have developed to help learners master a foreign linguistic code and its foreign pragmatic and sociolinguistic uses. Rather, by being given a glimpse at language as symbolic power, language educators are offered another pair of lenses through which to view what they and their students are in the business of doing. These lenses will enable them to see the language learning and teaching enterprise from a new, post-structuralist/post-modernist perspective. In this perspective, the focus will no longer be exclusively on the individual learner, striving to get his/her message across in a manner conforming to the normative grammar of the target language and to the predictable social conventions of the target culture; it will also include making the learners aware of the *effects* of their utterances, speech acts and politeness strategies on others; they will be made to reflect on the effects of style, register, topics and discourse strategies on the economy of symbolic power in poems, plays and prose. As we make learners aware of the symbolic power struggles that go on in the real world, both in face-to-face and online interactions, we will be raising their consciousness of the historical, social and cultural dimensions of the words they use. However, as we are also asking them to focus on a social symbolic context that is fundamentally indeterminate and on a contextual knowledge open to different interpretations, we will not be able to test their understanding of language as symbolic power and their ability to exercise that power through the usual multiple choice or fill-in-the-blank tests. A post-structuralist/post-modernist approach to language education will require developing learners' interpretive abilities, sensitivity to context and appreciation of symbolic complexity.[7]

It will be the teacher's responsibility to enlighten students about the symbolic conditions under which institutional teaching and learning takes place; remind them of the large amount of knowledge about language that cannot be taught within the institutional constraints of the language classroom, and yet that will be essential for them to have. Teachers will want to make time to share with them during a coffee hour or an informal chat after class the insights they themselves have gained through their own experience as multilingual instructors (Kramsch and Zhang 2018).[8] These are insights, not information; painful understandings, not knowledge; alien wisdoms, not personal data.

As members of the institution they serve, language teachers will also want to manage the politics of academia to raise the administration's awareness of the new nature of language education in a global economy and of the new challenges their students face. This might lead to a re-thinking of the purposes of language learning within a (post-) humanistic education and a recalibrating of the respective importance given to language, linguistics and literature study within departments of foreign language and literature (Warner 2018). Indeed, in both research and practice, applied linguists will have to grapple with issues of ethics and politics as never before.[9]

C.5   BACK TO ETHICS AND POLITICS

In the last chapter of *Language – the loaded weapon* (1980, see Introduction), titled "An ecology of language," Dwight Bolinger made four recommendations to counter (linguistic and political) abuses of language.

- "Messages must be clear [. . .] Clear language is palatable as well as understandable. An honest message does not have to sacrifice style or humor." (p.184)
- "The message must identify itself with what it says, not with who says it. We have no need of professional jargon as guarantee of the importance, authority, or authenticity of the source." (p.184)
- "The message has to be free of snares – shun biases as much as possible." (p.184) We shouldn't be taken in by advertisements and propaganda.
- Allow the free flow of messages in the public sphere: . . . "There should be no off-limits to language. To speak only half the truth is to speak in half-truths." (p.186)

Forty years later, we have to place these recommendations in their historical context – a time of staunch belief in the unproblematic relation of language and thought, where speaking clearly was synonymous with thinking well and behaving honestly ("clear language," "honest message"); where grammar itself was seen as incorruptible and containing its own source of authority ("what it says and not who says it"); and where truth was uncontrovertible, whether it be the truth of grammars and dictionaries, or the truth of social and scientific facts. Linguists like Bolinger were convinced that there was no truth that couldn't be captured in a linguistic system ("no off-limits to language"), and that despite their structural differences different languages were all able to express universal truths (Bolinger 1980:175). Indeed, language users had a moral responsibility to speak the whole truth, not "half-truths." These four recommendations corresponded to what Bolinger called an "ecology" in which "language must take its place alongside diet, traffic safety, and the cost of living as something that everyone thinks about and talks about." (p.188)

How things have changed! Today, language is being talked about more than ever in the mass and social media, and the concept of ecology is alive and well in applied linguistics (see e.g., Kramsch 2002; van Lier 2004), but it has difficulty being heard over the din of the other terms we have encountered throughout this book: scientific hoax, witch-hunt, disinformation, post-truth, symbolic violence and symbolic warfare, virality, consumerism, instrumentalization, weaponization, institutional crises and distrust of institutions, global inequalities – all terms that point to the major symbolic power struggles that are going on today around language and other symbolic systems, fueled in part by global information technologies beyond our control.

In this climate, most language instructors are careful not to enter the fray. They justifiably interpret their mandate as helping language learners acquire and use language accurately and appropriately, and they are held accountable for doing precisely that (see Kramsch and Zhang 2018). In so doing, they are responding also to their students' expectations of being rewarded for having acquired "useful skills" and being able to demonstrate these skills on the required test. But such a practice is justified by an educational ideology that is being seriously put into question now, albeit outside the very language instructional circles whose interests it claims to serve. Many language instructors have found their own ways of enriching their teaching beyond the expectations of their students and the constraints of their institution. They are aware that they are not only instructors, but educators, with an unspoken mandate to prepare adolescents and young adults for a world that is not the bland world presented in the textbook nor the romantic world dreamed of by their students. They know (for having been there themselves) that the "real-world" of language use is far more complex and more treacherous, but also more exciting, than their students expected. They are looking for ways to lift the veil on some of those complexities without disappointing their students' expectations of predictability and accountability.

Our discussion of the nature and the uses/abuses of language as symbolic power lead me therefore to the following reflections.

1) As we have seen again and again throughout this book, verbal interactions are not a matter of "deploying usable skills."[10] Speakers don't just want to make statements, they want to transform the state of knowledge, the perceptions, the feelings of their interlocutors. In turn they want to understand not just what their interlocutors said, but why they said this and not that, and what effect they intended their words to have. And in turn they want to be listened to, taken seriously and respected. Indeed, every interaction is an exchange of symbolic power: the power to speak or to remain silent, to use one linguistic code or another, to use gestures or not, to make meaning online through complete sentences or through emoticons, to use Facebook or Twitter, as well as the power to hedge, dodge, brag, obfuscate or manipulate.[11] The teaching and learning of language in classrooms is itself a prime example of symbolic power in action; it requires minute by minute decisions by both teacher and students on how to best use that power to foster insights into the language games we all play. How can such an important and all-pervasive dimension of language use be engaged with in the language classroom?

2) One way is to find examples of the exercise of symbolic power in literary and non-literary texts and discuss them with the class. These texts can be taken from dialogues in novels or news releases, but also from the very dialogues or essays written by students, as they try to inform, convince, persuade and warn others through their choice of words. Such meta-reflection on the choices made might be integrated into the teaching of authentic texts earlier than one thinks (Kramsch and Zhang 2018, chapters 7 and 8). If language teachers become aware of the symbolic dimensions of language learning, they will remember that adolescents and young adults learning languages have two contradictory needs. On the one hand, they are looking to "belong" to a group and be accepted by the group as one of them (social and economic capital); on the other hand, they are eager to distinguish themselves from groupthink, and to acquire a profit of distinction such as knowing a language that others don't know

(symbolic capital). They seek *conviviality* and teachers encourage participation, interaction, collaboration, use of the Internet, blogs, Facebook, Instagram, communication online and so on – but they also seek *distinction*, that is, originality, not being like everyone else. How can teachers encourage the acquisition of this paradoxical symbolic capital? They can do it through independent reading, exercising critical thinking, questioning authority, seeing the larger picture, understanding historic reasons and effects. They can help students see links between historical events and how the way they have been referred to, talked about, interpreted in various periods says something about the values of the period. They can systematically teach historic complexity.

3) But most of all, in our times of great uncertainty, language teachers are called upon to reflect and draw on their own subjective experience (e.g., Kramsch 2009a; McNamara 2019). Whether they are native or non-native speakers of the target language, they cannot take their own culture for granted. They are answerable to their students, their questions, their misunderstandings, their unusual insights. In turn, they realize that their power to transform their students' way of speaking and thinking does not necessarily entail words – a smile, a gesture, a side comment, a picture, a metaphor, a shift in tone, or a codeswitch can go a long way in modelling a response.[12]

4) Ethics always intersects with politics. However, ethics in language teaching is understood differently in different parts of the world (see Introduction). While in China, teaching Western languages is intended to give Chinese youngsters the means to make westerners understand Chinese culture in their own languages, in France, language teachers have an epistemological responsibility to build and broaden their students' minds through the acquisition of a foreign linguistic system; in Europe, Australia and Latin America, language teachers are enjoined to develop their students' intercultural awareness; in Singapore and the United States, language teachers understand their ethical mandate as helping their students to develop their full potential as productive members of a global economy.[13]

C.6 "LANGUAGE – THE MEASURE OF OUR LIVES": A TRIBUTE TO TONI MORRISON

Ultimately, the best way to illustrate the relevance of symbolic power for language educators is to listen to Toni Morrison's Nobel lecture of

1993[14] – a parable that still grabs us today, reminding us of the symbolic power we hold every time we use language in concert with others.[15]

"Once upon a time there was an old woman. Blind but wise." Thus begins Morrison's story about an old woman, the daughter of slaves, Black, American, who lives alone in a small house outside of town. Her reputation among her people is unquestioned and she is held in high esteem. One day, the woman is visited by some young people from the city "who seem to be bent on disproving her clairvoyance and showing her up for the fraud they believe she is." One of them says: "Old woman, I hold in my hand a bird. Tell me whether it is living or dead." The woman is blind and cannot see her visitors, but she knows their motive. After a long silence, she says: "I don't know whether the bird you are holding is dead or alive, but what I do know is that it is in your hands. It is in your hands." In other words, she makes the young visitors responsible for the life of the bird they claim to hold; either it is dead and they found it that way or they have killed it; or it is alive and they can still kill it.

The narrator chooses to interpret this story as an allegory: the bird as language itself and the old woman as a writer. As a writer "she thinks of language partly as a system, partly as a living thing over which one has control, but mostly as agency – as an act with consequences." She goes on to describe how language can die when it is abused, "censored and censoring," when it "thwarts the intellect, stalls conscience, suppresses human potential." Language, she argues, dies not only when it is no longer spoken, but also when speakers use it with "carelessness, indifference, or absence of esteem." All language users are then "accountable for its demise." Here, the narrator in the voice of the old woman:

> The systematic looting of language can be recognized by the tendency of its users to forgo its nuanced, complex, mid-wifery properties, replacing them with menace and subjugation. Oppressive language does more than represent violence: it is violence; does more than represent the limits of knowledge: it limits knowledge. Whether it is obscuring state language or the faux language of mindless media; whether it is the proud but calcified language of the academy or the commodity-driven language of science; whether it is the malign language of law-without-ethics, or language designed for the estrangement of minorities, hiding its racist plunder in its literary cheek – it must be rejected, altered and exposed. It is the language that drinks blood, laps vulnerabilities, tucks its fascist boots under crinolines of respectability and patriotism as it moves relentlessly toward the bottom line and the bottomed-out mind. Sexist language,

racist language, theistic language – all are typical of the policing languages of mastery, and cannot, do not, permit new knowledge or encourage the mutual exchange of ideas.

The old woman's prosecution of language abuses goes on for some time: eloquent, detailed and brutally honest. In the end, she sums up her view of language and language use: "We die. That may be the meaning of life. But we *do* language. That may be the measure of our lives."

In her book *Excitable Speech* (1997), Judith Butler uses this portion of Morrison's lecture to express her views on what she calls "a politics of the performative": although we do not have sovereignty over the language we use, we do have agency and are thus responsible for our verbal actions. But our linguistic vulnerability is also the condition of possibility of our resistance to abuses of power. The old woman thus teaches her young visitors a lesson and exhorts them to assume their responsibilities.

But the story does not end there. In fact, it starts anew.

> 'Once upon a time . . . 'Visitors ask an old woman a question. Who are they, these children? What did they make of that encounter? What did they hear in those final words: 'The bird is in your hands'?

In the second half of the story, the tables are turned around. Now it is the children's turn to chide the old woman. The narrator continues: "Suppose nothing was in their hands. Suppose the visit was only a ruse, a trick to get to be spoken to, taken seriously as they have not been before... Perhaps their question meant: 'Could someone tell us what is life? What is death?'". The old woman remains silent and the children get annoyed. So they start filling the silence with language invented on the spot.

> 'Is there no speech,' they ask her, 'no words you can give us that help us break through your dossier of failures? Through the education you have just given us that is no education at all because we are paying close attention to what you have done as well as to what you have said? [. . .] We have no bird in our hands, living or dead. We have only you and our important question [. . .] Don't you remember being young, when language was magic without meaning? When what you could say, could not mean? [. . .] When questions and demands for answers burned so brightly you trembled with fury at not knowing? [. . .]
>
> Why didn't you reach out, touch us with your soft fingers, delay the sound bite, the lesson, until you knew who we were? [. . .] We are young. Unripe. We have heard all our short lives that we have to be responsible. What could that possibly mean in the catastrophe this world has become? [. . .] How dare you talk to us of duty when we stand

waist deep in the toxin of your past? Is there no song, no literature, no poem full of vitamins, no history connected to experience that you can pass along to help us start strong? [. . .]

You are an adult. The old one, the wise one. Think of our lives and tell us your particularized world [. . .] Tell us what the world has been to you in the dark places and in the light. Don't tell us what to believe, what to fear [. . .] Tell us what it is to be a woman so that we may know what it is to be a man. What moves at the margin. What it is to have no home in this place. To be set adrift from the one you knew. What it is to live at the edge of towns that cannot bear your company.'

At this point the children start telling the very story they would have wanted to hear from the old woman. What it meant to be a Black woman having to give birth in a field, picking cotton. To be a Black man in a wagonload of slaves, freezing in the night, knowing that the next stop would be their last. When the children finish speaking, the woman breaks into the silence:

"Finally," she says, "I trust you now. I trust you with the bird that is not in your hands because you have truly caught it. Look. How lovely it is, this thing we have done – together."

For Morrison, the key to keeping the language alive is dialogue and the willingness to engage in the give and take that dialogue entails. The double movement of this story captures the vigilance required if one wants to avoid the trap of sanctimoniousness and sentimentality, the normative language of morals and the sensationalized language of the media. By having the children and the old woman construct a common narrative with different voices, and by allowing them to speak through each other's voice, the narrator enacts the very symbolic power that alone can counteract adults' abuses of symbolic violence. For, while the old woman is respected as a moral authority, the exercise of her authority is only legitimate to the extent that the young people buy into it – and for that she has to get to know them, with an open mind and an open heart. In turn the youngsters have to trust her to be interested in their story, *they* have to reach out to *her* despite their difference in age, and despite their differences in life experience, authority and institutional power.[16]

While such a reaching out might seem to be the easiest of linguistic gestures, it can be the most difficult symbolic gesture, because of the symbolic power of history, peer pressure and simple human pride and shame. Thus, as we teach speakers of one language to learn the language of others, it might be good to remember the wise comment of Erving Goffman:

These two tendencies, that of the speaker to scale down his expressions and that of the listeners to scale up their interests, each in the light of the other's capacities and demands, form the bridge that people build to one another, allowing them to meet for a moment of talk in a communion of reciprocally sustained involvement. It is this spark, not the more obvious kinds of love, that lights up the world. (Goffman 1967:116)

Glossary

Agency vs. sovereignty: The distinction between having the power to act and having the absolute power over one's decisions on how to act. As language users, we have agency but not sovereignty.

Algorithm: Series of instructions in programming language that is programmed into the computer in order to have the system process information in a certain way.

Arbitrariness: For structuralists such as Saussure, linguistic signs are arbitrary, that is, conventional, independent of individual speakers' will. For post-structuralists, the use of signs is non-arbitrary, that is, motivated, linked to a speaker's choice of what to say and how to say it. When Bourdieu says that *symbolic power can operate only if it is seen as arbitrary, he means if it is seen as natural (that's how the world is) rather than as a socially and historically contingent construction.

Cognitive category: A concept from cognitive linguistics referring to a unit in the organization of experience in the mind and its reflection in the language we use. We make sense of our experience through the construction of idealized cognitive models or meaning categories (e.g., INVASION) steeped in our bodily experience and shaped through imaginative mechanisms (metaphor, metonymy and imagery). Also called prototype.

Complicity: Term used by Bourdieu to refer to the fact that symbolic power cannot be exercised without agreement by all parties involved to play the social game. Bakhtin considers this complicity as the dialogic condition of our social existence.

Condensation symbol: A term used by Sapir to refer to "a highly condensed form of substitutive behavior for direct expression, allowing for the ready release of emotional tension in conscious or unconscious form." Anything can become a condensation symbol (e.g., a middle finger, a verbal insult, a shoe sole, the drawing of a heart). Related to what Barthes calls "myth."

Dialogism: Bakhtin's theory of language, which does not start with the linguistic sign as in Saussure, but with the duality of self and other (self in other and other in self) in every word that we utter.

Discipline: Self-regulation of the individual under a panoptic system of surveillance.

Discourse: For a structuralist, discourse is language in use, a process whereby we create and relate, organize and realize meaning. For a post-structuralist, a discourse is a way of thinking, knowing and using language and other symbolic systems to make sense of our social reality. Discourses represent political interests and are thus constantly vying for status and power.

Documediality: Power of the Web to transform any postings into permanent documents that can be reproduced, shared and multiplied virally ad infinitum on mass and social media.

Facework: Goffman's term for the work that participants in a verbal exchange have to do to save their own and the other's face. Also called politeness by Brown and Levinson.

Fundamental codes of a culture: Terms used by Foucault (1970:xx) to characterize the dominant discourses of a society at a particular time in its history.

Hurled speech: Discourse between two parties, "the instigator" and "the pivot," who utter damaging statements against a third party, called "the target," within earshot of that third party. Hurled speech is performed in the third-person singular.

Hyperreality: A life on the screen that is no longer distinguishable from life in the real world.

Illocution vs. perlocution: According to John Austin, illocution is the social action performed by a social actor's utterance (the illocutionary force of the speech act); perlocution is the effect of that utterance, either by virtue of the words spoken (as in "I hereby declare you husband and wife") or as their consequence (as in "please close the door" and you go and close the door).

Imposition: The degree of imposition or risk (R) is one of the three contextual variables in politeness theory, the others being social distance (D) and social power (P). Like the other two, the degree of imposition is a matter of perception by the participants in the verbal exchange.

Indexicality: A term used by linguistic anthropologists to refer not just to conventional semantic associations of the Saussurean kind, but to whole ways of talking that index or point to the social stratifications found in society and the social, cultural and political views that speakers and writers hold.

Intercultural mediation: Intercultural process of negotiation between cultures at various levels: the techno-economic level of institutions, the political-ideological level of individual entrepreneurship, the ethical level of human responsibility.

Interpellation: The act of hailing someone ("Hey, you...!"). Term used by Althusser to characterize the power of language to constitute us as social subjects, subjected to the order of discourse of our time and place.

Legitimacy: A dimension of language use that recognizes a language user's right to speak and be listened to based on that person's social, cultural, professional, demographic, political or religious/moral authority. The quest for legitimacy is at the root of many symbolic power struggles.

Linguistic survival: Term used by Butler to refer to the survival of language from misuses and abuses, and the survival of language users themselves from the effects of abusive language.

Metacultural model: A concept from anthropological linguistics referring to recognizable types of persons or objects in recognizable situations with which speakers frame their view of reality. Also called stereotype (but not necessarily with negative connotations).

Narrative: The transformation of lived experience into a discourse structured according to the rules of the narrative genre and according to a narrative mode of thought. The structure of a well-wrought story differs radically from that of a well-formed logical argument. Culture wars are fought over different national narratives.

Normativity: A characteristic of any educational project that has to socialize students into abiding by norms of language and language use that are not only acceptable to the educational institution itself, but are perceived as legitimate by other language users in the real world outside academia. Normativity is closely related to morality.

Oracle speech: Speech uttered not only as spokesperson for a group, but as the group itself. See the case of politicians who speak as delegates of the people ("they"), then switch to speaking as the very will of the people ("we").

Order of discourse: For Foucault, our ways of thinking, valuing, speaking and understanding events shape and are shaped by discourses (e.g., academic, political, ideological discourses) that are consistent with one another and are characteristic of the time and place in which we live. Today, several orders of discourse coexist in our lives at any given time. Also called Discourse (with a big D) by James Gee.

Order of indexicality: Stratified patterns of social meanings to which people orient (which they index) when communicating. The way that people talk indexes who they are and how they position themselves in society.

Panoptic: The all-seeing gaze of one over many.

Participation framework: Term used by Goffman to denote the different roles that participants may assume in an interaction (animator, author, principal).

Performance vs. performativity: The acting out of a given social role vs. the construction of the social role through words.

Perspectivism: A post-modern ethical stance that believes that norms of behavior are socially and historically contingent. It is opposed to moral relativism, according to which anything goes as norms are "up for grabs." Perspectivists like Ricoeur and Bakhtin differentiate between a modernist morals of conviction, based on institutional laws and norms, and a post-modernist ethics of responsibility, based on individual answerability.

Politics: By contrast with *la politique* or party politics, *le politique* is the exercise of symbolic power in the micro-world of everyday life.

Post-structuralism vs. post-modernism: Two theories that go beyond studying the structures of the social world and seek to reveal the historicity and subjectivity of social phenomena. Post-modernism as represented by Foucault, Butler, Cameron and Weedon insists in addition on the performative, that is, constructivist nature of discourse in the social world.

Representation: Symbolic processing of experience as 1) embodied mental perceptual schema of knowledge, or, 2) staged performance of speech acts, or, 3) delegation, that is, speaking for someone else as in vicarious speech, hurled speech or speech with oracle effect.

Ritual: Set of traditional actions, gestures and words performed in specific situations, that express and confirm the solidarity of the group and its symbolic power.

Securitization: Management of large flows of population for safety and surveillance purposes.

Security: 1) Safety (as in "national security") 2) police 3) evidence of investment, stocks and bonds.

Shibboleth: Word or object used to test your legitimacy and exert control over you as a member of a social group.

Signification: Relation of signifier and signified in Saussure's definition of the linguistic sign.

Simulacrum: Copy of the real thing for which the original no longer exists.

Social magic. The power of institutions to create differences where there were none, for example, with two applicants of equal excellence, admitting one and rejecting the other.

Speech act: Social action performed by an utterance (e.g., when I say: "Drop this case!" I am issuing an order).

Surveillance: The permanent observation and monitoring of individuals as a way of managing multiplicity. Applies to the external visible presence of guards, supervisors and administrative apparatuses that monitor our daily lives, as well as to the invisible algorithms that structure our Google searches and our Facebook likes.

Surveillant media: Media like Google or Facebook that exercise surveillance of its users, that is, tracks their search patterns and imposes on users its own way of inferencing, organizing, classifying and storing knowledge.

Symbolic: Non-material process of making meaning through the use of signs that represent (icons), point to (indices) or stand for (symbols) social reality. Symbolic relations are relations constructed by humans and addressed to other humans in order to mobilize their attention, beliefs, opinions and so on.

Symbolic capital: A person's source of symbolic power based on the social, cultural or economic capital that is particularly valued in that person's social group or society.

Symbolic power: The power to constitute reality through language and other symbolic systems, to make people see and believe in this reality, and to confirm or transform their vision of the world and thereby their action on the world.

Symbolic self: A person's social image, source of dignity and self-respect.

Symbolic system: A body of signs and symbols that combine together in a rule-governed, systematic way to make meaning. Language, music and the visual arts are symbolic systems.

Symbolic violence: The social pressure exerted on others that obligates them to conform to the norms of expectation in a given society. This social pressure can "do violence" to a person's autonomy and sometimes even do harm to a person's symbolic self.

Timescale: Concept used in the social sciences to characterize different ways of looking at time: as an event (e.g., the French revolution), as a conjuncture (the time of a particular political regime like the monarchy) or as a structure (slow development of the structure of government).

Vicarious speech: Speech uttered for someone else, such as a mother speaking for her infant.

Endnotes

Introduction

1 The American Association for Applied Linguistics was founded in 1978 in San Francisco by Wilga Rivers, Professor of French at Harvard University.

2 The cover blurb of Bolinger's 1980 book showed language to be" the vital agent with which we build our worlds: truth, class and dialect, manipulation through advertising and propaganda, sexual and other discrimination, official obfuscation and the maintenance of power." It was addressed to language studies scholars and language educators who valued its many insights into the nature of language and language use. It was believed that if teachers were given a critical insight into the workings of language, they would better know how to immunize their students against its manipulating and obfuscating effects. It has not worked that way. Global media and the Internet have democratized language use but they have brought with them their own manipulation and obfuscation. This book is an attempt to document these complexities to help language educators and their students understand the educational challenges and opportunities presented by looking at language as symbolic power.

3 See, for example, Osnos, E. 2018. Can Mark Zuckerberg fix Facebook before it breaks democracy? *New Yorker*. Sept. 17, p.39.

4 See Chapter 1. See also Deacon 1997, chapters 2 and 3. For the notion of "interpellation," see Althusser 1971) and the discussion in Butler 1997, p.2.

5 Here is the French original: "Le pouvoir symbolique comme pouvoir de constituer le donné par l'énonciation, de faire voir et de faire croire, de confirmer ou de transformer la vision du monde et, par là, l'action sur le monde, donc le monde, pouvoir quasi magique qui permet d'obtenir l'équivalent de ce qui est obtenu par la force (physique ou économique) grâce à l'effet spécifique de mobilisation, ne s'exerce que s'il est reconnu, c'est-à-dire méconnu comme arbitraire. Ce qui fait le pouvoir des mots et des mots d'ordre, pouvoir de maintenir l'ordre ou de le subvertir, c'est la croyance dans la légitimité des mots et de celui qui les prononce, croyance qu'il n'appartient pas aux mots de produire" (p.410) (Bourdieu, Pierre. 1977. Sur le pouvoir symbolique. In: *Annales. Economies, sociétés, civilisations.* 32e année. N.3, 1977, pp.405–411)

6 See the study on the social symbolic nature of "compliance" reported on in Sommers and Bohns. 2019. Mind if I search your phone?, *New York Times*. May 1, A23. Bohns shows how hard it is to refuse consent when asked by a police officer or a researcher to hand over your phone for a minute. "Telling people about their rights addresses information deficits, but the real reason people comply is social, not informational. The social imperatives to comply with a police officer's request persist even when people are properly informed of their rights or given a consent form to sign – or just asked politely." (see also Pavlenko 2008)

7 Loss of symbolic power is most on display when someone's reputation or social face is at stake. See, for example, Arthur Miller's *The Crucible* (1953/1971), a play written at the height of the McCarthy era.

8 Legitimacy is not a psychological notion such as "being liked," or "being popular" – it has to do with your social persona, your self-esteem, reputation, social worth. You can be a legitimate leader and yet be hated; you can be liked and yet not be seen as a legitimate leader. Legitimacy is an institutional category that refers to an entity that is larger than the individual, whether it be a political, a demographic, a professional, a religious/moral, a social or a cultural entity. The crucial importance of *legitimacy* over correctness, appropriateness and other forms of communicative competences in language use was vividly expressed a few years ago when a visiting scholar from Romania came to visit one of our German classes at University of California Berkeley. She was surprised that the instructor did not immediately correct every grammatical error the students made but let them talk, fluently but incorrectly. She added sadly: "This must be because they are Americans. If I appear at the German border with my black hair and dark eyes, my only legitimacy as a speaker of German is my knowledge of German grammar!"

9 For comprehensive reviews of the history of the field, see, for example, Brumfit 1997, Davies and Elder 2004, and Li Wei 2014.

10 One day, a German undergraduate student at a seminar I was teaching in Germany raised his hand and took me to task for claiming that the German language belonged to whoever was motivated enough to learn the language (Kramsch 1996). "I totally disagree!" he exclaimed. I smiled. He was putting into question my right, as a non-native speaker of German, to "own" the German language, thus countering Henry Widdowson's claim that non-native speakers of English had a right to "own" the English language (Widdowson 1994). I found myself put back in my place by a member of the German native speech community, the same way as Bichsel's old man was rejected by his compatriots for inventing a new language (see Chapter 1). "Oh yeah?" I said. "So who does the German language belong to?" – "It belongs first to the Ministry of Foreign Affairs that finances the Goethe Institute; secondly to the Goethe Institute that decides which German grammar and vocabulary to teach around the world; and third to the Klett publishing house that publishes German language textbooks." Faced with this impeccable logic, I could only laugh and congratulate the student. He had perfectly internalized the hierarchy of symbolic power that controls the teaching and learning of German as a Foreign Language around the world and that makes any German teacher complicit in upholding this hierarchy.

11 This political responsibility is viewed differently in various educational cultures. One of the major unexpected findings of the Kramsch and Zhang survey (2018) of foreign language teachers at the University of California was their almost unanimous view that it is not their role to "change the worldview of their students." By contrast, French language educators consider themselves to play a transformative role vis-à-vis their students. For example, in the edited volume *Ethique et politique en didactique des langues* (Beacco 2013) Francine Cicurel writes: "Let us not forget that the pedagogic act includes a will to transform the other or at least to act upon his/her knowledge" (Cicurel 2013:184 my translation). This transformative goal is, according to Cicurel, forward-looking in time and is bound to the prospective development of the learner in the future. For a transformative view of language education, see also Crozet and Diaz (2020).

Chapter 1

1 See Hirschfeld Davis, J. and Baker, P. 2019. How the border wall is boxing Trump in. *New York Times*. Jan. 5.

2 See Baker, Kevin 2019. Speaker Pelosi returns. *New York Times*. Jan.5.
3 See Bruni, Frank. 2019. The wall is a symbol of Donald Trump's neediness. *New York Times*. Jan.9, A23.
4 See Tackett, Michael and Edmondson, Catie. 2019. Trump offers steel wall; Democrats are unmoved. *New York Times*. Jan.7, A15. See also Gunderman, Dan. 2016. President-elect Donald Trump's "big, beautiful wall" may end up just being a modest, double-layered fence. *New York Daily News*, Nov.10.
5 The fight over the wall had become a fight about symbolism, not policy. As one critic puts it, "Liberals object less to aggressive border security than to the wall's xenophobic imagery, while the administration openly revels in its political incorrectness" (Abrahamian 2019).
6 See Cohen, Roger. 2018. A contagious and insidious American presidency. *New York Times*. 6 Oct. A18) and Tackett, Michael. 2019. It's a wall, but it's not that wall. *New York Times*. 22 Feb. A16).
7 For examples of the difficulties journalists have in naming the people who seek to cross national borders, for example, immigrants, migrants, asylum seekers, refugees, foreigners, aliens, see Dickerson, Caitlin. 2019. The tricky language of border-speak. *New York Times*. 20 May, A2.
8 See the famous passage in Benjamin Whorf: "*We dissect nature along lines laid down by our native languages.* The categories and types that we isolate from the world of phenomena we do not find there because they stare every observer in the face; on the contrary, the world is presented in a kaleidoscopic flux of impressions which has to be organized by our minds – and this means largely by the linguistic systems of our minds. *We cut nature up, organize it into concepts, and ascribe significances as we do, largely because we are parties to an agreement to organize it in this way – an agreement that holds throughout our speech community and is codified in the patterns of our language.* The agreement is, of course, an implicit and unstated one but its terms are absolutely obligatory. We cannot talk at all except by subscribing to the organization and classification of data which the agreement decrees. Users of markedly different grammars are pointed by their grammars toward different types of observations and different evaluations of events." (Whorf 1991: 213–214, my emphasis)
9 An idealized cognitive model becomes a frame through which we interpret the world. A wall thus represents an exclusionary frame that keeps people from "invading" our country. When that frame leads people to action, it turns into a metapragmatic model for acting in the world. For language learners, acquiring the power to signify means not just learning the referential signification of words and their value as part of a system of linguistic structures, but internalizing their cognitive categories, together with their frames and how these frames fit into larger orders of indexicality (Silverstein 2003).
10 Language learners feel most secure learning the type-level forms of the foreign language, and they accept the arbitrariness of those forms as one of the challenges of learning a new language. But learning only the symbolic types without their iconic and indexical relations to other tokens can only get them that far in communicating with other speakers of the language. For example, for linguists and American learners of German, the word "*das Volk*" may mean the same as the word "*the people*," that is, the members of a national community; and yet it might have a different value for Germans and Americans because they might interpret this word differently depending on their national history. An American might associate "people" with the Bill of Rights ("We, the people") or with a term used by politicians ("the American people"), or with the more informal meaning of "a group". A German might associate "*das Volk*" with its use in the Third Reich or

the German Democratic Republic. While Americans and Germans might understand each other's use of the type-level form "people," they might have quite a different interpretation of a token utterance like "the American people," especially if translated into current German as "das amerikanische Volk" – a linguistically accurate, but culturally inappropriate translation (except for the 1787 translation of the U.S. Constitution into German where "the people" was translated as "das Volk"). A more appropriate term today would be "die U.S. amerikanischen Bürger" [U.S.-American citizens].

11 The recent case of the Thai singer wearing a swastika T-shirt to a performance and the outcry this produced on social media is a case in point (see Ives, Mike. 2019. Did a Thai singer's swastika represent hate or ignorance? *New York Times* Jan.29, A12). Globalized media trade in cultural symbols that are not necessarily familiar to everyone. While Nazi imagery has been widely shunned in the West since World War II, it is not necessarily perceived as offensive in other parts of the world.

12 See Peters, Jeremy, Grynbaum, Michael, Collins, Keith, Harris, Rich and Taylor, Rumsey. 2019. How El Paso killer echoed the incendiary words of conservative media stars. *New York Times*, 11 Aug.

13 Associated Press April 10, 2007. Obama stops wearing American flag pin.

14 See *Paris Match* no. 326 of June 25–July 2, 1955. This photograph on the front page of the famous French weekly seemed to promote French imperial power at a time when the debate was raging in France about the viability of the French colonial empire after World War II. Indeed, Burkina Faso became independent five years later in 1960 as Upper Volta.

15 The challenge posed by globalization and the danger it poses to international understanding lies precisely in the mixture of genres exercised by such populist presidents intent on dismantling not only the traditional institutions of democracy but the discourse genres that make democratic discourse possible. By mixing the business hyperbole, the poetic flourish, the political report, the temper tantrum, the theatrical bombast of Reality TV, and the inflammatory tweet, Donald Trump disorients his listeners and keeps everyone guessing (see Chapter 6).

16 For a relevant discussion of the social construction of "mugs, rocks and tables," see Pennycook (2018:111 ff) and Hacking (1999a), to which we return in Chapters 7 and 9.

Chapter 2

1 The use of "her" for the frog is deliberate. Note that in French "frog" (*la grenouille*) is feminine, "ox" (*le boeuf*) masculine; "fox" and "crow" are masculine as are "wolf" and "lamb" – thus making it easier for readers to attribute gender related properties to these animals in the first fable, and, when gender is not an issue as in the other two fables, to focus instead on age and political power differential. Translators have been careful to retain the human personal pronoun to acknowledge the anthropomorphic nature of these animals.

2 Kramsch (forthcoming) offers a political analysis of La Fontaine's "The fox and the crow." For a discussion of representation in some of La Fontaine's fables and Perrault's folktales, see Marin (2002).

3 Today we would add that he has to follow the opinion of Fox News, his "friends" on Facebook, and perhaps his electoral "base," who all urge him to take action against those who dare put into question his legitimacy.

4 Marin relies here on the argumentation of Blaise Pascal in his major treaty *Pensées* (1976), where he writes:

Justice, force. It is just that what is just be obeyed, it is necessary that the most forceful [i.e. powerful] be obeyed. Justice without force is powerless: force without justice is tyrannical. Justice without force will be contradicted, because there will always be bad people; force without justice will be accused [of injustice]. Justice and force thus must be put together; and in order to achieve this what is just must be made forceful or what is forceful must be made just. [However], justice is subject to dispute, whereas force is very recognizable and indisputable. Thus it has not been possible to give force to justice, because force has contradicted justice and has said that it was unjust and that force was itself just. Thus, faced with the impossibility of making what is just forceful, one has made what is forceful just. (Pascal 1976:137 my translation)

The interesting logic here is that symbolic power has the power not only to impose its will, but to redefine the word "justice" to fit its (unjust) interests. Which is what we have in the logic of the wolf, who not only cloaks his actions under the name of (retributive) justice but redefines the very concept of "justice" at every step of his argument.

5 Today's readers might think that Marin's argument says nothing more than that dictators have always had a need to "rationalize" their acts of power (like the wolf). Indeed, throughout history, dictators have either manufactured crises or taken advantage of and magnified existing crises to show that their actions are right, that is, justified. But this is not quite what Marin is arguing. Those in power, says Marin, have not only to show that their actions are *justified*, that is, logical and rational, and therefore necessary, but that they are *morally just* and that their power is therefore *legitimate*. Some might argue that it is difficult to see dictators as "moral." And yet even Kings like Louis XIV need the recognition by their people of their legitimacy, that is, a shared vision of what is morally good. When the wolf says: "I must take revenge," he is saying that he must save his honor, his reputation, his good name against the temerity, the audacity of the lamb and his shepherds to challenge his legitimate authority and the authority of the system he represents. And the readers of the fable must agree with him. Likewise, when George W. Bush said that Saddam Hussein tried to kill his father and therefore he had to take revenge on him, or that Saddam had more weapons of mass destruction than the United States (the audacity!) and therefore had to be crushed, he was seeking to assert his symbolic and moral power, not just his military power, in retaliation for the humiliation inflicted upon him and the United States by Saddam Hussein. This discussion about the relationship of justice and power is the topic of the dialogue between Socrates and Thrasymachus in Book I of Plato's *Republic*.

6 Some readers might ask: "How should the lamb have acted instead?" One can imagine him threatening the wolf with the nearby presence of his shepherd and dogs; one can envisage the lambs even banding together against the wolves; or, as the play *Gutmenschen* (dir. Yael Ronen, Volkstheater Wien) humoristically suggests, trying to make wolves into vegetarians. But all these suggestions remain at the level of the plot. At the level of the story and why La Fontaine tells it that way, one needs to understand that the rational logic of the lamb serves to transform the wolf's brute force into legitimate power. Thus the fable is not about a lamb being devoured by a wolf but about monarchical power that cannot exist without the complicity of its subjects.

7 A cartoon by Paul Noth in the *New Yorker* of August 18, 2016 captures pretty well the relevance of this story to the populist governments of the present day. It features a herd of sheep grazing on a hill, on top of which stands a large billboard featuring a head-and-shoulders photograph of a wolf dressed in suit and tie, next to a caption in big letters: "I am going to eat you." All the sheep are busy grazing

with their backs turned. But two sheep are turned towards the billboard and one says to the other: "He tells it like it is."

8 An interesting social psychological analysis of shame can help to understand why the wolf needs to shame the lamb into feeling guilty and to take revenge to save his honor, that has been "shamed" by the negative image promoted by shepherds against wolves. Once disseminated in public, "his image of himself is put beyond his own power of forgetting and remembering. One cannot prevent from knowing unless one possesses the power of killing. A powerful man, wishing to save his own image of himself, may on that ground alone cause another man to die" (Riezler 1943:458).

9 Opening lines of the YouTube video *"What kind of Asian are you?"* (Zhu Hua and Li Wei 2016).

10 The French term *"représentation"* is used in French applied linguistics to denote not only individual beliefs and mindsets but also preconstructed social and cultural knowledges that play themselves out in the behaviors and attitudes of social actors (see, e.g., Moscovici 2003; Jodelet 2003). Bourdieu characterizes the first as "mental representations," the second as "objectified representations" (Bourdieu 1991:220). These two kinds of representation have been conflated into one by cognitive scientists, who show that all mental representations are socially constructed. I follow their lead here. I further include the French term *"représentation"* as show or performance, especially as in "performance on a stage" (play, musical, or any other entertainment show), to which I add the English concept of "performativity" (Butler 1997; Pennycook 2007, chapter 4). Finally, I include representation as delegation, as in "citizens' representation in parliament," that is, a delegate who speaks for the citizens. These three meanings of the term have been researched from various disciplinary angles. Representation as social embodied cognitive schema has been investigated by American psychologists, psycholinguists and cognitive scientists like Dan Slobin, George Lakoff and Mark Johnson. Representation as staged performance has been studied by philosophers and cultural critics like Michel Foucault and Judith Butler. Representation as social and political ritual has been researched by sociologists, sociolinguists and linguistic anthropologists like Pierre Bourdieu, Erving Goffman and William Hanks.

11 Schema theory, originally developed in work on artificial intelligence (Kintsch 1974; Minsky 1977; Rumelhardt 1980) was a forerunner for research in cognitive science with its discourse frames and idealized cognitive models, and in linguistic anthropology with its metapragmatic models, both discussed in Chapter 1.

12 See the work of Gumperz and Levinson (1996), Slobin (1996) and many others.

13 As we shall see in Chapter 7, the addiction to symbolic representation in a spectacle society includes: peer pressure and the power of mimesis, identification and desire, as well as the quest for symbolic distinction. This last aspect points to one of the paradoxes of symbolic power. While many users of social media are addicted to acceptance and validation by the group, they also seek to stand out, that is, to be distinct from or even better than the other members of the group.

14 Note that the use of Twitter as hurled speech to someone in the presence of 58 million other Twitter users can make the addressee lose face in front of his own people (e.g., Trump's tweet to his supporters expressing hope or expectation that President Xi from China do this or that was perceived as an insult in China). See Chapter 8.

15 In Chapter 5 I show how the use of neoliberal keywords like *sustainability, empowerment* and so on in statements of mission or applications for funding, are used to give additional legitimacy to a candidate's discourse because it is

seen as being delegated by a higher institutional authority such as The Market, The Corporation or The Economy. See Schmenk et al. (2019) on sloganization.

16 In particular, there is a danger that researchers impose their representations on the collective belief of applied linguistic researchers and teachers, and that, as Bourdieu says,

> they create, by their mobilizing capacity, the conditions of their own realization. But they do no better, when, giving up the distance of the observer, they adopt the representation of the agents and participants, in a discourse which, by failing to provide itself with the means of describing the game in which this representation is produced and the belief which underlies it, is nothing more than one contribution among many to the production of the belief whose foundations and social effects should be described (Bourdieu 1991:226).

Chapter 3

1 The book has been translated into over forty languages including a variety of German dialects and is still widely read around the world. It has spawned mock versions at various points in history, such as: Spence, P. and R. *Der Struwwel Hitler. A Nazi storybook by Dr Schrecklichkeit*, published in 1941 by the British national tabloid newspaper *The Daily Sketch* during World War II; Bernstein, F.W. 1994. *Der Struwwelpeter – umgetopft.* Berlin: Rütten & Loening; and F. K. Waechter's *Der Anti-Struwwelpeter oder listige Geschichten und knallige Bilder*, published in 1970 in the anti-authoritarian spirit of the sixties. There is a popular Struwwelpeter Museum in Frankfurt.

2 See Lyman, R. 2006. In many public schools, the paddle is no relic. *New York Times.* Sept.30, A1; and Caron, C. 2018. Spanking is ineffective and harmful to children, pediatricians' group says. *New York Times.* Nov.5.

3 Variation on the famous saying in the French comic Astérix: *"Ils sont fous ces Romains!"* [They are crazy, those Romans!]

4 Gayatri Chakravorty Spivak argues that the narrative genre is ideally suited to transmit moral values through the "uncoercive re-arrangement of desires" (Spivak 2004:526).

5 See Jost Hermand (1958).

6 Such non-conformist behaviors can have a washback effect on those in power. For example, in the Fidgety Phil story, the picture of the father stomping the floor with his foot leads the reader to interpret his anger as a tantrum rage that in fact indexes weakness. The more the father rages against his son, the greater the likelihood that the son not only will seek to resist his father's symbolic violence, but might later reproduce with his own children the cycle of violence he was raised in. Many of the French children's stories of that time feature the tactics used by both "good" and "bad" children to avoid corporal punishment or to take revenge on their abusive parents. See, for example, the novels by La Comtesse de Ségur *Les petites filles modèles* (1857), *Un bon petit diable* (1865) or *Les bons enfants* (1893) in the collection *La Bibliothèque Rose*, started in 1856 by the Paris publisher Hachette for children between the ages of 6–12 years old.

7 An informal survey among the some 100 students of the *Language and Power* class given at University of California Berkeley regarding their experience with corporal punishment revealed that 1) quite a few students had received corporal punishment from their parents when they were young (with their mother's ladle or their father's leather belt) but these were mostly foreign-born students, 2) many felt they would prefer to receive a corporal punishment and be done with it than be subjected to a guilt trip and reeducation practices.

8 One prime example of this is Pierre Bourdieu himself, who, from a modest family background in the Béarn, was raised and schooled in the French national educational system that enabled him to move up the echelons of French academia and attain the highest distinctions in the French academic world (see Bourdieu 1990, 1998, 2008). He achieved all this, and revolutionized the field of sociology, even though he systematically criticized the very educational institution that had enabled him to do so. He gained his world-wide scholarly fame through the multiple followers he gained abroad, in particular in Germany and the United States, but he remained a controversial figure in the French intellectual landscape.

9 However, see Francine Cicurel's attempt to bring back the singularity of the teacher's person behind the academic persona in Cicurel (2013).

10 In this "America First" narrative, Trump has used shaming and punishing strategies on his political opponents that are reminiscent of *Struwwelpeter*, e.g., pillorying, name-calling from Crooked Hillary (Clinton) to Sloppy Steve (Bannon) and Little Rocket Man (Kim Jong-Un); hurled speech in tweets; and other humiliating and stigmatizing practices (see Editorial. 2018. Mr. Trump's foes by any other name, *New York Times*. Nov.20, A22)

Chapter 4

1 See Schmidt. M. 2017. Comey memo says Trump asked him to end Flynn investigation. *New York Times*. May 6.

2 A year later, Michael Cohen, Trump's lawyer, testified before Congress to the same effect, saying that the president never explicitly instructed him to lie. Rather, Cohen said he understood the president's directions without specific words, saying Mr. Trump spoke in "code" and he understood "the code" from having worked for him for ten years. (Tackett, M. 2019. Five Takeaways from the hearing. *New York Times*. Feb.28, A15)

3 Kamala Harris, a 2020 Democratic presidential contender, started her five minutes with Republican Attorney General William Barr with one question: "Has the president or anyone at the White House ever asked or suggested that you open an investigation of anyone? Yes or no?" Barr stumbled for a second, asked Harris to repeat the question, and then hesitated some more and finally said he was "trying to grapple with the word 'suggest.'" So Harris provided a few synonyms ("asked"? "hinted"?) – and Barr ended up saying that he didn't know.

4 One could say that Donald Trump himself cultivates an ambiguous subject position here: is he speaking to Comey as the legitimate president of the United States, or as a godfather-like mafia boss? (see Graff, G. 2019. Treat Trump like a mafia boss *New York Times*. Mar.5, A27.) Considering that the day before he had explicitly asked Comey for his loyalty ("I need loyalty"), Comey could have thought that by not interpreting the president's "I hope" as an indirect order he would be perceived as being disloyal. But it must be noted that in the United States, the Justice Department is not under the jurisdiction of the Executive, thus the Director of the FBI does not take any orders from the president, even though he can be fired by the president.

5 The question is still open as to whether Trump committed "obstruction of justice" – an impeachable offense – in this incident or not. What satisfies the *linguistic/pragmatic* felicity conditions of the speech act "giving an order" are not the same as the *legal* truth conditions necessary to charge Trump with the crime of obstruction of justice, nor are they the same as the *political* conditions necessary to make this speech act an impeachable offense of disrespect for the Constitution. This came to light dramatically in April 2019 upon the release of the Mueller report and the debates that ensued between Republicans and Democrats in the House of Representatives (see Section 8.5, Post-truth and disinformation in the information age).

6 As Searle points out, a representing intention, by lowering the degree of imposition on the hearer, lowers at the same time the degree of responsibility of the speaker for the perlocutionary effect of his/her utterance. But, whatever the President had intended to say by these words, his subsequent firing of James Comey showed retroactively that he had indeed meant it to be a directive. For a deeper analysis of the perlocutionary effect of Trump's utterance, see Kramsch 2020.

7 See the testimony of Christine Blasey Ford at Brett Kavanaugh's nomination hearing for the Supreme Court on September 27, 2018. When asked what most traumatic memory she had of the evening when she was abused by Kavanaugh and his friends, she answered it was their laughter as they were trying to rape her. The memory of the humiliation caused by that laughter was enough to make her cry.

8 The possibility of challenging those beliefs, that is, of putting into question their "institutional" character, is not equally shared among scholars. Pierre Bourdieu and Judith Butler had an historic debate about this when Bourdieu visited UC Berkeley shortly before his death in 2001. Bourdieu had a much more pessimistic view than Butler about the possibility of institutional change.

9 See the breakdown of the legitimacy of public institutions under Trump (Brooks, D. 2018. A complete national disgrace. *New York Times*. Oct.5, A27) and of the political independence of the judiciary (Cohen, R. 2018. A contagious and insidious American presidency. *New York Times*. Oct.6, A18.)

10 I called this kind of competence "symbolic competence" to supplement the notion of communicative competence with a dimension of symbolic power that I felt it had lost in language education over the several decades of communicative language teaching (see Kramsch 2006, 2009a, 2011; Kramsch and Whiteside 2008). For the use of speech acts in literary discourse, see Felman 1983.

11 SPEAKING stands for: Setting-Participants-Ends-Acts-Key-Instrumentalities-Norms of interaction and interpretation-Genre (see Hymes 1986:59–65).

Chapter 5

1 These anecdotes were collected by Tomajin Morikawa, a student in the *Language and Power* class I taught at University of California Berkeley in spring 2018, who wrote his term paper on "'I love you' as symbolic violence." He found the quotes online at www.buzzfeed.com/skarlan/people-share-the-story-of-their-first-i-love-you. I reproduce excerpts from his paper here with his permission.

2 Tomajin Morikawa comments:

> When the girl explained that she wanted to show that she "cared about him and that he was a big part of my life," perhaps the receiver interpreted the illocutionary force as a declarative rather than an expressive. Yet, there is an alternative possibility: perhaps the receiver exploited the girl's explanation to render the utterance as a declarative rather than an expressive to escape the girl's desired perlocutionary effect of establishing a romantic relationship. This example is crucial in understanding one way to resist symbolic violence.

3 In this case, the young man severed the link between the woman's intended illocutionary intention (i.e., to elicit a reciprocal "I love you too") and the perlocutionary effect of the man actually saying the words. The woman doesn't begrudge him his avoidance tactic but she acknowledges having been hurt by it.

4 In fact, Bourdieu's theory of symbolic power, despite its commercial metaphors (e.g., capital, marketplace) is not a theory of economic class structure (or socio-economic status) as much as it is a theory of symbolic value. In France, some aristocratic families with high symbolic status because of their lineage may have

very little economic capital and, vice-versa, some very wealthy families may never gain the recognition of the aristocratic elite because of their low symbolic capital.

5 As we saw in the last chapter, an institution in Bourdieu's sense is not necessarily a particular organization, but "any relatively durable set of social relations which *endows* individuals with power, status and resources of various kinds" (Thompson 1991:8). Thus endowed, individuals reproduce the power of these social relations in their very actions *as individuals*. It then becomes difficult to tell whether these individuals are speaking as "authors" in Goffman's sense (see Chapter 4) or as "principals."

6 Learning a foreign language means learning when to use such euphemisms. Early in my career as a French academic in the United States, I used to recommend that "the teacher should do this" and "the teacher should not do that," when in a research paper I had written in English one of the reviewers corrected my English, suggesting I write: "the teacher may choose to do this," "the teacher may want to avoid doing that" – euphemisms more in line with the English publication context.

7 I experienced such a dilemma when I was in a foreign country at a conference and a male colleague handed me a chocolate truffle at breakfast one morning. I thanked him and placed the truffle in front of my plate when another female colleague came in and sat down next to me. Not wanting to be indebted to the male colleague nor wanting to exclude my female colleague, I cut the truffle in half and offered her the other half. The reproaches my male colleague made to me after breakfast for having shared his gift with a third party and the lecture he gave me on the proper cultural etiquette showed me retrospectively that my intuition had been correct and that his gift might have had a deeper meaning than just a piece of chocolate.

8 Not all cultures find it appropriate for parents to say "I love you" to their children. Some Asian parents would find it superfluous and face-threatening to do so; the sacrifices they make to ensure a better life for their children is how Asian parents say "I love you" without having to say it. Similarly they expect their children to express love through gratitude, for example by obeying their parents and following their wishes on how they should live their lives (see Viet Thanh Nguyen. 2019. The three words we can't say. *New York Times*. Jan.13, SR p.6).

9 In California, such friendly compliments by strangers are not unusual. I was accosted the other day on the street by two women who told me with a smile that they liked my hair. Although their remark was most friendly, my French habitus felt slightly aggressed. My first impulse was to downplay the compliment by treating it as a statement of fact. But then I remembered that I am in the United States, where compliments are perceived as gifts, so I returned the gift with a smile and a simple "Thank you."

10 The ambiguous nature of gifts and of the time-lag between gift and counter-gift is perfectly illustrated in current politics by the case of politicians possibly being the target of what the Russians call "kompromat," that is, compromising gifts or favors that seem like disinterested generosity at the time, but are based on the expectation of a counter-gift at some point in the future. Here an account of how Russian gifts, having bailed Donald Trump out of bankruptcy, are now obligating him to deliver counter-gifts of various kinds and are causing him political trouble for having possibly "colluded with a foreign power" during his 2016 campaign for the presidency.

> [The Russian oligarch] Rybolovlev's purchase of [Trump's] Florida mansion put about $74 million in Trump's pocket. Trump suddenly had oxygen.

What had Trump done to earn such a favor? It may seem surprising, but the answer could be nothing. At least not then. Trump was being enrolled in the Russian system of *kompromat*, of which Putin is a master. Grant a favor, ask for nothing. Both parties understand that someday something may be expected in return (Speier, J. 2018. Strange real estate deal raises specter of Putin buying Trump. *San Francisco Chronicle*. Dec.14).

The gift by Trump to Putin of a $50 million penthouse in his planned Moscow Trump Tower would be a counter-gift in kind, but the pledge by the president never to say a bad word about Vladimir Putin on the world stage would certainly be another more symbolic one. These examples show how the gift system described by Mary Douglas, which forms much of the basis for networking in the business world, can collide with a political rule-of-law system based not on personal favors but on laws that are not up to negotiation once they have been codified in a country's democratic constitution.

11 The story of many college graduates these days is not the happy story it was meant to be but is often a grueling confrontation with economic disparity and social privilege. "It is a dispiriting confirmation of the bragging rights and brand obsession that pervert higher education today." (Bruni, F. 2019. When did college turn so cruel? *New York Times*. Sept.4, A23)

12 Confronted with conflict talk, sociolinguists may either focus their analysis on the symbolic power being exercised (e.g., Cameron 1998), or on the differences in conversational style (Tannen 1993). For an interesting comparison between the two approaches, see Cameron 1998 and 2005.

13 Other evidence of symbolic violence might be less subtle: interrupting, hogging the floor; not engaging the other; the silent treatment; the cold shoulder; avoidance tactics, switching topics. Put-downs (Man: "I love your necklace," when the woman is trying to make a point) (Cameron 1998); "Where's your coat?" – "Thanks, Mom" (Tannen 1993), talking in the presence of others in a language that others don't understand, or about things that some people don't know anything about, behaviors labelled "inconsiderate," "insensitive," "tactless" are all manifestations of symbolic violence. If not picked up on, it's because complicity is the easier way to buy harmony and peace within a group, but it tends to marginalize, minimize individuals and ultimately make them invisible.

14 Because many language teachers are native speakers of the language they teach, they are often immigrants with uncertain immigration status; they have temporary appointments and are heavily dependent on good student evaluations to retain their job. They are thus particularly keen on meeting the expectations of their students and avoiding difficult topics like politics, religion, history or culture that might create controversy in the classroom and prompt the students to drop their courses.

Chapter 6

1 Baker, P. and Sang-Hun, C. 2017. Trump threatens 'fire and fury' against North Korea if it endangers the U.S. *New York Times*. Aug.8.

2 By using the case of Donald Trump yet again to illustrate the uses and abuses of symbolic power, I do not wish to give preference to controversial political figures over everyday occurrences of such power. If, in this third and last example, I draw on the president's verbal behavior it is not only because it is overwhelmingly in the news these days, but because it holds up as in a distorting mirror many of the bullying and manipulating behaviors each of us has encountered in various forms in playgrounds, schoolrooms, boardrooms and workplaces – stigmatizing practices described in Goffman (2009).

3 I use here the notion of "symbolic warfare" differently from Brooks. While Brooks interprets Bourdieu's very notion of symbolic power as symbolic warfare, I apply the term only to the abuse of power to crush opponents through symbolically violent means.

4 The double meaning of the French *reconnaissance* has been overlooked by the translator of Bourdieu (1994), I therefore offer my own translation in this quote.

5 Donald Trump's way of talking has been analyzed by linguists and psychiatrists alike. See, for instance, the interview of linguist John McWhorter by MSNBC Brian Williams on Sept.15, 2017, which focuses on Trump's exclusively casual way of talking, that McWhorter finds "extremely artful," but "narcissistic and oddly adolescent." The adolescent feel of Trump's way of talking might, however, be the result of years playing "The Apprentice" in a Reality TV show that transformed a real adolescent into "a character on TV without an off-switch," as described by the television critic James Poniewozik in Poniewozik (2019b).

6 See Cottle, M. 2018. The Chuck and Nancy and Donald Show, Editorial, *New York Times*. Dec.12, A26. See also Hirschfeld Davis, J. 2018. Clash on camera as Trump warns of a shutdown. *New York Times*. Dec.12, A1.

7 The outcome of this meeting was: The government was shut down for thirty-five days, then both Republicans and Democrats in Congress passed a bi-partisan bill to strengthen border security without the wall that Trump wanted; Trump signed the bill but simultaneously declared a "state of emergency" that would allow him to get money elsewhere.

8 It has also been viewed as characteristic of the kind of mobster talk studied by Jacquemet (2009) and others on the discourse of the Italian mafia .

9 Landler, M. and Roberts, K. 2019. Trump's aides have followed their leader on twitter, *New York Times*. Mar.8, A10. See also the devastating special issue of the *New York Times* of Nov.3, 2019 on "The Twitter presidency" that explains the economy of tweets and retweets shaping the political landscape in the United States today.

10 Mayer, J. 2019. The making of the Fox News White House. *New Yorker*. Mar.4, p.51.

11 See Twitter vs. Facebook politics in Pucciarelli, M. 2019. Anatomy of a populist. The true story of Matteo Salvini. *New Left Review*, no.116–117. March–June. According to Pucciarelli, Matteo Salvini, then Italy's prime minister, benefitted from the advice of Luca Morisi, his digital advisor, on how to perfect his communication style. Salvini was on Twitter, but on Morisi's advice, switched to Facebook. "Twitter is too constraining. The platform is autoreferential and favors messages of confirmation. Most people in Italy are on Facebook, not on Twitter, so we have to be on Facebook." As a result, the number of Salvini's followers grew to more than 3 million on Facebook, from 18,000 in 2013 and 1.5 million in 2015.

12 One example of such hurled speech is the way one of the president's sons, Eric Trump, who was attending Michael Cohen's testimony to Congress, took to Twitter while Cohen was still seated at the table in the hearing room, to dispute Cohen's claim that he never wanted to go to the White House.
"Michael was lobbying EVERYONE to be 'Chief of Staff,'" he tweeted. "It was the biggest joke in the campaign and around the office. Did he just perjure himself again?" Other members of the 2016 Trump campaign backed him up.
Assuming that Eric Trump's Twitter feed reached as many people as his father's, such a tweet was likely to have enormous perlocutionary effects on the way that Congress' investigation into the conduct of Donald Trump got perceived by the American electorate. See Fandos, N. and Haberman, M. 2019. Hearings are over, but the testimony has a life of its own, *New York Times*. Mar.8, A19.

13 Comey, J. 2019. How Trump co-opts leaders like Barr, *New York Times*. May 2, A25.

14 See also Shteyngart, G. 2019. Must see TV? *New York Times* Sunday Book Review. Sept.7, p.11. Trump has been compared with Ronald Reagan, another entertainer who applied his acts to politics and became president of the United States. But, as Poniewozik argues, "there is a crucial difference between what 'playing a character' means in the movies and what it means on reality TV." Ronald Reagan was an actor, with the ability to "believe deeply in the authenticity and interiority of people besides [himself]." Being a reality star like Donald Trump is antithetical to movie acting. "Playing a character on reality TV means being yourself, but bigger and louder." (Poniewozik 2019b)

15 "The Apprentice" is a global reality TV series that ran for fourteen seasons in which contestants compete for a job as an apprentice to billionaire American Donald Trump. For Trump's career in television, see Nussbaum, E. 2017. Guilty pleasure. The TV that created Donald Trump, *New Yorker*. July 31. To understand the quintessentially American imagination behind the brutality, recklessness and greed of reality TV, see Bouie, J. 2019. America holds onto an undemocratic assumption from its founding: that some people deserve more power than others, *New York Times Magazine*. Aug.4).

16 At his campaign rallies Trump likes to highlight the fact that he is not a 'real' president, he is only impersonating the office. At a campaign rally for Rick Saccone in Pennsylvania on Mar.11, 2018, he told the crowd that they would all be really bored if, heaven forbid, he ever decided to act "presidential." "You know how easy it is to be presidential? But you'd be so bored, right?" Then stiffening up and speaking somewhat nasally, he launched into an impression of a more formal politician. "Ladies and gentlemen, thank you for being here tonight. Rick will be a great, great congressman. He will help me very much. He's a fine man and Yong is a wonderful wife. I just want to tell you on behalf of the United States of America that we appreciate your service. We appreciate your service," Trump said in his 'presidential' voice. "See, that's easy. That's much easier than doing what I have to do. But this is much more effective. If I came like a stiff, you guys wouldn't be here tonight," he said as himself again. But where is his real self?

Chapter 7

1 I wish to thank Michael Bronstein, a student in my *Language and Power* class in Spring 2018, for giving me permission to reproduce this passage from his term paper on "The power of memes."

2 For a similar incident, see de Leon, C.. 2019. Woman is clawed by Jaguar after reaching zoo's barrier. *New York Times*. Mar.12, A18.) A woman apologizes to officials at an Arizona zoo after she climbed over a barrier while trying to take a photo and was attacked by a jaguar. "Life threatening and fatal incidents in recent years have highlighted the dangers that people will accept for a photo, especially a selfie. According to a 2018 study, 259 deaths from October 2011 to Nov.2017 were a result of attempted selfies, most while the person was engaging in risky behavior like standing on the slippery edge of a cliff."

3 See "The 50 greatest Harambe memes of all time." https://thoughtcatalog.com/jacob-geers/2016/08/the-greatest-harambe-memes-of-all-time.

4 See, for example, McPhate, M. 2016. Gorilla killed after child enters enclosure at Cincinnati zoo. *New York Times*. May 29.

5 See Goldberg, M. 2019. Toxic nostalgia breeds derangement. *New York Times*. Aug.20, A22 where she argues that our "post fact society emerges from despair and cynicism about the future" and that the biggest challenge for educators "may

be to create belief in a future that doesn't seem nightmarish, to restore faith in a rational path forward, to give people a sense of control over their destiny."

6 In his book *Absurd drama* (1965), the literary critic Martin Esslin wrote: "[The Theatre of the Absurd] is a challenge to accept the human condition as it is, in all its mystery and absurdity, and to bear it with dignity, nobly, responsibly; precisely *because* there are no easy solutions to the mysteries of existence, because ultimately man is alone in a meaningless world. The shedding of easy solutions, of comforting illusions, may be painful, but it leaves behind it a sense of freedom and relief. And that is why, in the last resort, the Theatre of the Absurd does not provoke tears of despair but the laughter of liberation." (p.23)

7 The feminist movement of the sixties and seventies in particular (e.g., Betty Friedan's 1963 *Feminine mystique*), drawing on the early writings of Simone de Beauvoir's *The second sex* (1949), lay the ground for a social constructivist view of gender that first held the modern view that "one is not born, but becomes a woman" through socialization and observance of social sexual norms. it then grew into the late modern feminist approach developed by Chris Weedon, Deborah Cameron and others.

8 In applied linguistics, the terms post-structuralism and late modernism have become blurred (see Morgan 2007; Angermüller 2018); they are used interchangeably by various scholars to draw attention to the socially constructed nature of truth and the complexity of linguistic and social phenomena (e.g., Pavlenko and Norton 2007:669; McNamara 2012). Because the term "late modern" has been used to describe phenomena associated with symbolic power in late modernity (e.g., Giddens 1991; Rampton 2006; Kramsch 2012a; McIntyre 2018, chapter 6), I will refer to late modernism (also called post-modernism) throughout this and the next chapter.

9 In addition to social constructionism, late modernists highlight a theory of subjectivity that is discursively produced in the social interactions between culturally produced, contradictory subjects. Just as discourse is seen here as the very condition that makes it possible for us to know, think and speak at all within a given historical time period, in the same way our subjectivity is not totally under our control. Foucault, writing in the 1960s and 1970s, was the first to describe the order of discourse (Foucault 1971) that regulates our existence as speaking subjects – an eminently late modern stance.

10 The American notion of a "college campus," picked up by such giants of data surveillance as Facebook's "campus" in Menlo Park, Google's "campus" in Mountain View or Apple's "campus" in Cupertino, evokes a secure, reassuring environment in which surveillance and monitoring are taken for granted.

11 See Foucault, M. 1995. *Discipline and punish*, pp. 6–7, 170–173, 183–192.

12 See Foucault, M. 2004. *Sécurité, territoire, population: Cours au Collège de France* (1977–1978), ed. Michel Senellart. Paris: Gallimard/Le Seuil.

13 The notion of spectacle society is echoed in the latest French hit song: "*Paraître ou ne pas être / Ouh la la la question que voilà / Paraître ou ne pas être / La question fait débat*" [to appear or not to be, oooh what a question!, to appear or not to be, the question is up for debate] by Maxime Le Forestier, French singer and songwriter, in his album *Paraître ou ne pas être*, released in 2019. The song plays on the French pun: *paraître* (to appear) *ou ne pas être* (or not to be) and alludes of course to Hamlet's dilemma.

14 Reality TV is another manifestation of Debord's spectacle society. Critics have suggested that Trump's success as a businessman was built on the bet that it is far more important to appear to be like a thing than to actually be that thing. In his interview with *Playboy* magazine in 1990, Glenn Paskin asks Trump: "What

does all this – the yacht, the bronze tower, the casinos – really mean to you?" Trump answers: "Props for the show" – "And what is the show?" – "The show is 'Trump' and it is sold-out performances everywhere." ("Paskin, G. 1990. Interview with Donald Trump." *Playboy*. Mar.1. www.playboy.com/articles/playboy-interview-donald-trump-1990).

15 Much of what the mass media decry about Donald Trump's disrespect of truth is in fact the world of hyperreality in which he established himself as a powerful businessman, and from which he now governs a real world in which threats and promises, executive orders and violations of the law have real consequences.

16 See Danah Boyd, principal researcher at Microsoft Research, author of *It's complicated. The social life of networked teens*. Newhaven: Yale University Press, 2014. See also Senior, J. 2019. "Our neurotic "privacy paradox." *New York Times*. May 19, SR 5. This phenomenon is not restricted to networked teens. Trump's economic capital is not the source of his symbolic capital, which relies on his Twitter feed, directly addressed to his supporters ("he speaks like us"). For Trump, as for his supporters, economic capital is less important than symbolic capital (the equivalent of social elite/TV celebrity). He has replaced the social status that he lacks in real life by online visibility and TV celebrity.

17 See Poniewozik, J. The real Donald Trump is a character on TV, *New York Times*. Sept.8, 2019, SR4–5. See also Poniewozik, J. 2019. A titan of business (at least that's who he played on TV), *New York Times*. May 9, A16.

18 According to Ferraris and Martino 2018, the two main features of documediality are the following: 1) documents, that is, legal or codified documents like testaments and degree certificates, or non-codified documents like conversational patterns or shopping behaviors, can be stored without the knowledge of the subject that produces them; 2) the novelty of a product, picture or document is not as important as their large quantity.

19 The notions of re-entextualization and re-semiotization were coined by Silverstein and Urban (1996) to refer to the processes whereby texts are formed and performed, crystallized and destabilized, and social categories are a product of such textual practices, not sediments of social life. In their view, processes of (re) entextualization and (re)contextualization lie at the heart of cultural dynamics.

Chapter 8

1 I wish to thank Jian Gao for giving me permission to reproduce this passage from his term paper on "Foucault: Understanding power."

2 In *Society must be defended: Lectures at the College de France 1975–1977*. New York: Picador, 2002, Foucault wrote:

> Power must [...] be analyzed as something that circulates [...] It is never localized here or there [...] Power is exercised through networks, and individuals do not simply circulate in those networks; they are in a position to both submit to and exercise this power. They are never the inert or consenting targets of power; they are always its relays [...] Power passes through individuals. It is not applied to them (p.29)

3 "The new organizational and technological context derived from the rise of global digital networks of communication is the fundamental symbolic-processing system of our time" (Castells 2009:4).

4 Poster (1990) was one of the few scholars to consider how the post-structuralist position illuminates the decentering effect of electronically mediated communication on the speaking subject and its power to impose the global social context as a decentering ground for theory. Since 1990, electronic communication has become so widespread that the link between post-structuralism and our current

digital era has become largely forgotten. As we shall see in this chapter, the decentered post-structuralist/late modern condition has ironically given way to a recrudescence of structuralism and authoritarianism in a different form.

5 The historian Robert Darnton disputes Poster's idea that the mode of information is something new. He wrote in 2000: "Standing here on the threshold of the year 2000, it appears that the road to the new millennium leads through Silicon Valley. We have entered the information age, and the future, it seems, will be determined by the media. In fact, some would claim that the modes of communication have replaced the modes of production as the driving force of the modern world. I would like to dispute that view [. . .] I would argue that every age was an age of information, each in its own way, and that communication systems have always shaped events" (Darnton 2000b: p.1). And he goes on to suggest that "the Paris of Louis XV may help us gain some perspective on the Washington of Bill Clinton." (p.35)

6 The relation between the material and the symbolic has become the object of heated debates today as some of the perpetrators of mass shootings explicitly relate their action to the words they have heard populist politicians campaign on (see Peters, J., Grynbaum, M., Collins, K and Harris, R. 2019. How the El Paso Gunman echoed the words of right-wing pundits. *New York Times*. Aug.12, A1).

7 For an example of this idealism, see Google's "Ten things we know to be true" philosophy, accessible at www.google.com/about/philosophy.html

8 It is against that aspect of digital technologies that countries with different cultural traditions are pushing back. Europeans are particularly concerned about the ethical issues raised by digital technologies regarding the increase in social and economic inequalities, the regulation and instrumentalization in the transfer of knowledge, and the increased commercialization of the Internet. New privacy laws in Europe as of May 2018 require companies to provide a plain-language description of their information-gathering practices, including how the data is used, as well as have users explicitly "opt in" to having their information collected. The rules also give consumers the right to see what information about them is being held, and the ability to have that information erased ("right to be forgotten"). In addition, some European countries like France, Italy, and Spain are contemplating imposing taxes on the income raised by the giant digital companies Google, Apple, Facebook and Amazon (GAFA) to compensate for the enormous profits they make through their online publicity, their sale of personal data and the activities on their platforms. See Vaidhyanathan (2011, chapter 1).

9 Wasik, B. 2015. Welcome to the age of digital imperialism. *New York Times Magazine*. June 7, pp.16–20.

10 Hughes, C. 2019. It's time to break up Facebook. *New York Times*, May 12, SR2.

11 On Trump's political use of social media, see Lakoff 2017, Montgomery 2017, Ott 2016, Kreis 2017, Blommaert 2017, 2018.

12 Scholars have uncovered the subtle ways in which our participation online is tracked to market products targeted toward our preferences (Zuboff 2019), where filter bubbles are created based on our viewing/reading habits (Pariser 2011), and where our emotions are strategically manipulated through the content of our newsfeeds (Goel 2014). Critical applied linguists like Macedo (2019), Kubota (2016, 2019), or Kramsch (2019) have recognized such practices as neocolonial practices and called for "decolonizing foreign language education." For recent work on "surveillant media" and how they are shaping our experiences and the way we form knowledge, see Beer (2009) and Jones (2016, 2019a, b, 2020a, b and in press)

13 see Vivion Brooks, B. 2019. Our fear of being a nobody. *New York Times*. Oct.4, A.27. ""With the rise of automation, a widening wealth gap and an unstable political climate, it is easy to feel unimportant [...] Social media is no longer a mere public extension of our private socialization; it has become a replacement for it. What happens to our humanity when we relegate our real lives to props for the performance of our virtual ones?"

14 Recent misuses or abuses of the Facebook platforms for ideological or political purposes have prompted Facebook to delete offensive postings and videos, but not without soul-searching debates about freedom of expression and Facebook's reluctance to exercise panoptic surveillance.
   Part of the dignity we seek to maintain as individuals is what has been called *le droit à l'oubli* [the right to be forgotten], a human right guaranteed by a EU law as the right of people to "determine the development of their life in an autonomous way, without being perpetually or periodically stigmatized as a consequence of a specific action performed in the past." This law, adopted in the EU in 2010, and that is basically a right to privacy, has been seen in the United States as possibly clashing with the First Amendment on freedom of expression. The goals of Facebook and Google, to "connect the world," to "bring people together" are readily recognizable and accepted as good by most American consumers. But they are not necessarily a response to the anguished questions posed by Europeans: "*Pourrons-nous vivre ensemble? Égaux et différents* [Will we be able to live together? Equal and different] (Touraine 1997) or "*Où atterrir? Comment s'orienter en politique* [Where to land? How to orient yourself in politics] (Latour 2017).

15 See Warzel, C. 2019. Our post-truth information system. *New York Times*. Aug.13, A20. See also Davis (2017).

16 According to an article by John Gray in *The Guardian*, 20 May 2017, facts have been irrelevant in politics for a while. Why are liberals so shocked by fake promises? Gray reviews two books: Matthew d'Ancona *Post-Truth: The new war on truth and how to fight back*, and Evan Davis *Post-Truth: Why we have reached peak bullshit and what we can do about it*. See also: R. Lakoff 2017; Montgomery 2017.

17 I draw here on Benkler, Y., Faris, R. and Roberts, H. 2018. *Network propaganda: Manipulation, disinformation and radicalization in American politics* (esp. chapter 1 Epistemic crisis), referenced by Mayer, J. 2019. Trump TV (Fox News) in *The New Yorker*. March 11. See also Apuzzo, M. and Satariano, A. 2019. Hackers spread disinformation as European Parliament vote looms. *New York Times*. May 12, p.1.

18 See Chomsky, N. 2019. Interview with C.J. Polychroniou *Truthout*. July 3, and Brooks (2019).

19 See also Peter Pomerantsev, British journalist born in the Soviet Union: *Nothing is true and everything is possible* (2014) and *This is not propaganda: Adventures in the war against reality* (2019). Also, see Andrew Marantz, *Antisocial: Online extremists, techno-utopians and the hijacking of the American conversation* (2019). For the paradox of anonymity on the Internet that facilitates both disclosure and surveillance, see Warzel 2019.

20 See Marcus, G. and Davis, E. (2019a) as discussed in their article, Build A.I. we can trust. *New York Times*. Sept.7, A23.

Chapter 9

1 One can find the same kind of cunning in the wonderful 1983 Hungarian film *The revolt of Job* (Hungarian: Jób lázadása) directed by Imre Gyöngyössy and Barna Kabay, which was nominated for the Academy Award for Best Foreign Language Film about a Jewish couple who, unable to have children of their own, "trick" God by adopting a non-Jewish Hungarian orphan in Nazi-occupied Hungary in 1943.

2 It is worth noting that Boccaccio wrote this story in the middle of generalized extreme physical violence, as the plague epidemic was raging in Florence at the time; and that Bakhtin read Boccaccio when in exile in equally violent times in the Soviet Union.

3 See also Butler (2014, 2016).

4 Butler has much more faith than did Bourdieu in the individual's ability to respond to institutional power and to resist the symbolic warfare waged by populist politicians. As we will see, the much longer timescale on which Bourdieu operates is the product of a different biographical trajectory and different geographical conditions of possibility.

5 I wish to thank Christine Freyche from the Conservatoire National des Arts et Métiers in Paris for alerting me to Diderot's strategies in his *Encyclopédie*.

6 For a discussion of simultaneity inspired by Bakhtin, see Jan Blommaert (2005a:126). The question raised by Bakhtin: "How can I be both an independent self and a member of a social group?" is the same paradox we encountered in Chapter 4 when we discussed the paradoxical demands of face studied by sociolinguists. In order to save one's sacred face, one has to juggle the contradictory demands of power and solidarity, independence and involvement, closeness and distance.

7 For the phrase "traffic in meaning," see Pratt, M.L. 2002. The traffic in meaning: translation, contagion, infiltration. *Profession*, 25–36.

8 Boyer and Yurchak (2010) describe the practice of *Stiob* in the last two decades of the Soviet Union – a form of humor characterized by an overidentification with the person or idea at which it is directed. It is often impossible to tell whether *stiob* is sincere support, ridicule or a mixture of the two.

9 In his senior thesis: "Culture jamming: The playful political uses of humor" (2010, Dept of Anthropology, University of California Berkeley), Chris Hebdon defines culture jamming as "a type of cultural resistance that involves a contestation of hegemonic power," "a controlling process to create change" (p.xvi). Hebdon applies this notion to forms of political activism from civil rights demonstrations to Freeway Bloggers who use highway bridges to display billboards in support of various causes for all automobilists to see. See also: Dery, M. 1993. Culture Jamming: Hacking, slashing and sniping in the empire of signs. Accessed at www.markdery.com/culture_jamming.html; Nomai, A. 2008. Culture Jamming: Ideological struggle and the possibilities of for social change. PhD dissertation, University of Texas at Austin, Dept of Communications; Egan, T. We need to keep laughing. *New York Times*. Jan.5, 2019, A18. For laughter in activist movements: https://foreignpolicy.com/2013/04/05/why-dictators-dont-like-jokes/ See also the work of political comedians: Stephen Colbert, Jimmie Kimmel, Bill Maher, Seth Myers, Trevor Noah, John Oliver.

10 The use of a language by non-native speakers (NNSs) in a native environment is a case in point. The NNSs insert into the native environment ways of speaking that come from elsewhere. In so doing, they slowly change the local pragmatics, interaction rituals and social expectations of the native speech community, as can be seen in the global spread of English.

11 Outsideness is an important concept that should not be confused with indifference, detachment or fatalism. For Bakhtin, it is the necessary subject position from which one can view events within the larger scheme of things: as having happened before, and likely to happen again; as in proportion to other events; as having both good and bad effects. Outsideness is the condition for humor, understood not as comedy, but as irony and an ability to smile at human foibles without ceasing to work to make things better.

12 In the section of the *Pensées* titled "*La justice et la raison des effets*" [justice and the reason of effects], Pascal argues that, unlike the scholastically educated elite, common people have a practical sense that leads them to sound judgment and appropriate social behavior. Real savviness, he says, is not to look down on the common people in the name of some higher rationale, nor to espouse their purely practical sense, but to speak like them while judging actions and events from a larger perspective that he calls "*la pensée de derrière*" [thought from behind], or holding a [bigger] understanding of things in the back of your head. "*Raison des effets. – Il faut avoir une pensée de derrière et juger de tout par là, en parlant cependant comme le peuple*" (p.145).

13 The scholars I have drawn on in this chapter are discussed only from the perspective of the argument made in this book. Their immensely rich and complex body of work certainly warrants further reading. Some readers will disagree with my interpretations of their theories. Indeed, the work of these scholars has been the object of many debates regarding the relation of language and symbolic power. See for example, de Certeau (1984b) who criticized both Bourdieu and Foucault for different reasons than Butler (1997:180–181) who heavily disagreed with Bourdieu. See Calhoun et al. 1993; see also the debate between Chomsky and Foucault (Mortensen 1971) on YouTube. If Bourdieu's sociolinguistic framework was chosen for this book it is because it seemed to be the most appropriate to construct a bridge between the micro-level of signs and speech acts and the macro-level of social media and politics. It is also the most suited to illuminate the workings of language as symbolic power from the interdisciplinary perspective adopted here.

Conclusion

1 See Robinson's criticism of "constative" linguistics vs. "performative" linguistics in Douglas Robinson (2003).

2 For example, mastery of a symbolic system does not index the same proprietary power for native and non-native speakers.

3 Such destruction of one's legitimacy is called humiliation, stigmatization or "social death" (hence the phrase "I was mortified" to characterize the deadly effect of a humiliating comment).

4 These writings formed the syllabus of the undergraduate course *Language and Power*, on which this book is based.

5 The change in the symbolic status of language teachers in various countries is a case in point. In France, a teacher used to be a professional who had both teaching experience and a deep knowledge of education and the transmission of knowledge. Nowadays, a professional is someone who is an expert in the management of knowledge, and the teacher is reduced to being a technician who applies the procedures developed by the expert. This has led to the de-skilling or de-professionalizing/devaluing of language teachers and to enhancing the symbolic power of the second language acquisition expert (Martine Derivry, pers. comm.).
In the United States, a professional used to be a scholar who had a deep understanding of literature or linguistics – two domains of language study, and who taught both language and literature, or language and linguistics. Nowadays, the two domains have a significantly different symbolic value: a scholar is someone who engages in scholarship in literary or linguistic studies, while the language teacher has become a methodologist who engages in curricular research and practice (Warner 2018).

6 Jürgen Moltmann was a German Protestant theologian who in his book: *The Trinity and the kingdom: The doctrine of God* (New York: Harper and Row, 1981) argued that

in the dialogue between the three persons of the Trinity (the Father, the Son and the Holy Spirit) God suffers with humanity.

7 Hence the difficulties encountered when trying to fit the notion of "symbolic competence" (Kramsch 2006, 2011) into a structuralist syllabus.

8 The course *Language and Power* on which this book is based included two 90-minute lectures plus a 1-hour recitation section a week for fifteen weeks. Every week, I held a 1–2-hour coffee hour directly after lecture at a near-by café. This coffee hour was assiduously attended each week by fifteen to twenty students who were eager to share their thoughts and experiences and to hear how I myself had dealt with the various aspects of language as symbolic power.

9 Many teachers have accepted the reductionist view of language and language learning offered by the textbook and the devalued image of their profession offered by their institution and the public at large. They might, therefore, resist any suggestion that language could be taught as symbolic power rather than merely as a linguistic system. Some might fear losing students if they seem to be destroying their romantic view of the speakers of the language by mentioning symbolic power. They also fear being dragged into a political discussion in which they might lose control of their classrooms – and their jobs.

10 The call in the 1980's by the American Council for the Teaching of Foreign Languages for teaching a "usable skill" instead of the ability to translate foreign texts was in this sense already indexing not the use-value, but the exchange-value of knowing foreign languages. Indeed, in Duchêne and Heller (2012), Monica Heller and Alexandre Duchêne discuss the transformation of language seen as an object of national pride in traditional nation-states into an "added value" in a global economic world order. From older discourses that treat language as a political and cultural asset, associating it with the formation of the nation-state, we have moved since the 1990s towards seeing language and culture primarily in economic terms. Authenticity is a source of value. Pride is put in the service of economic and symbolic profit.

11 The power of the computer as cultural homogenizer makes it easy to forget that, as discussed in Chapter 8, technology must be understood within its culturally specific political economy. The use of Twitter or Facebook by French users is different from their use by American users. The ethical responsibility of the language teacher is seen differently in France (see, e.g., Beacco 2013; Coste 2013) than in Anglo-Saxon countries (see, e.g., Byram 2008; Byram et al. 2017).

12 See Crozet and Diaz (2020), especially p.117 on political and ethical engagement as choice and responsibility for university language teachers/researchers (see also O'Sullivan 1999; Crozet 2006; Macedo 2019; Phipps 2019). For the move from education for information to education for transformation, see Crozet and Diaz (2020). "The introduction of inner/subjective knowledge in education for current times could assist in making the shift from education for information to education for transformation" (Crozet and Diaz, 2020:265).

13 For China, see Gao, S. (2018a, 2018b) who discusses how multilingualism is used to serve the goals of neo-nationalism. Wen Qiufang's (2016) practice-oriented approach focuses on production/output to make westerners understand Chinese culture through English. For France, see: Beacco, J.-C. (ed). 2013. *Ethique et didactique dans l'enseignement des langues*, in particular Daniel Coste's description in that volume of what French educators value as "epistemological ethics" rather than social ethics. For intercultural education as promoted in Europe, Australia and Latin America, see: Byram 2008; Byram et al. 2017 for the civic dimension of intercultural education; Crozet 2006 for its spiritual dimension; Guilherme 2002; and Guilherme and de Souza 2019 for its sociopolitical dimension.

14 As I write these lines, Toni Morrison has just died on August 5, 2019 at the age of eighty-eight. A discussion of her Nobel lecture was the subject of the last class in the course *Language and Power* on which this book is based. It can serve to tie many of the strings together that we have explored in *Language as symbolic power*, and is presented here as a tribute to the great writer who has accompanied so many of that course's students on their life journey after they left Berkeley.

15 The following discussion draws on Judith Butler's interpretation of the first half of this parable in her book *Excitable Speech* (1997) and expands on it to include the second half, not mentioned in Butler. The audio recording of Toni Morrison delivering this lecture can be accessed on YouTube http://nobelprize.org/nobel_prizes/literature/laureates/1993/ morrison-lecture.html.

16 Morrison taps here into the three axes of human existence – time, space and causality. Time: the African American woman is older, her experience spans several decades. Space: she lives outside of town, and is from a different race, a different culture; being blind, she is deprived of her young visitors' apprehension of space, but she knows their reality, that is, their motive. Causality: the children ask the old woman: "tell us how we got to where we are," but rather than just asking her to remember her painful past as the daughter of slaves, the children ask her to project herself into *their* future and to find the reason of effects in the future, not in the past ("Tell us what it is to be a woman, so that we may know what it is to be a man"). The children's suggestion that they can learn more from the old woman's acknowledgement of her vulnerability than from her admonishments is echoed in Butler 2014 and Butler et al. 2016.

References

Abrahamian, A. A. (2015). *The cosmopolites: The coming of the global citizen.* New York: Columbia University Press Global Report.

(2019, January 26). The real wall isn't at the border: It's everywhere, and we're fighting against the wrong one. *New York Times.* Retrieved from: www.nytimes.com/2019/01/26/opinion/sunday/border-wall-immigra tion-trump.html

Albright, J. and Luke, A. (eds.). (2008). *Pierre Bourdieu and literacy education.* London: Routledge.

Althusser, L. (1971). Ideology and ideological state apparatuses (B. Brewster, trans.). *Lenin and Philosophy* (pp.170–186). New York: Monthly Review Press.

Anderson, B. (1991). *Imagined communities. Reflections on the origins and spread of nationalism.* London: Verso.

Angermüller, J. (2018). *Why there is no poststructuralism in France: The making of an intellectual generation.* London: Bloomsbury.

Auden, W. H. (1940). In memory of W. B. Yeats. *Another Time.* New York: Random House.

Austin, J. (1962). *How to do things with words.* Cambridge, MA: Harvard University Press.

(1979). Performative utterances. *Philosophical Papers* (pp.233–252). Oxford: Oxford University Press.

Bakhtin, M. (1981). *The dialogic imagination* (M. Holquist, trans.). Austin: University of Texas Press.

(1984). *Rabelais and his world* (H. Iswolsky, trans.). Bloomington: Indiana University Press.

(1990). Art and answerability. *Early philosophical essays.* M. Holquist and V. Liapunov (eds. and trans). Austin: Texas University Press.

Barad, K. (2007). *Meeting the universe halfway: Quantum physics and the entanglement of matter and meaning.* Durham: Duke University press.

Barney, D. (2004). The vanishing table, or community in a world that is no world. In A. Feenberg and D. Barney (eds.), *Community in the digital age* (pp.31–52). Oxford: Rowman & Littlefield.

Barthes, R. (1972). *Mythologies* (J. Cape, trans). New York: Hill and Wang. (Original work published 1957.)

(1977). Rhetoric of the image (S. Heath, trans.). *Image-Music-Text* (pp.32–51). New York: Noonday Press.

(1982). *Empire of signs* (R. Howard, trans). New York: Hill and Wang. (Original work published 1970.)

Basso, E. (1990). The trickster's scattered self. *Anthropological linguistics, 30*, (3:4), 292–318.

Baudrillard, J. (1983). *Simulations* (P. Beitchman, P. Foss and P. Patton, trans.). New York: Semiotext.

Beacco, J-C. (ed.). (2013). *Ethique et politique en didactique des langues*. Paris: Didier.

Beckett, S. (2012). *Waiting for Godot*. London: Faber & Faber. (Original work published 1953.)

Beer, D. (2009). Power through the algorithm? Participatory web cultures and the technological unconscious. *New Media and Society, 11*(6), 985–1002.

Berenstain, S. and Berenstain, J. (1994). *The Berenstain Bears' new neighbors*. New York: Random House.

Berger, P. and Luckman, T. (1966) *The social construction of reality: A treatise in the sociology of knowledge*. New York: Doubleday.

Bettelheim, B. (1975). *The uses of enchantment: The meaning and importance of fairy tales*. New York: Vintage.

Bichsel, P. (1969). *Kindergeschichten*. Neuwied: Luchterhand.

Block, D. (2007). *Second language identities*. London: Continuum.

(2018). *Political economy and sociolinguistics. Neoliberalism, inequality and social class*. London: Bloomsbury.

(2019). *Post-truth and political discourse*. London: Palgrave Macmillan.

Block, D., Gray, J. and Holborow, M. (2012). *Neoliberalism and applied linguistics*. London: Routledge.

Blommaert, J. (2005a). *Discourse. A critical introduction*. Cambridge, UK: Cambridge University Press.

(2005b). Difference and value: Orders of indexicality and pretextuality. *Discourse* (pp.73–78). Cambridge, UK: Cambridge University Press.

(2010). *The sociolinguistics of globalization*. Cambridge, UK: Cambridge University Press.

(2017). Small genres of veridiction: The Twitter profile. Retrieved from https://alternative–democracy-research.org/2017/04/28/small-genres-of-veridiction-the-twitter-profile/.

(2018). Trump's Tweetopoetics. Tilburg papers in Culture Studies, Paper 203, 1–5. Retrieved from http://137.56.247.223/upload/983ecbaf-bcfe-4dcc-b167-f52aae4ed3fc_TPCS_203_Blommaert.pdf

Bolinger, D. (1980). *Language. The loaded weapon*. New York: Longman.

Bourdieu, Pierre. 1977a. Sur le pouvoir symbolique. In: *Annales. Economies, sociétés, civilisations*. 32e année. 3, 405–411.

(1977b). *Outline of a theory of practice* (R. Nice, trans.). Cambridge, UK: Cambridge University Press. (Original work published 1972.)

(1977c). The economics of linguistic exchanges (R. Nice, trans.). *Social Science Information*, *16*, 645–668.

(1982). *Ce que parler veut dire: L'économie des échanges linguistiques*. Paris: Fayard.

(1990). Fieldwork in philosophy (M. Adamson, trans.). In *Other Words: Essays towards a reflexive sociology* (pp.3–33). Stanford, CA: Stanford University Press.

(1991). *Language and symbolic power* (G. Raymond and M. Adamson, trans.). Cambridge, MA: Harvard University Press.

(1994). *Raisons pratiques: Sur la théorie de l'action*. Paris: Seuil.

(1996). *The state nobility. Elite schools in the field of power* (L. Clough, trans.). Stanford, CA: Stanford University Press.

(1998). *Practical reason: On the theory of action*. Stanford, CA: Stanford University Press

(2000). Introduction (R. Nice, trans.). *Pascalian Meditations* (pp.1–8). Stanford, CA: Stanford University Press.

(2000). *Pascalian meditations* (R. Nice, trans.). Stanford, CA: Stanford University Press. (Original work published 1997.)

(2008). *Sketch for a self–analysis*. Chicago: University of Chicago Press. (Original work published 2004.)

Bourdieu, P. and Passeron, J.–C. (1990). *Reproduction in education, society and culture* (R. Nice, trans.). London: Sage. (Original work published 1970.)

Boyer, D. and Yurchak, A. (2010). American Stiob: Or, what late socialist aesthetics of parody reveal about contemporary political culture in the West. *Cultural Anthropology 25*(2), 179–221.

Brockmeier, J. and Carbaugh, D. (eds.) (2001). *Narrative and identity: Studies in autobiography, self and culture*. Amsterdam: John Benjamins.

Brooks, D. (2017a, May 26). Four American narratives. *New York Times*. Retrieved from www.nytimes.com/2017/05/26/opinion/the-four-ameri can-narratives.html.

(2017b, July 18). Getting radical about inequality. *New York Times*. Retrieved from www.nytimes.com/2017/07/18/opinion/inequality-pierre-bourdieu.html.

(2018, November 19). Fighting America's spiritual void. *New York Times*. Retrieved from www.nytimes.com/2018/11/19/opinion/mental-health-ptsd-community.html.

(2019, May 30). When trolls and crybullies rule the earth. *New York Times*. Retrieved from www.nytimes.com/2019/05/30/opinion/online-trolling-empathy.html.

Brown, P., and Levinson, S. (1978). *Politeness: Some universals in language usage*. Cambridge, UK: Cambridge University press.

Brown, R., and Gilman, A. (1960). The pronouns of power and solidarity. In T. A. Sebeok (ed.), *Style in language* (pp.252–281). Cambridge, MA: MIT Press.

Brumfit, C. (1997). How applied linguistics is the same as any other science. *International Journal of Applied Linguistics*, 7(1), 86–94.

Bruner, J. (1986). *Actual minds, possible worlds*. Cambridge, MA: Harvard University Press.

(1990). *Acts of meaning*. Cambridge, MA: Harvard University Press.

(2001). Self-making and world-making. In J. Brockmeier and D. Carbaugh (eds.), *Narrative and identity: Studies in autobiography, self and culture* (pp.25–37). Amsterdam: John Benjamins.

(2002). The narrative construction of reality. In M. Mateas and P. Sengers (eds.), *Narrative intelligence* (pp.41–62). Amsterdam: John Benjamins

Bucher, T. (2018). *If...then. Algorithmic power and politics*. Oxford: Oxford University Press.

Butler, J. (1997). *Excitable speech: The political promise of the performative*. London: Routledge.

(2014). Vulnerability and resistance. *Profession 2014*. Retrieved from https://profession.mla.org/vulnerability-and-resistance/

(2016). Rethinking vulnerability and resistance. In J. Butler, Z. Gambetti and L. Sabsay (eds.), *Vulnerability in resistance* (pp.12–27). Durham, NC: Duke University press..

Butler, J., Gambetti, Z., and Sabsay, L. (eds.) (2016). *Vulnerability in Resistance*. Durham, NC: Duke University Press.

Byram, M. (2008). *From foreign language education to education for intercultural citizenship: Essays and reflections*. Clevedon, UK: Multilingual Matters.

Byram, M., Golubeva, I., Hui, H. and Wagner, M. (eds.) (2017). *From principles to practice in education for intercultural citizenship*. Clevedon, UK: Multilingual Matters.

Byrd Clark, J. and Dervin, F. (eds.). (2014). *Reflexivity in language and inter-cultural education*. London: Routledge

Calhoun, C., LiPuma, E. and Postone, M. (eds.). (1993). *Bourdieu: Critical perspectives*. Chicago: University of Chicago Press.

Cameron, D. (1997). Performing gender identity: Young men's talk and the construction of heterosexual masculinity. In S. Johnson and U. Mein-hof (eds.), *Language and masculinity* (pp.47–64). Oxford: Blackwell.

(1998). "Is there any ketchup, Vera?": Gender, power and pragmatics. *Discourse & Society, 9*(4), 437–455.

(2000). *Good to talk? Living and working in a communication culture*. London: Sage.

(2005). Language, gender, and sexuality: Current issues and new direc-tions. *Applied Linguistics, 26*(4), 482–502.

Camus, A. (1946). *The stranger* (S. Gilbert, trans.). New York: Alfred Knopf. (Original work published 1942.)

(1955). *The myth of Sisyphus and other essays* (J. O'Brien, trans.). New York: Alfred Knopf. (Original work published 1942.)

Cardon, D. (2015). *A quoi rêvent les algorithmes: Nos vie à l'heure des big data*. Paris: Seuil.

Carles, P. (2001). *La sociologie est un sport de combat [Sociology is a martial arts] [Video]*. France: C-P Productions et VF Films.

Carnegie, D. (1936). *How to win friends and influence people*. New York: Simon & Schuster.

Castells, M. (2009). *Communication power*. Oxford: Oxford University Press.

de Certeau, M. (1984a). *The practice of everyday life*. Berkeley: University of California Press.

(1984b). "Foucault and Bourdieu" and "Walking in the City." *The practice of everyday life* (pp.45–60, 91–110) Berkeley: University of California Press.

Chapelle, C. (ed.). 2012. *Encyclopedia of applied linguistics*. Oxford: Wiley-Blackwell.

Charaudeau, P. (2011). Réflections pour l'analyse du discours populiste. *Mots: Les Langages du Politique, 97*. Retrieved from http://mots.revues .org/20534

Chun, C. (ed.) (forthcoming). *Applied linguistics and politics*. London: Bloomsbury.

Cicurel, F. (2013). Culture professorale et singularité: Une lecture de Bergson pour aborder la fabrique de l'action d'enseignement. In J.-C.. Beacco (ed.), *Ethique et politique en didactique des langues* (p.169–190). Paris: Didier.

Cook, G. (1994). A basis for analysis: Schema theory, its general principles, history and terminology. *Discourse and literature* (pp.9–22). Oxford: Oxford University Press.

(2010). *Translation in language teaching.* Oxford: Oxford University Press.

Coste, D. (2013). La didactique des langues entre pôles d'attraction et lignes de fracture. In J.-C. Beacco (ed.), *Ethique et politique en didactique des langues* (pp.38–75). Paris: Didier.

Crozet, C. (2006). The spiritual dimension of intercultural education. *International Journal of the Humanities*, 4(3), 119–124.

Crozet, C., and Diaz, A. (2020). *Tertiary language teacher-researchers between ethics and politics. Silent voices, unseized spaces.* New York: Routledge.

Culler, J. (1982). *On deconstruction: Theory and criticism after structuralism.* Ithaca: Cornell University Press.

Curran, A. (2019). *Diderot: The art of thinking freely.* New York: Other Press.

D'Ancona, M. (2017). *Post-truth: The new war on truth and how to fight back.* London: Ebury.

Darnton, R. (2000a). Paris: The early internet. *The New York Review of Books*, 47(11), 42–47.

(2000b). An early information society: News and the media in 18th century Paris. *The American Historical Review*, 105(1), 1–35.

Davies, A. and Elder, C. (eds.). (2004). *The handbook of applied linguistics.* Oxford: Blackwell.

Davis, E. (2017). *Post-truth: Why we have reached peak bullshit and what we can do about it.* London: Little Brown Books.

Deacon, T. (1997). *The symbolic species.* New York: Norton

Debord, G. (1983). *Society of the spectacle* (D. Nicholson-Smith, trans.). Detroit, MI: Black & Red. (Original work published 1967.)

De Costa, P., Park, J. and Wee, L. (2016). Language learning as linguistic entrepreneurship: Implications for language education. *The Asia Pacific Education Researcher*, 25(6), 695–702.

De Francisco, V. L. (1991). The sounds of silence: How men silence women in marital relations. *Discourse & Society*, 2(4), 413–423.

De la Peña, M. (2015). *Last stop on Market Street.* New York: Penguin Books.

Delbanco, A. (2018, November 2). The long struggle for America's soul. *New York Times.* Retrieved from www.nytimes.com/2018/11/02/opinion/the-long-struggle-for-americas-soul.html.

Derrida, J. (1977). Signature Event Context. In G. Graff (ed.), *Limited, Inc.* (pp.1–24) Evanston, IL: Northwestern University Press.

(1978). Structure, Sign and Play in the Discourse of the Human Sciences (A. Bass, trans.). *Writing and Difference* (pp.278–294) Chicago: University of Chicago Press.

Descartes, R. (1911). *Meditations: The philosophical works of Descartes* (E. S. Haldane, trans.). Cambridge, UK: Cambridge University Press. (Original work published 1641).

Dewaele, J.-M. (2010). *Emotions in multiple languages*. London: Palgrave Macmillan.

Dickinson, E. (1993). A word is dead. *Poems* (p.13). New York: Alfred Knopf.

Douglas, M. (1990). Foreword: No free gift. In M. Mauss, *Essay on the gift* (p.i–x). London: Routledge.

Dretzin, R. (Producer), Goodman, B. (Producer) and Rushkoff, D. (Producer). (2004). *The persuaders*. Boston: WGBH.

Duchêne, A. and Heller, M. (eds.). (2012). *Language in late capitalism: Pride and profit*. London: Routledge.

Duranti, A. and Goodwin, C. (eds.). (1992). *Rethinking context: Language as an interactive phenomenon*. Cambridge, UK: Cambridge University Press.

Dürrenmatt, F. (1973). *The visit*. London: Penguin. (Original work published in 1956.)

Esslin, M. (1965). Introduction. *Absurd drama* (pp.7–23). New York: Penguin Books.

Fairclough, N. (2014). *Language and power* (3rd ed.). London: Routledge.

Feldman, C. F. (1987). Thought from language: The linguistic construction of cognitive representation. In J. Bruner and H. Haste (eds.), *Making sense: The child's construction of the world* (pp.133–146. New York: Methuen.

(2001). Narratives of national identity as group narratives: Patterns of interpretive cognition. In J. Brockmeier, and D. Carbaugh (eds.), *Narrative and identity* (pp.129–144). Amsterdam: John Benjamins.

Felman, S.(1983). *The literary speech act: Don Juan with J. L. Austin, or seduction in two languages* (C. Porter, trans.). Ithaca: Cornell University Press.

Ferraris, M. (2019). Du postmoderne à la postvérité (M. Orcel, trans.). *Post–vérité et autres énigmes* (pp.21–74). Paris: Presses Universitaires de France. (Original work published 2017.)

Ferraris, M., and Martino, V. (2018). What is documediality and why traces, documents and archives are normative. *Law Text Culture, 22*, 21–30. Retrieved from https://ro.uow.edu.au/ltc/vol22/iss1/3

Fishman, P. (1978). Interaction: The work women do. *Social problems, 25*(4), 397–406.

Foucault, M. (1970). *The order of things. An archeology of the human sciences*. New York: Vintage.

(1971). *L'ordre du discours*. Paris: Gallimard.

(1979). Governmentality. *Ideology and consciousness, 6*, 5–21.

(1995). *Discipline and punish* (2nd ed.). (A. Sheridan, trans.). New York: Vintage. (Original work published 1977.)

(2005). *The hermeneutics of the subject: Lectures at the College de France* (G. Burchell, trans.). New York: Palgrave MacMillan. (Original work published 1981–1982.)

Fowler, R. (1996). *Linguistic criticism* (2nd ed.). Oxford: Oxford University Press.

Freadman, A. (2014). Fragmented memory in a global age: The place of storytelling in modern language curricula. *Modern Language Journal,* **98** (1), 373–385.

Freud, S. (1946). *Totem and Taboo* (A.A. Brill, trans.). New York: Vintage.

Gainous, J. and Wagner, K. M. (2013). *Tweeting to power. The social media revolution in American politics.* New York: Oxford University Press.

Gao, S. (2018a). Multilingualism and good citizenship: The making of language celebrities in Chinese media. *Multilingua,* **37**(6), 541–559.

(2018b, March). The neoliberal moralization of language learning: Stories of a tour guide in Chinese media. *Paper presented at conference of American Association of Applied Linguistics,* Chicago.

Gee, J., Hull, G. and Lankshear, C. (1996). *The new work order: Behind the language of the new capitalism.* Boulder, CO: Westview press.

Giddens, A. (1991). The contours of high modernity. *Modernity and self-identity: Self and society in the late modern age* (pp.10–34). Stanford, CA: Stanford University Press.

Goel, V. (2014, June 29). Facebook tinkers with users' emotions in newsfeed experiment, stirring outcry. *New York Times.* Retrieved from www .nytimes.com/2014/06/30/technology/facebook-tinkers-with-users-emo tions-in-news-feed-experiment-stirring-outcry.html.

Goffman, E. (1959). *The presentation of self in everyday life.* New York: Doubleday.

(1967). *Interaction ritual: Essays on face-to-face behavior.* New York: Pantheon Books.

(1981). *Forms of talk.* Cambridge MA: Harvard University Press.

(2009). *Stigma: Notes on the management of spoiled identity.* New York: Simon and Schuster.

Gordon, C. (1991). Governmental rationality: An introduction. In G. Burchell, C. Gordon and P. Miller (eds.), *The Foucault effect: Studies in governmentality* (pp.1–52). Chicago, IL: University of Chicago Press.

Gramling, D. (2019). Supralingualism and the translatability industry. *Applied Linguistics,* 1–20. doi:10.1093/applin/amz023

Gray, J. (2017, May 19). Post-truth by Matthew d'Ancona and Post-truth by Evan Davis review – is this really a new era of politics? *The Guardian.*

Retrieved from www.theguardian.com/books/2017/may/19/post-truth-matthew-dancona-evan-davis-reiews.

Gray, J. and Block, D. (2012). The marketization of language teacher education and neoliberalism: Characteristics, consequences and future prospects. In D. Block, J. Gray and M. Holborow, *Neoliberalism and applied linguistics* (pp.114–143). New York: Routledge.

Grice, P. (1975). Logic and conversation: In P. Cole, and J. L. Morgan. (eds.), *Syntax and semantics*, Vol. 3, Speech Acts (pp.41–58). New York: Academic Press.

Grimshaw, A. (ed.). (1990). *Conflict talk: Sociolinguistic investigations of arguments in conversations*. Cambridge, UK: Cambridge University Press.

Guilherme, M. (2002). *Critical citizens for an intercultural world: Foreign language education as cultural politics*. Clevedon: Multilingual Matters.

Guilherme, M. and de Souza, L. (2019). *Glocal languages and critical intercultural awareness: The South answers back*. New York: Routledge.

Gumperz, J. and Levinson, S. (eds.). (1996). *Revisiting linguistic relativity*. Cambridge, UK: Cambridge University Press.

Gumperz, J., Jupp, T. C. and Roberts, C. (1979). *Cross-talk: A study of cross-cultural communication*. London: National Center for Industrial Language Training.

Gunderman, D. (2016, November 10). President elect Donald Trump's big beautiful wall may end up just being a modest, double-layered fence. *New York Daily News*.

Habermas, J. (1970). Towards a theory of communicative competence. *Inquiry*, *13*, 360–375.

    (1984). *Theory of communicative action* (T. McCarthy, trans.). Boston: Beacon Press.

Hacking, I. (1999a). *The social construction of what?* Cambridge, MA: Harvard University Press.

    (1999b). Kind-making: The case of child abuse. *The social construction of what?* (pp.125–162). Cambridge, MA: Harvard University Press.

Hall, G. (2015). *Literature in language education*. London: Palgrave Macmillan.

Hanks, W. (1996). *Language and communicative practices*. Boulder, CO: Westview Press.

    (2005). Pierre Bourdieu and the practices of language. *American Review of Anthropology*, *34*, 67–83.

Harcourt, B. E. (2014). Digital security in the expository society: Spectacle, surveillance, and exhibition in the neoliberal age of big data. *Columbia Public Law Research Paper*, No. 14–404. http://dx.doi.org/10.2139/ssrn.2455223

Harcourt, B. (2015). *Exposed: Desire and disobedience in the digital age.* Cambridge, MA: Harvard University Press.

Hathaway, J. (2017). Mourning Harambe, the last great meme. *The Daily Dot* www.dailydot.com/unclick/harambe-memes.anniversary.

Heath, S. B. (1983). *Ways with words.* Cambridge, MA: Harvard University Press.

Heller, M. and McElhinny, B. (2017). *Language, capitalism and colonialism: Toward a critical history.* Toronto, CA: University of Toronto Press.

Hermand, J. (1958). *Die literarische Formenwelt des Biedermeiers.* Giessen: W. Schmitz.

Hoffmann, H. (1986). Der Struwwelpeter oder lustige Geschichten und drollige Bilder. Münster: F. Coppenrath Verlag. (Original work published 1845.)

Holborow, M. (2012). Neoliberal keywords and the contradictions of an ideology. In D. Block, J. Gray and M. Holborow, *Neoliberalism and applied linguistics* (pp.33–55). London: Routledge.

Holquist, M. (1981). The politics of representation. In S. Greenblatt (ed.), *Allegory and representation* (pp.163–183). Baltimore: John Hopkins University Press.

(1990). *Dialogism: Bakhtin and his world.* London: Routledge.

Hunston, S. (2017). Donald Trump and the language of populism. Retrieved from www.birmingham.ac.uk/research/perspective.

Hyde, L. (1998). *Trickster makes this world: Mischief, myth, and art.* New York: Farrar, Straus and Giroux.

Hymes, D. (1972). On communicative competence. In J. B. Pride and J. Holmes (eds.), *Sociolinguistics* (pp.269–293). Harmondsworth: Penguin.

(1986). Models of the interaction of language and social life. In J. J. Gumperz and D. Hymes (eds.), *Directions in Sociolinguistics: The ethnography of communication* (pp.35–71). Oxford: Basil Blackwell.

(1987). Communicative competence. In U. Ammon, N. Dittmar and K. Mattheier (eds.), *Soziolinguistik/Sociolinguistics Vol.1* (pp.219–229). Berlin: Walter de Gruyter.

Jackson, S. (2008). *The lottery.* New York: Wildside Press. (Original work published in 1948.)

Jacquemet, M. (2009). *Credibility in court: Communicative practices in the Camorra trials* (2nd ed.). Cambridge, UK: Cambridge University Press.

Jakobson, R. (1960). Linguistics and poetics. In T. Sebeok (ed.), *Style in language* (pp.350–377). Cambridge, MA: MIT Press.

Jodelet, D. (ed.). (2003). *Les représentations sociales.* Paris: Presses Universitaires de France.

Johnson, M. (1987). *The body in the mind: The bodily basis of meaning, imagination, and reason.* Chicago: University of Chicago Press.

(1993). *Moral imagination: Implications of cognitive science for ethics.* Chicago: University of Chicago Press.

Johnstone, B. (2018). *Discourse analysis* (3rd ed.). Oxford: Wiley-Blackwell.

Jones, R. (2016). Surveillance. In A. Georgakopoulou and T. Spilloti (eds.), *The Routledge handbook of language and digital communication* (pp.408–411). London: Routledge.

(2019a). The text is reading you: Teaching language in the age of the algorithm. *Linguistics and Education.* https://doi.org/10.106/j.linged.2019.100750.

(2019b). Surveillant media. Technology, language and control. In C. Cotter and D. Perrin (eds.), *The Routledge handbook of language and media* (pp.244–262). London: Routledge.

(2020a). The rise of the pragmatic web: Implications for rethinking meaning in interaction. In C. Tagg and M. Evans (eds), *Historicising the digital. English language practices in new and old media.* Amsterdam: Walter de Gruyter.

(2020b). Mediated discourse analysis and the digital humanities. In S. Adolph and D. Knight (eds.), *Routledge handbook of English language and digital humanities.* Ch.12. London: Routledge.

(in press). Discourse analysis and digital surveillance. In A. de Fina and A. Georgakopoulou (eds.), *Cambridge handbook of discourse studies.* Cambridge, UK: Cambridge University Press.

Jones, R. and Hafner, C. (2012). *Understanding digital literacy: A practical introduction.* London: Routledge.

Jones, R., Chik, A. and Hafner, C. (eds.). (2015). *Discourse and digital practices: Doing discourse analysis in the digital age.* London: Routledge.

Kafka, F. (1971). The judgment; In the penal colony; A report to an academy. In N. N. Glazer, *Kafka: The complete stories* (pp. 77–88; 140–167; 250–258). New York: Schocken Books.

Kaminski, M. (2018 August 16). Toward defining privacy expectations in an age of oversharing. Open Future. *The Economist.* Retrieved from www.economist.com/open-future/2018/08/16/toward-defining-privacy-expectations-in-an-age-of-oversharing

Kaplan, A. (1993). *French Lessons: A memoir.* Chicago: University of Chicago Press.

Kearney, E. (2016). *Intercultural learning in modern language education: Expanding meaning-making potentials.* Bristol, UK: Multilingual Matters.

Kerlan, A. and Simard, D. (eds.). (2012.) *Paul Ricoeur et la question éducative.* Lyon: ENS de Lyon.

Kern, R. (2015). *Language, literacy, and technology.* Cambridge, UK: Cambridge University press.

Khan, K. (2014). Citizenship, securitization and suspicion in UK ESOL policy. *Working Papers in Urban Language and Literacies*, Paper 130. London: King's College Centre for Language Discourse & Communication.

Kintsch, W. (1974). *The representation of meaning in memory*. Potomac: Lawrence Erlbaum.

Klein, N. (2017). *No is not enough: Resisting Trump's shock politics and winning the world we need*. Chicago: Haymarket books.

Klemperer, V. (2000). *The language of the Third Reich: LTI – Lingua Tertii Imperii. A philologist's notebook* (M. Brandy, trans.). London: Continuum.

Kramsch, C. (1996). Wem gehört die deutsche Sprache? *Die Unterrichtspraxis*, **29** (1), 1–11.

Kramsch, C. (ed.). (2002). *Language acquisition and language socialization: Ecological perspectives*. London: Continuum.

(2004). Language, thought, and culture. In A. Davies and C. Elder (eds.), *The handbook of applied linguistics* (pp.235–261). Oxford: Blackwell.

(2006). From communicative competence to symbolic competence. *Modern Language Journal*, *80*(2), 249–251.

(2008). Pierre Bourdieu: A biographical memoir. In J. Albright and A. Luke (eds.), *Pierre Bourdieu and literacy education* (pp.33–49) London: Routledge.

(2009a). *The multilingual subject*. Oxford: Oxford University Press.

(2009b). La circulation transfrontalière des valeurs dans un projet de recherche international. *Le Francais dans le monde*, *46*, 66–75.

(2011). The symbolic dimensions of the intercultural. *Language Teaching*, 44(3), 354–367.

(2012a). Imposture: A late modern notion in poststructuralist SLA research. *Applied Linguistics*, *33*(5), 483–502.

(2012b). Symbolic mediation. In P. Robinson (ed.), *Routledge encyclopedia of second language acquisition* (pp.620–622.). London: Routledge

(2014). Introduction: Teaching foreign languages in an era of globalization. *Modern Language Journal*, *98*(1), 296–311.

(2015). What can the native language instructor contribute to foreign language education in an era of globalization? *ADFL Bulletin*, *43*(2), 88–101.

(2019). Between globalization and decolonization: Foreign languages in the cross-fire. In D. Macedo (ed.), *Decolonizing foreign language education: The misteaching of English and other colonial languages* (pp.50–72). London: Routledge.

(2020). "I hope you can let this go"/"Ich hoffe, Sie können das fallen lassen" – Focus on the perlocutionary in contrastive pragmatics. *Journal of Contrastive Pragmatics*, *1* (1), 1–24.

(2019). Educating the global citizen or the global consumer? *Language Teaching*. https://doi.org/10.1017/S026144 4819000363

(forthcoming). The politics of culture. In C. Chun (ed.), *Applied linguistics and politics*. London: Bloomsbury

Kramsch, C. and Huffmaster, M. (2008). The political promise of translation. *Fremdsprachen Lehren und Lernen*, 37(1), 283–297.

Kramsch, C. and Whiteside, A. (2008). Language ecology in multilingual settings: Towards a theory of symbolic competence. *Applied Linguistics*, 29(4),645–671.

Kramsch, C. and Zhang, L. (2018). *The multilingual instructor: What foreign language teachers say about their experience and why it matters*. Oxford: Oxford University Press.

Kreis, R. (2017). The 'Tweet politics" of President Trump. *Journal of Language and Politics*, 14(4), 607–618.

Kress, G. (1993). Against arbitrariness: The social production of the sign as a foundational issue in critical discourse analysis. *Discourse and Society*, 4 (2), 169–191.

Kubota, R. (2016). The multi/plural turn, postcolonial theory, and neoliberal multiculturalism: Complicities and implications for applied linguistics. *Applied Linguistics*, 37, 474–494.

(2019). Confronting epistemological racism, decolonizing scholarly knowledge: Race and gender in Applied Linguistics. *Applied Linguistics*. doi:10.1093/applin/amz033.

Lakoff, R. (1975). *Language and woman's place*. New York: Harper & Row.

(1990). *Talking power: The politics of language*. New York: Basic Books.

(2017). The hollow man: Donald Trump, populism and post-truth politics. *Journal of Language and Politics*, 16(4), 595–606.

Lakoff, G. (1987). *Women, fire and dangerous things: What categories reveal about the mind*. Chicago: University of Chicago press.

Larsen-Freeman, D. and Cameron, L. (2008). *Complex systems and applied linguistics*. Oxford: Oxford University Press.

Latour, B. (1999). *Pandora's hope: Essays on the reality of science studies*. Cambridge, MA: Harvard University Press.

(2017). *Où atterrir? Comment s'orienter en politique*. Paris: La Découverte.

Laviosa, S. (2014). *Translation and language education: Pedagogic approaches explored*. London: Routledge.

Li, W. (ed.). (2014). *Applied linguistics*. Oxford: Wiley Blackwell.

Liddicoat, A. (2011). *An introduction to conversation analysis*. London: Continuum.

(2016). Native and non-native speaker identities in interaction: Trajectories of power. *Applied Linguistics Review*, 7(4), 409–430

Lipton, S. 2017. Trump's meddlesome priest. *New York Times.* June 8.

Luntz, F. (2008). *Words that work: It's not what you say, it's what people hear.* New York: Hyperion.

Lyotard, J.-F. (1984). *The postmodern condition: A report on knowledge* (G. Bennington and B. Massumi, trans.). Minneapolis: University of Minnesota Press. (Original work published 1979.)

Macedo, D. (ed). (2019). *Decolonizing foreign language education: The misteaching of English and other colonial languages.* London: Routledge

Mao, L. (1994). Beyond politeness theory: "Face" revisited and renewed. *Journal of Pragmatics, 21*(5), 451–486.

Marcus, G. and Davis, E. (2019a). *Rebooting AI: Building artificial intelligence we can trust.* New York: Penguin.

Marcus, G., and Davis, E. (2019b, September 7). How to build artificial intelligence we can trust. *New York Times.* Retrieved from www .nytimes.com/2019/09/06/opinion/ai-explainability.html

Marin, L. (1988). *Portrait of the King* (M.M. Houle, trans.). Minneapolis: University of Minnesota Press. (Original work published in 1981.)

(2002). *On representation* (C. Porter, trans.). Stanford, CA: Stanford University Press.

Marwick, A. E., and boyd, d. (2010). I tweet honestly, I tweet passionately: Twitter users, context collapse, and the imagined audience. *New Media & Society, 13*(1), 114–133.

Mathias, P. (2009). *Qu'est-ce que l'internet?* Paris: Vrin.

Mauss, M. (1990). *The gift: The form and reason for exchange in archaic societies.* (W.D. Halls, trans.). London: Routledge. (Original work published 1950.)

McIntyre, L. (2018). *Post-Truth.* Cambridge, MA: MIT Press.

McNamara, T. (2012). Poststructuralism and its challenges for applied linguistics. *Applied Linguistics Special Issue, 33*(5), 473–482.

(2019). *Language and subjectivity.* Cambridge, UK: Cambridge University Press.

McWhorter, J. (2018, July 20). The unmonitored president. *The Atlantic.* Retrieved from www.theatlantic.com/ideas/archive/2018/07/trump–speech/565646/

Meyrowitz, J. (1985). *No sense of place: The impact of electronic media on social behavior.* New York: Oxford University Press.

Miller, A. (1971). *The crucible.* Harmondsworth: Viking Press. (Original work published in 1953.)

Minsky, M. (1977). Frame theory. In P. N. Johnson-Laird and P.C. Wason (eds.), *Thinking: Readings in cognitive science* (pp.355–376). Cambridge, UK: Cambridge University Press.

Mishler, E. (2006). Narrative and identity: the double arrow of time. In A. de Fina, D. Schiffrin and M. Bamberg (eds.), *Discourse and identity* (pp.30–47). Cambridge, UK: Cambridge University Press.

Montgomery, M. (2017). Post-truth politics?: Authenticity, populism and the electoral discourses of Donald Trump. *Journal of Language and Politics*, *16*(4), 1–21.

Morgan, T. (2007). Discussion of poststructuralism vs. postmodernism. In J. Cummins and C. Davison (eds.), *International handbook of English language teaching* (pp.669–680). New York: Springer.

Morozov, E. (2012). *The net delusion: The dark side of internet freedom*. London: Penguin.

Morrison, T. (1993). *The Nobel lecture in literature*. New York: Knopf.

Mortensen, M. (1971). Noam Chomsky – Michel Foucault. Human nature: justice versus power. Youtube video.

Morville, P. and Rosenfeld, L. (2006). *Information architecture for the World Wide Web: Designing large scale websites* (3rd ed.). Sebastopol, CA: O'Reilly Media.

Moscovici, S. (2003). Des représentations collectives aux représentations sociales. In D. Jodelet (ed.), *Les représentations sociales* (pp.79–103). Paris: Presses Universitaires de France.

New London Group. (2000). A pedagogy of multiliteracies. Designing social futures. In B. Cope and M. Kalantzis (eds.), *Multiliteracies: Literacy learning and the Design of Social Futures* (pp.9–37). London: Routledge.

Nissenbaum, H. (2009). *Privacy in context: Technology, policy and the integrity of social life*. Stanford, CA: Stanford Law Books.

Norton, B. (1995). Social identity, investment, and language learning. *TESOL Quarterly*, *29*(1), 9–31.

Norton, B. (2001). Non-participation, imagined communities and the language classroom. In M. Breen (ed.), *Learner contributions to language learning: New directions in research* (pp.159–171). London: Longman.

Norton, B. (2010). *Identity and language learning: Extending the conversation* (2nd ed.). Bristol, UK: Multilingual Matters.

Ong, W. (1982). *Orality and literacy: The technologizing of the word*. New York: Methuen.

Oren, I. and Solomon, T. (2014). WMD, WMD, WMD: Securitization through ritualized incantation of ambiguous phrases. *Review of International Studies*, *41*(2), 313–336.

Orwell, G. (2017). *1984*. New York: Houghton Mifflin. (Original work published 1949.)

Osborne, J. (1993). *Look back in anger*. In *Plays*. New York: Faber & Faber. (Original work published in 1957.)

O'Sullivan, E. (1999). *Transformative learning: Educational vision for the 21st century*. London: Zed Books.

Ott, B. L. (2016). The age of Twitter: Donald J. Trump and the politics of debasement. *Critical Studies in Media Communication*, 34(1), 59–68.

Packard, V. (1957). *The hidden persuaders*. New York: D. McKay Co.

(1964). *The naked society*. New York: D. McKay Co.

Packer, G. (2019, August 6). The left needs a language potent enough to counter Trump. *The Atlantic*. Retrieved from www.theatlantic.com/ideas/archive/2019/08/language-trump-era/595570/.

Pan, Y. (2000). *Politeness in Chinese face-to-face interaction*. Greenwich: Ablex.

Paran, A. and Robinson, P. (2016). *Literature*. Oxford: Oxford University Press.

Pariser, E. (2011). *The filter bubble: What the internet is hiding from you*. New York: Penguin.

Pascal, B. (1976). *Pensées*. Paris: Flammarion. (Original work published 1670.)

Pavlenko, A. (2004). 'The making of an American': Negotiation of identities at the turn of the 20th century. In A. Pavlenko and A. Blackledge (eds.), *Negotiation of identities in multilingual contexts* (pp.34-67). Cambridge, UK: Cambridge University Press.

(2005). *Emotions and multilingualism*. Cambridge, UK: Cambridge University Press.

(2008). "I'm very not about the law part": Non-native speakers of English and the Miranda warning. *TESOL Quarterly*, 42(1), 1–30.

Pavlenko, A. and Norton, B. (2007). Imagined communities, identity, and English language learning. In J. Cummins and C. Davison (eds.), *International handbook of English language teaching* (pp.669–680). New York: Springer.

Peirce, C.S. (1992 and 1998). *Selected philosophical writings, Vol.1 and 2*. Bloomington, Indiana University Press. Vol.1 edited by N. Houser and C. Kloesel, 1992; Vol.2, edited by The Peirce Edition Project, 1998.

Pennycook, A. (2001). *Critical applied linguistics*. Mahwah, NJ: Lawrence Erlbaum.

(2007). *Global Englishes and transcultural flows*. London: Routledge.

(2018). *Posthumanist applied linguistics*. London: Routledge.

Philips, S. U. (1972). Participant structures and communicative competence: Warm Springs children in community and classroom. In C. Cazden, V. John and D. Hymes (eds.), *Functions of language in the classroom* (pp.370–394). New York: Teachers College Press.

Phipps, A. (2019). *Decolonising multilingualism: Struggles to decreate*. Bristol: Multilingual Matters.

Picketty, T. (2014). *Capital in the 21st century* (A. Goldhammer, trans.). Cambridge, MA: Harvard University Press.

Pinter, H. (1988). *Mountain language*. New York: Grove Press.

Piper, W. (1930). *The little engine that could*. New York: Penguin Random House.

Politico Staff. (2017). Full text: James Comey testimony transcript on Trump and Russia. www.politico.com/story/2017/06/08/full-text

Poniewozik, J. (2019a). *Audience of one: Donald Trump, television and the fracturing of America*. New York: Liveright.

(2019b, September 8). The real Donald Trump is a character on TV. *New York Times*. Retrieved from www.nytimes.com/2019/09/06/opinion/sunday/trump-reality-tv.html.

Poster, M. (1990). *The mode of information: Poststructuralism and social context*. Chicago: University of Chicago Press.

(2006). *Information please. Culture and politics in the age of digital machines*. Durham, N.C.: Duke University Press.

Radeska, T. (2018, January 27). The fun but morbid Struwwelpeter is a 19th century German children's book in which the children suffer bizarre punishments. *The Vintage News*. Retrieved from: www.thevintagenews.com/2018.01.27/struwwelpeter-german-childrens-book

Ramos, J. (2019, January 9). Trump is the Wall. *New York Times*.

Rampton, B. (2006). *Language in late modernity: Interaction in an urban school*. Cambridge, UK: Cambridge University Press.

(2016). Foucault, Gumperz and governmentality: Interaction, power and subjectivity in the 21st century. In N. Coupland (ed.), *Sociolinguistics: Theoretical debates* (pp.303–328) Cambridge, UK: Cambridge University Press.

Rancière, J. (1998). *Autour du politique*. Paris: Folio.

Reddy, M. (1993). The conduit metaphor: A case of frame conflict in our language about language. In A. Ortony (ed.), *Metaphor and thought* (2nd ed.) (pp.164–201). Cambridge, UK: Cambridge University Press.

Rettberg, J. W. (2014). *Seeing ourselves through technology: How we use selfies, blogs and wearable devices to see and shape ourselves*. Basingstoke: Palgrave Macmillan.

Ricoeur, P. (1980). Narrative time. In W. J. T. Mitchell (ed.), *On narrative* (pp.165–186). Chicago: University of Chicago Press.

(1991). *Tâches de l'éducateur politique. Lecture I: Autour du politique*. Paris: Seuil.

(2016). *Philosophical anthropology: Writings and lectures* (Vol. 3) (D. Pellauer, trans.). Cambridge, UK: Polity Press.

Rieffel, R.(2014). *Révolution numérique, révolution culturelle?* Paris: Gallimard.

Riezler, K. (1943). Comment on the social psychology of shame. *American Journal of Sociology* **48**(4), 457–465.

Robinson, D. (2003). *Performative linguistics: Speaking and translating as doing things with words*. London: Routledge

Rogers, R. (2014). Debanalising Twitter: The transformation of an object of study. In K. Weller, A. Bruns, J. Burgess, M. Mahrt and C. Puchmann (eds.), *Twitter and society* (pp.ix–xxvi). New York: Peter Lang Publishing.

Rumelhart, D. (1980) Schemata: The building blocks of cognition. In R. J. Spiro, B. C. Bruce and W. F. Brewer (eds.), *Theoretical issues in reading comprehension* (pp.33–58). Hillsdale, NJ: Lawrence Erlbaum.

Sacasas, L.M. (2019). The inescapable town square. *The New Atlantis*, **58**, 47–53.

Sacks, H., Schegloff, E. and Jefferson, G. (1974). A simplest systematics for the organization of turn-taking in conversation. *Language*, **50**(4), 696–735.

Sapir, E. (1934). Symbolism. *Encyclopedia of the Social Sciences*, **14**, 492–495. Retrieved from: www.brocku.ca/MeadProject/Sapir/Sapir_1934_a.html

(1949). *Culture, language and personality: Selected essays*. Berkeley: University of California Press.

Saussure, F.de (1959) *Course in general linguistics* (W. Baskin, trans.). New York: McGraw Hill. (Original work published 1916.)

Schmenk, B., Breidbach, S. and Küster, L. (eds.). (2019). *Sloganization in language education discourse*. Clevedon, UK: Multilingual Matters.

Schultz, E. A. (1990). *Dialogue at the margins: Whorf, Bakhtin, and linguistic relativity*. Madison, WI: University of Wisconsin Press.

Sclafani, J. (2018). *Talking Donald Trump: A sociolinguistic study of style, metadiscourse, and political identity*. London: Routledge.

Scollon, R. and Scollon S. (2001). Interpersonal politeness and power. *Intercultural Communication. A discourse approach* (2nd ed.) (pp.43–59). Oxford: Basil Blackwell.

Scollon, R., Scollon, S. W. and Jones, R. (2012). *Intercultural communication: A discourse approach* (3rd ed.). Oxford: Wiley-Blackwell.

Sealey, A. (2007). Linguistic ethnography in realist perspective. *Journal of Sociolinguistics*, **11**(5), 641–60.

Searle, J. (1969). *Speech acts*. Cambridge, UK: Cambridge University Press.

(1979). *Expression and meaning*. Cambridge, UK: Cambridge University Press.

(1983). *Intentionality: An essay in the philosophy of mind*. Cambridge, UK: Cambridge University Press.

Seuss, Dr (1953). *The Sneetches and other stories*. New York: Random House.

(1957). *The cat in the hat.* New York: Random House.

Short, M. (1996). *Exploring the language of poems, plays and prose.* London: Longman.

Silverstein, M. (1976). Shifters, linguistic categories, and cultural description. In K. Basso and H. Selby (eds.), *Meaning in Anthropology* (pp.11–55). Albuquerque, NM: University of New Mexico Press.

(2003). Indexical order and the dialectics of sociolinguistic life. *Language and Communication,* **23**, 193–229.

Silverstein, M. and Urban, G. (1996). *Natural histories of discourse.* Chicago: University of Chicago Press.

Simpson, P. (1997). *Language through literature: An introduction.* London: Routledge.

Simpson, J. (ed.). (2011). *The Routledge handbook of applied linguistics.* London: Routledge.

Slobin, D. (1996). From "thought and language" to "thinking for speaking." In J. J. Gumperz and S. Levinson (eds.), *Rethinking linguistic relativity* (pp.70–96). Cambridge, UK: Cambridge University Press.

Spivak, G. C. (2004). Righting wrongs. *South Atlantic Quarterly,* **103**(2–3), 523–581.

Statistic Brain – Twitter statistics. (2017, May 28). Retrieved from: www .statisticbrain.com/twitter-statistics

Swaffar, J., Arens, K. and Byrnes, H. (1991). *Reading for meaning: An integrated approach to language learning.* Englewood Cliffs, NJ: Prentice-Hall.

Swartz, D. (1997). *Culture & power: The sociology of Pierre Bourdieu.* Chicago: University of Chicago Press.

Tannen, D. (1984). *Conversational style: Analyzing talk among friends.* Norwood, NJ: Ablex.

(1990). *You just don't understand: Women and men in conversation.* New York: Ballantine.

(1993). The relativity of linguistic strategies: Rethinking power and solidarity in gender and dominance. In D. Tannen (ed.), *Gender and Conversational interaction* (pp.165–188). Oxford: Oxford University Press.

(2001). *He said, she said: Gender, language and communication with Deborah Tannen [video].* San Francisco: Kanopy.

Terkel, S. (1964, October 22). "Dr. Martin Luther King discusses civil rights in regards to his 'I have a Dream' speech" [Audio Recording]. Retrieved from https://studsterkel.wfmt.com/programs/dr-martin -luther-king/jr-discusses-civil-rights.

Teubert, W. (2013). Was there a cat in the garden? Knowledge between discourse and the monadic self. *Language and Dialogue,* **3**(2), 273–297.

Thompson, J. B. (1984). Symbolic violence: Language and power in the writings of Pierre Bourdieu. *Studies in the theory of ideology* (pp.42–72). Berkeley: University of California Press.

(1991). Editor's introduction. In P. Bourdieu, *Language and symbolic power* (pp.1–31). Cambridge, MA: Harvard University Press.

Touraine, A. (1997). *Pourrons nous vivre ensemble? Egaux et différents.* Paris: Fayard.

Turner, V. (1975). Symbolic studies. *Annual Review of Anthropology*, **4**, 145–161.

Vaidhyanathan, S. (2011). *The googlization of everything (and why we should worry).* Berkeley: University of California Press.

(2019). *Antisocial media: How Facebook disconnects us and undermines democracy.* Oxford: Oxford University Press.

Van Lier, L. (2004).*The ecology and semiotics of language learning. A sociocultural perspective.* Dordrecht: Kluwer Academic.

Varela, F., Thompson, E., and Rosch, E. (1991). *The embodied mind: Cognitive science and human experience.* Cambridge, : MIT Press.

Varis, P. and Blommaert, J. (2015). Conviviality and collectives on social media: Virality, memes, and new social structures. *Multilingual margins*, **2**(1), 31–45.

Voloshinov, V. N. (1973). *Marxism and the philosophy of language* (L. Matejka and I. R. Titunik, trans.). Cambridge, MA: Harvard University Press.

Warner, C. (2018). Transdisciplinarity across two-tiers: The case of applied linguistics and literary studies in U.S. foreign language departments. *AILA Review*, **31**, 29–52.

Warzel, C. (2019, October 29). Pierre Delecto, QAnon and the paradox of anonymity. *New York Times*. Retrieved from www.nytimes.com/2019/10/29/opinion/pierre-delecto-qanon-anonymous-anonymity.html

Weedon, C. (1997). *Feminist practice and post-structuralist theory* (2nd ed.). Oxford: Blackwell.

Wen, Q. (2016). The production-oriented approach to teaching university students English in China. *Language Teaching*, **51**(4), 526–540. doi10.1017/S026144481600001X

Wenger, E. (1999). *Communities of practice: Learning, meaning and identity.* Cambridge, UK: Cambridge University Press.

White, H. (1980). The value of narrative in the representation of reality. In W. J. T. Mitchell (ed.) *On narrative* (pp.1–24). Chicago: University of Chicago Press.

Whorf, B. L. (1991). Science and linguistics. In J. B. Caroll (ed.), *Language, thought and reality: Selected writings of Benjamin Lee Whorf* (pp.207–219). Cambridge, MA: MIT Press. (Original work published 1956.)

Widdowson, H. G. (1994). The ownership of English. *TESOL Quarterly, 28*(2), 377–389.

(2018). Applied linguistics as transdisciplinary practice: What's in a prefix? *AILA Review, 31*(1), 135–142.

Wodak, R. (2015). *The politics of fear: What right-wing populist discourses mean.* London: Sage.

Wolff, M. (2018). *Fire and fury: Inside the Trump White House.* New York: Henry Holt & Co.

(2019). *Siege: Trump under fire.* New York: Henry Holt & Co.

Woodward, B. (2018). *Fear in the Trump white house.* New York: Simon & Schuster.

Wortham, J. (2019, March 7). Jenna Wortham on the exhilarating work that leaves her 'naked and shivering'. Interview by Lara Takenaga. *New York Times.* Retrieved from: www.nytimes.com/2019/03/07/reader-center/jenna-wortham-new-york-times-magazine-still-processing.html.

Wortham, S. (2006). Social identification and local metapragmatic models. *Learning identity: The joint emergence of social identification and academic learning* (pp.29–89). Cambridge, UK: Cambridge University Press.

Young, J. (1991). *Totalitarian language: Orwell's newspeak and its Nazi and Communist antecedents.* Charlottesville: University of Virginia Press.

Yurchak, A. (2006). *Everything was to be forever, until it was no more: The last Soviet generation.* Princeton: Princeton University Press.

Zarate, G. and Liddicoat, A. (eds.) (2009). La circulation internationale des idées en didactique des langues. *Le Francais dans le Monde, 46,* 66–75

Zhu, H., and Kramsch, C. (eds.). (2016). Symbolic power and conversational inequality in intercultural communication. *Applied Linguistics Review, 7*(4), 375–383.

Zhu, H., and Li, W. (2016). "Where are you really from?" Nationality and ethnicity talk in everyday interactions. *Applied Linguistics Review, 7*(4), 449–470.

Zuboff, S. (2019). *The age of surveillance capitalism. The fight for a human future at the new frontier of power.* New York: Public Affairs

Index

1984 (Orwell), 129

abuse of language
  in communicative practice, 83–84, 86
  countering, 204–205
  as infelicitous speech act, 83
  insincere declarations of love as, 98
  in marketing and propaganda, 1–2
  as symbolic violence, 199, 208–209
  in symbolic warfare, 119, 121–123
abuses of power, resistance to, 128–129,
    167, 183–184, 209
accountability, 10, 205–206, 208–209
action, symbolic
  communicative action as, 82–88,
    93–95
  in dialogism, 185–186
  economy of symbolic exchange in,
    91–93
  in everyday life, 15
  interaction rituals as, 88–91
  knowledge and recognition in, 12
  language as, 2–3, 195
  in narratives of power, 74–75
  performatives in, 81–89
  and symbolic representation, 22,
    29–30
  Trump's "hope" as, 79
  use of "code" as, 224n2 *see also* speech
    acts; violence, symbolic; warfare,
    symbolic
actors, social
  in construction and manipulation of
    social reality, 142–143, 197
  in dialogism, 184, 186–188
  in engaging with symbolic violence,
    191
  Facebook as, 154–157

in power struggles, 196
in symbolic power, 7, 155
and symbolic representation, 55
in symbolic systems, 196–199
in symbolic violence, 103–104,
    198–199
in symbolic warfare, 119
addressees
  in engaging with symbolic violence,
    72–74
  for narratives of power, 70–71
  of performative speech acts, 83–84
  in semiotic relations, 27–28
  and symbolic representation, 31,
    33–34, 93
  in symbolic warfare, 118–119
addressivity, 175–184
advertising/advertisements, 145–146,
    156–157
affect/affectivity, 43–44, 46–48,
    120–121
agency
  in discourse, 94
  in narrative, 54
  in perlocutionary effects, 178–179
  in postmodernism, 142–143
  in use of digital symbolic systems, 200
agents
  in symbolic relations, 27–28
  in symbolic violence, 99, 101–102
ahistoricity. *see* history/historicity
alchemy, symbolic, 120
algorithms, 160, 163–166, 170–171
alignment, 89–90, 151–152
alternative symbolic universe, 138
Althusser, Louis, 72–74
ambiguity
  in manipulation, 30–31, 122–123

259

For EU product safety concerns, contact us at Calle de José Abascal, 56–1°,
28003 Madrid, Spain or eugpsr@cambridge.org.

www.ingramcontent.com/pod-product-compliance
Ingram Content Group UK Ltd.
Pitfield, Milton Keynes, MK11 3LW, UK
UKHW020350140625
459647UK00020B/2376

* 9 7 8 1 1 0 8 7 9 8 8 9 1 *